T0032635

Praise for *The Seven Necess* ▊▊▊▊▊▊▊▊ *rls*

LISTED IN **Ms. Magazine**'s READS FOR THE REST OF US
AND **Bustle**'s 10 NEW #MeToo MOVEMENT BOOKS TO READ

"A sharp manifesto for fighting the patriarchy . . . Brilliant and electrifying."

—COURTNEY EATHORNE, *Booklist*, STARRED REVIEW

"A vociferous, highly motivational call to arms for the feminist movement."

—*Kirkus Reviews*

"Eltahawy's arguments come through with as much intelligence and clarity as passion and evocative imagery; they are built on facts about racism, capitalism, and homophobia, as well as her own and others' experiences."

—*Publishers Weekly*

"Eltahawy's book is an enormously valuable accounting of the work of patriarchy-smashers who are not white or rich or famous."

—MRILL INGRAM, *The Progressive*

"The fierce Mona Eltahawy is back with the feminist manifesto of the year. Inspired by #MeToo and more, this book provides readers with everything they need to launch their latest and greatest assault on the patriarchy."

—KARLA STRAND, *Ms.*

"Memoir, historical record, and manifesta, the book offers an enraged testimony of injustice and misogyny, as well as a tribute to women fighting both."

—RACHEL DEWOSKIN, *Women's Review of Books*

"Mona Eltahawy's *The Seven Necessary Sins for Women and Girls* is shocking, brave, gloriously unfeminine, and right on time. This global MeToo is the ultimate and intimate TimesUp for patriarchy. Reading it will free you, and acting on it will free us all."

—GLORIA STEINEM

"The world-renowned feminist anarchist Mona Eltahawy returns with her incredibly direct and fiercely intelligent writing in this ever timely feminist guide from the future. A future where we are all free. *The Seven Necessary Sins for Women and Girls* is a book for those who don't wait for permission."

—MARWA HELAL, author of *Invasive species*

"Mona Eltahawy reminds me that when I was young we called it women's liberation: she is here for your liberation and that of every woman and girl, from Nunavut to Namibia. *The Seven Necessary Sins for Women and Girls* is a manifesto book that exhorts and advocates for more confidence, more clarity, more of a sense of value and rights, more pleasure and joy for women. With its gloriously energetic, rampaging prose, it also inspires those things, because those good things are also contagious."

—REBECCA SOLNIT, author of *Men Explain Things to Me*

"Mona Eltahawy's womxnifesto thrills me. Eltahawy is serious about revolutionizing reality. I love serious women, especially when they champion fun and vital things like ambition, lust, and violence, and . . . she speaks directly to women like me, who experience multiple marginalizations."

—MYRIAM GURBA, author of *Mean*

"An incendiary, searing manifesto by one of the most important feminist activists of our time. Mona Eltahawy writes with urgency and passion about women around the world, calling on us to banish self-doubt and shame—all the traits that so many have been taught from childhood—and heed her battle cry against the patriarchy. She has written a wildly inspiring, brave book that commands our attention."

—LETA HONG FINCHER, author of *Betraying Big Brother: The Feminist Awakening in China*

"*The Seven Necessary Sins for Women and Girls* is a clarion call to action and a declaration of independence from patriarchal oppression. It is an homage to the girls we were and the girls we could have been. Mona Eltahawy writes with bracing wit and fierce intelligence, with unapologetic fury and an expansive heart. In these pages you will find yourself again and again, and you will see who you can become. This book is fucking brilliant."

—MAAZA MENGISTE, author of *The Shadow King*

THE SEVEN NECESSARY
SINS FOR WOMEN AND GIRLS

ALSO BY MONA ELTAHAWY

Headscarves and Hymens:
Why the Middle East Needs a Sexual Revolution

THE SEVEN NECESSARY SINS FOR WOMEN AND GIRLS

MONA ELTAHAWY

BEACON PRESS
BOSTON

BEACON PRESS
Boston, Massachusetts
www.beacon.org

Beacon Press books
are published under the auspices of
the Unitarian Universalist Association of Congregations.

© 2019 by Mona Eltahawy
All rights reserved
Printed in the United States of America

23   8 7 6 5 4

This book is printed on acid-free paper that meets the uncoated paper
ANSI/NISO specifications for permanence as revised in 1992.

Text design and composition by Kim Arney

Library of Congress Cataloging-in-Publication Data

Names: Eltahawy, Mona, author.
Title: The seven necessary sins for women and girls / Mona Eltahawy.
Description: Boston : Beacon Press, 2019. | Includes bibliographical
references and index.
Identifiers: LCCN 2019006195 (print) | LCCN 2019013006 (ebook) |
ISBN 9780807013823 (ebook) | ISBN 9780807002582 (paperback)
Subjects: LCSH: Feminism. | Women's rights. | BISAC: SOCIAL SCIENCE /
Feminism & Feminist Theory. | SOCIAL SCIENCE / Women's Studies. |
SOCIAL SCIENCE / Essays.
Classification: LCC HQ1155 (ebook) | LCC HQ1155 .E48 2019 (print) |
DDC 305.42—dc23
LC record available at https://lccn.loc.gov/2019006195

*Make your heart too rebellious for patriarchy
to plant itself within you.
Make your mind too free for fascism
to chain your imagination.*

CONTENTS

THE SEVEN NECESSARY
SINS FOR WOMEN AND GIRLS

Defying, Disobeying, and Disrupting the Patriarchy

I **WROTE THIS BOOK** with enough rage to fuel a rocket. I knew I had to write it while I was still high on the glory of beating up a man who had sexually assaulted me. Who was this woman I had become, who looks men in the eye, seizing their gaze with my fury until their fear tells me they understand not to fuck with me? I wanted to figure her out. For years I had been shedding shame and gaining fury. For years I had been thumping away at patriarchy, like a piñata hanging tantalizingly just out of reach. It was stubborn, but my tenacity and ferocity became my ladder. This book is my instruction manual for smashing that piñata.

Once upon a time, in 1982, I was a fifteen-year-old girl sexually assaulted twice at Islam's holiest site in Mecca, Saudi Arabia, as I performed hajj, the Muslim pilgrimage that is the fifth pillar of Islam. I had never been sexually assaulted before, and I froze and burst into tears. I was ashamed and traumatized, and, most crucially, I was silent.

It took me years before I could tell anyone what had happened when I was on my first hajj. I did not know of the writer and poet Audre Lorde's work when I was assaulted, but as my feminism grew, I began to understand what she meant when she said, "Your silence will not protect you."[1] And so I began to speak. The first time I shared my hajj story it was with an international group of women in Cairo. An Egyptian Muslim woman took me aside and warned me to stop sharing what had happened in front of foreigners because it would "make Muslims look bad." I told her it was not I but the men who assaulted me who "make Muslims look bad."

The next time I spoke publicly about my assault it was in Arabic on an Egyptian prime-time television show in 2013. The segment producer told me I was the first person who had ever shared a story like this on Egyptian television. It was such a taboo that he was lucky he still had a job after the backlash that followed. As I continued to quietly share with fellow Muslim women my experience of sexual assault during the hajj, the stories started to flow, with more and more women saying, "Me too!" All those years of silence were for the same reason: we thought it was impossible that anyone else had gone through a violation at such a sacred place. I also had to mature into the understanding that the men who assaulted me had abused the sanctity of a sacred space to ensure the silence of their victim. They knew that no one would believe me.

I wanted a permanent record of what had happened to me, so I wrote about my sexual assault in my 2015 book *Headscarves and Hymens: Why the Middle East Needs a Sexual Revolution*.[2] Muslim women from all over the world wrote to tell me that reading about my experience made them cry. Two years later, as Muslims from around the world were again preparing to converge on Mecca for the hajj, I posted a series of tweets about being sexually assaulted during the pilgrimage because I wanted to warn fellow Muslim women. Until the Saudi authorities who administer the holy sites take concrete steps to ensure that female pilgrims can perform pilgrimage free from sexual harassment and assault, we must protect each other. And so there I was, at my computer in February 2018, sharing once again that I had been sexually assaulted twice during pilgrimage in 1982 to support Sabica Khan, a Pakistani woman who had shared on Facebook her own assault in Mecca. I asked fellow Muslim women who felt safe enough to share their own experience of sexual harassment or assault either while performing hajj or in a Muslim sacred place. I added a hashtag to my post: #MosqueMeToo. Over two days my Twitter thread was retweeted and liked thousands of times. It was shared in Indonesian, Arabic, Turkish, French, German, Spanish, and Farsi. I had never before seen such a response.

At first men demanded, "Why didn't you make more of a fuss?" Soon after, men went into full-gaslighting mode: anything to persuade me I had not experienced what I had experienced or else questioning my character as a way to undermine my story. I could write a whole other book called

"Things You Will Hear When You Say You've Been Sexually Assaulted."
Observe:

- You are too ugly to be sexually assaulted.
- You are being paid to say this.
- You just want to be famous.
- You just want attention.
- You want to destroy Islam.
- You want to make Muslim men look bad.
- You are a whore.
- You imagined it; it was crowded.
- Why didn't you report it?
- You waited all that time. Why?
- What do you expect? Sexual assault happens everywhere.
- Why aren't you talking about sexual assault in New Zealand?
- You should have yelled and made a fuss.

For five days, women from around the world had shared with me their most harrowing experiences of sexual harassment and assault at pilgrimage or other sacred spaces. Reading their stories undid something that had broken in me as that young pilgrim in 1982 that I thought I had stitched together: I had not fully grasped the magnitude of being sexually assaulted at the site toward which Muslims pray five times a day. The experience of telling stories, and especially men's refusal to believe them, was as if I were standing in pouring rain—I could feel it drenching every part of me, only to hear the weather forecast on television confidently explaining that it was sunny and dry with not a drop of rain expected. Being forced to absorb the terrible violation of being sexually assaulted, but also to be robbed of a spiritual experience that so many long to experience, forced me to connect that violation with the many other violations I have been subjected to. How could all of that have happened to me? How have I absorbed it, been forced to accept it so that I could go on every day, and how had I learned to get on with my life?

For one night I wanted some respite from that reckoning, so, five days after I launched #MosqueMeToo, my beloved and I went to a club in Montreal to dance it off, to revel in the sensual delight of moving my body to music, in the hope that all those beats per minute would be a balm to my traumatized heart.

And there, in the middle of a crowded and sweaty dance floor, at age fifty, I felt a hand on my ass.

I had exactly two thoughts: "You've got to be fucking kidding me" and "This is still happening?" I remembered my fifteen-year-old self at hajj, covered from head to toe with just my face and hands showing. Now, on that dance floor in Montreal, I was wearing a tank top and jeans. It did not matter—hijab or tank top – a man's hands still found me.

And I was done.

But unlike in 1982 when I could not turn around to find my assaulter, I immediately spotted my creep, who had started to walk away. As if on autopilot, I followed him and tugged so hard at the back of his shirt that he stumbled.

When he fell, I sat on top of him and I punched and punched and punched his face. Once was not enough. And each time I punched him, I yelled, "Don't you ever touch a woman like that again!" While I was punching the man who had assaulted me, I could see from my peripheral vision my beloved talking to two men who had been dancing when I started beating the man and who were now preparing to pull me off my assaulter. My beloved later told me the two men had wanted to stop me from punching the man who had groped me. "No, no, he assaulted her," he told the two men; let's call them the chorus for patriarchy. "She's got this."

It had been a long time since I had experienced as much clarity as I did in those moments. I knew exactly what I was doing—defending myself—and exactly why I was doing it. I was done with men who gave themselves the right to do as they wished with my body. If at that most sacred of temples—the holiest site of my religion—I am not safe from predatory hands, where am I safe? If at that most secular of temples—a dance club—predatory men also insist on assaulting us, where are we safe?

My beloved and I went to the bar to get some water. A man who appeared to be from club management approached us and asked me to tell him what had happened. After I explained that I had beaten a man who had sexually assaulted me, he looked at my beloved and asked me, "Why didn't you let your husband take care of it?"

At what age does my body belong just to me?

Patriarchy is so universal and normalized that it is like asking a fish *What is water?* It enables and protects men who sexually assault women, and it demands that only other men "protect" us. As long as we obey and behave in ways it approves, it will "protect" us. And if we disobey, you can be sure that that protection will be revoked quicker than you can say "patriarchy." But I don't want to be protected. I just want patriarchy to stop protecting and enabling men. I don't want to be protected. I want to be free.

Regardless of whether you live in an absolute monarchy like Saudi Arabia or in a liberal democracy like Canada or the United States, regardless of what your religion is or if you are atheist or secular, regardless of whether your country has been colonized or itself once colonized and exploited others, patriarchy lives everywhere. It controls how our society and institutions are organized and run, and it has legal implications for women, nonbinary people, and children, who have less power than men.

I was born in Egypt, moved to the United Kingdom when I was seven years old, moved to Saudi Arabia when I was fifteen, lived in Jerusalem for fourteen months as a reporter when I was in my thirties, and moved to the United States in 2000 after I married an American. My reporting and public speaking have taken me to Central and South America, Asia, Australia, Europe, and Africa. Patriarchy lives in every single one of those countries and on each continent. Whether you live in the best country to be a woman—Iceland and neighboring Scandinavian countries usually top those lists—or the worst, patriarchy is clear: No country has achieved political equality. Many countries have never had a female head of state. No country pays men and women equally for work they do. In every country it is fact that most acts of domestic, intimate-partner, and sexual violence pose significant threats to women and girls, and that the majority of such acts are perpetrated by men. Some religions still refuse to ordain women to holy orders. And men by and large control and are disproportionately represented in the media, the arts, and the cultural landscapes that shape our tastes and ideas.

Patriarchy is universal.

Feminism must be just as universal. I want patriarchy and all who benefit from it to have the same look of terror as that man in the Montreal club who, before he ran away, took a look at me so that he could see the woman who had dared strike back. I want patriarchy to know that feminism is rage unleashed against its centuries of crimes against women and girls around the world, crimes that are justified by "culture" and "tradition" and "it's just the way things are," all of which are euphemisms for "this world is run by men for the benefit of men." We must declare a feminism that is robust, aggressive, and unapologetic. It is the only way to combat a patriarchy that is systemic.

I also want feminism to be led by the nonwhite and the queer, who don't have the luxury of fighting *only* misogyny. We must fight the multiple systems of oppressions that patriarchy often intertwines itself with: racism, bigotry, homophobia, transphobia, classism, ableism, and ageism. There is much work to do.

After the fight at the club, and astonished at how my attempt to take care of myself after the intensity of #MosqueMeToo had unfolded, I shared what had happened on Twitter under a new hashtag: #IBeatMyAssaulter. All that weekend I was icing my bruised knuckles and hearing from women around the world who sent me their #IBeatMyAssaulter experiences. As with #MosqueMeToo, so many women wrote to me and said, "Me too": "I was in a club/at a bus stop/in school, here, there, and #IBeatMyAssaulter." Much like with #MosqueMeToo, it was a global chorus of women who saw each other and recognized what it means to be done with the fuckery of patriarchy.

As women sent me examples of how they had beaten their assaulters, men were showing me how easily the goal posts can move. Under #MosqueMeToo men asked me, "Why didn't you make more of a fuss?" Under #IBeatMyAssaulter men said, "You made too much of a fuss. You were too violent. Don't you think you overreacted?" And more audaciously: some men asked, "What if the situation were reversed?" As if women make a habit of groping men at clubs; as if centuries of patriarchy had not enabled and protected men's entitlement to women's bodies, and so therefore the situation cannot be reversed; as if the power of violence and assault had not historically always been and continues to be in the hands of men.

Whatever a woman does, she will always be victim-blamed. My message was clear: "Women, do whatever you need to at the moment." This is self-defense. This is putting patriarchy on notice that we will fight back. This is warning patriarchy that it should fear us.

All those women who shared their experiences under #MosqueMeToo and #IBeatMyAssaulter did so understanding the power of saying "Me too." And, more likely than not, they had heard of the now global movement called MeToo. Like many revolutionary moments, MeToo is the latest iteration of many years of work by activists. Black feminist Tarana Burke originated #MeToo in 2006 to show solidarity with survivors of sexual violence. When famous actresses began to use it in 2017 to expose sexual assault by powerful producers, MeToo gained exposure and a massive platform that has helped it resonate globally.

I am deeply grateful to Burke for supporting and amplifying voices of survivors, who are too often marginalized and silenced. I appreciate the courage of anyone who is able to expose her assaulters. But we cannot allow MeToo be conflated with powerful white men and the ways they abuse famous, privileged white women. We must make sure that MeToo breaks the race, class, gender, abilities and faith lines that make it so hard for marginalized people to be heard. MeToo is at its heart a movement that fights patriarchy and the ways it enables and protect men who abuse. When famous actresses began sharing their #MeToo stories, their courage and fame propelled MeToo into international headlines. But MeToo must not remain stuck in their rarefied world, otherwise we risk losing this revolutionary moment wherein we can see each other across the whole world, whether performing hajj in Mecca or dancing in Montreal. Me Too must remain a movement about justice, not about protecting power and the privileges it bestows.

This is a revolutionary moment in which we are connecting and exposing the ways patriarchy has enabled and protected so many, daily, in every aspect of our lives: from Donald Trump, the president of the most powerful country in the world, who has been accused of sexual assault by more than a dozen women,[3] and other politicians who shape policy and law; to filmmakers and other creatives who have shaped our culture and our music and our economies; to journalists who have shaped the news and the agendas that consume us; to the priests and pastors and clerics and religious scholars who shape our consciences and act as the gatekeepers of god; to the sports coaches who train our athletes; to the more everyday examples of what we are finally calling toxic masculinity and the ways it has socialized men and boys into believing they are entitled to women's attention, affection, and more.

This is a revolutionary moment in which women from Egypt to the United States to Argentina to India to Ireland to China to South Korea and across the world are reading, sharing, and echoing stories of abuse, survival, and resilience. It is a revolutionary moment of women's rage. Men cannot sit back and say, "Well, I'm not rich and powerful; that's not me." It is you—if you are not actively dismantling the patriarchy, you are factually benefiting from it. Are you uncomfortable? Good. You should be. Discomfort is a reminder that privilege is being questioned, and this revolutionary moment is one in which we must defy, disobey, and disrupt the patriarchy, everywhere.

With #MosqueMeToo, I wanted to end the silencing and shaming of women who have been exposed to violence and abuse in sacred spaces and to say, "My body is sacred too." With #IBeatMyAssaulter, I wanted to fight back, to say, "If you grope me, I will beat the fuck out of you." It is my right to be free of sexual assault, and it is my right to fight back if I am assaulted. Ultimately it is my right to defy, disobey, and disrupt.

Thirty-five years separate me at fifteen and me at fifty. But one week in Montreal collapsed that distance and reminded me that regardless of age or location, sacred or secular, patriarchy socializes men to believe they are entitled to women's bodies. And patriarchy not only fails to teach us how to fight back, but it actively encourages our acquiescence and fear.

I made a list of milestones, from #MosqueMeToo to #IBeatMyAssaulter, partly as my way of acknowledging events that had shaped my evolution from fifteen to fifty, and partly honoring what I had learned and survived.

For example, in March 2011, less than a month after the Egyptian revolution forced Hosni Mubarak, our dictator of more than thirty years, to step down, the Egyptian military subjected at least seventeen female activists to "virginity tests," a form of sexual assault. I wrote in the *Guardian* at the time that Egypt needed another revolution, a feminist one that placed gender equality front and center, as a form of protest against those violations.[4] It didn't happen and still hasn't happened, although we sorely need it in Egypt. Eight months later, in November 2011, during a protest I joined against the police and army near Tahrir Square, Egyptian riot police beat me, broke my left arm and right hand, sexually assaulted me, and threatened me with gang rape. I was detained incommunicado for six hours by the Interior Ministry and another six by military intelligence during which I was blindfolded and interrogated. I was denied medical attention for my fractures during my twelve hours in detention. I required surgery to help align the fractured bone in my left arm, and I spent three months with a cast on each arm, unable to perform many simple tasks such as washing and brushing my own hair. The head of Egyptian military intelligence at the time of the "virginity tests" and my assault and detention was a man called Abdel-Fattah el-Sisi. He is now the president of my country of birth.

Sisi has a great ally in Donald Trump, who was elected US president in November 2016. Trump has called Sisi a "fantastic guy."[5] After Trump's inauguration, in January 2017, I wrote in the *New York Times* that the nationalism and authoritarianism evident in Trump's ceremony rendered him the American Sisi. A month later, an Egyptian newspaper ran a banner headline about my column on its front page above a picture of me from the days when I had a cast on both of my arms. The caption called me a "sex activist," and the editor in chief of the newspaper devoted the entire second page—this is a broadsheet newspaper—to denouncing me, complete with a picture of my tattoos and an allegation that I was a spy. The message was clear: we broke your arms and we can do that again. "Sex activist" was code for "whore," a way to use my feminist work for women's sexual rights to discredit and shame me.

In 2016 I was invited to speak at a literary festival in Sarajevo. I spent my last day in Bosnia paying respect to victims of that country's war. A feminist journalist took me to Visegrad, where a hotel and spa that had been used as a rape concentration camp now boasts "healing spa waters." There is no mention at all of the horrors that were perpetrated against the two hundred Bosnian Muslim women and girls who were sexually enslaved there. My journalist friend also took me to Srebrenica, where a genocide committed by the Serbs killed eight thousand Muslim men and boys. There is a memorial there, as there should be, with the names of the more than six thousand victims already identified. But there is no memorial for the women and girls in Visegrad. Men and boys get memorials, women and girls get nothing—no plaque, no sign of remorse, and no accountability. Neither the Serbian militia nor any of its soldiers have been held accountable for the atrocities they committed there.

The next year, in 2017, I joined a group of France-based antiracist activists in Rwanda for a commemoration of the genocide against the Tutsis. The Bosnian War and the genocide against the Tutsis in Rwanda happened at around the same time. I was a journalist at Reuters News Agency in Cairo then and never imagined I would one day go to either of those countries about which I read news as it came across the wires. Those two wars shamed the international community so deeply, because the atrocities committed there were so clear and known and yet nothing was done to prevent them. And those wars were reminders that sexual violence against women was an integral part. Rape has always been used as a weapon of war; expected and too often accepted as such. The brave women who survived and spoke out about it forced us to reckon with horrors that too many prefer not to see.

My visits to sites of horrific violence in Bosnia and Rwanda shattered my heart. The sexual violence in Bosnia and Rwanda were extreme versions of the systemic nature of patriarchy, but they must be connected to the violence inflicted on female activists in Egypt soon after our revolution, as well as what happened to me in Cairo on Mohamed Mahmoud Street in 2011. Sexual violence is an extreme manifestation of patriarchy, but women and girls around the world are subjected to more quotidian forms, of course. There aren't enough pages to list all the "less extreme" examples of patriarchy I or other women and girls experience daily.

For a story that starts at pilgrimage, it was "sin" that brought fifteen-year-old me full circle: the sin of blaspheming against the god of Patriarchy. Christianity preaches the Seven Deadly Sins. The Gospel of Mona presents instead the seven necessary sins women and girls need to employ to defy, disobey, and disrupt the patriarchy: anger, attention, profanity, ambition, power, violence, and lust.

I call them "sins," but of course they are not. They are what women and girls are not supposed to be or do or want. They are condemned as "sins" by a patriarchy that demands we acquiesce to, not destroy, its dictates.

In the chapter on anger, I ask what the world would look like if girls were taught that they were volcanoes that could and should erupt to

disrupt patriarchy. I examine how anger and rage are discouraged and broken out of girls and the ways in which that anger and rage are important
in the fight against patriarchy. I also ask who is allowed to be angry, and
I analyze how, depending on their race and class, some girls are punished
for behavior that is tolerated in others.

In my examination of attention, I insist that women and girls demand
attention because we deserve it and must not shy away from it. The quickest and laziest way to discredit a woman is to accuse her of "attention
seeking." I explain the importance of defiantly declaring that we deserve
attention, and why such a declaration is a powerful tool for disrupting patriarchy's demands that we remain "modest" and "humble."

We must say "Fuck." In the chapter on profanity, I insist on the power
of profanity as a force in disrupting, disobeying, and defying patriarchy
and its rules. In understanding why profanity is off-limits to women, I un-
pack the ways that girls are socialized into the straitjacket of being "nice"
and "polite," and recognize the absurdity of patriarchy's claim that our
profane words are worse than the violence it subjects us to.

Why is ambition considered a "dirty" word for women? Why does
patriarchy teach girls and women that it is wrong to openly declare they
want to be better than everybody else at something? And why—when
they *are* better, when they are recognized as experts *who are better than
everybody else*, must women play down or diminish their expertise and the
ambition that propelled them to those levels?

What is a powerful woman? In the chapter on power, I insist on dif-
ferentiating between power that dismantles patriarchy from power that
is used in the service of patriarchy. Patriarchy has often thrown women
crumbs in return for a limited form of power that often replicates the hierarchies that patriarchy has created. We must refuse those crumbs. We must
bake our own cake. And we must define power in a way that liberates us
from patriarchy's hierarchies.

In the chapter on violence, I examine the right of women and girls to
fight back against the crimes of patriarchy. Violence is a legitimate form of
resistance in struggles against colonization and occupation; it has long been
accepted as just and necessary in such struggles. What about the struggle
against a form of oppression that hurts half the world's population? This

book is not a road map for making peace with patriarchy. It is a manifesto to dismantle patriarchy and to end its crimes.

And finally, in examining lust, I emphasize the importance of a deceptively simple but revolutionary insistence: I own my body. Nobody else owns it: not the state, the street, or the home, not the church, mosque, or temple. I examine the importance and the power of expressing and insisting on desire, pleasure, and sex on our own terms. Wanting sex and expressing sexuality outside the teachings of heteronormativity are about a chaos and liberation that deeply threatens patriarchy. I examine the centrality of consent and agency to challenging patriarchy's stranglehold over our bodies, and how queerness upends patriarchy's insistence that it alone dictates not only who can have sex and how they can have it, but who can express desire and lust.

This is a moment for those who are not rich, white, or famous to be heard. It is a moment in which we must have a reckoning with patriarchy and in which we recognize how normalized its crimes are, as well as a reckoning with how it intersects with other forms of oppression like racism, classism, ableism, homophobia, transphobia, and bigotry. I am from many worlds, and I travel between many places. Throughout this book I will share voices and stories from across the world about the ways women and queer people yell a big fuck-you to the patriarchy. We must listen and learn when women in South Korea hold monthly protests against "molka" or spycam videos, which involve men secretly filming women in schools, offices, trains, toilets, and changing rooms. Those protests became the biggest ever women's protest in South Korea, and we must listen and learn, especially to their placards that affirm "Angry women will change the world."[6] We must listen and learn when Argentinian women hold a general strike to protest violence against women, which has spread across Latin America and connects our right to be free from all forms of violence as well as our right to autonomy over our bodies, whether in sexual desire or access to safe and legal abortions. We must listen and learn when feminists and queer activists in Uganda march against murder and abduction. We must listen and learn when Irish feminists spark a revolution against the Catholic Church in their country by galvanizing a nation to vote for abortion rights, and we must listen and learn when LGBTQ activists in

India work across religious, ethnic, and caste lines to push their supreme court to finally decriminalize homosexuality by overturning an article in their penal code that was a legacy from the British colonial era.

We must listen and learn, and we must connect all these struggles as part of the global feminist revolution—what Argentinian activists call feminist internationalism.[7]

My work is about dismantling patriarchy everywhere. We must not waste this revolutionary moment fighting with each other about whose men are the worst or allowing bigots, racists, or misogynists of any side to silence women. It has been good to see #ChurchToo expose sexual harassment and abuse in Christian sacred spaces in the United States. There have been similar exposés under #AidToo of men who work in the aid sector and also in the music and media industries, academia, and other fields.

I am not naive. I know too well that Muslim women are caught between a rock and a hard place. On one side are Islamophobes and racists who are all too willing to demonize Muslim men by weaponizing my testimony of sexual assault. On the other side is the "community" of fellow Muslims who are all too willing to defend all Muslim men—they would rather I shut up about being sexually assaulted during the hajj than make Muslims look bad. Neither side cares about the well-being of Muslim women.

In a world in which the president of the United States of America is a man who has boasted that when you are famous, women let you "grab them by the pussy," and who maintains the support of white Evangelical Christians, it is dangerously delusional for his supporters to write to me—as they do—that Islam is to blame for the sexual assault I expose as part of #MosqueMeToo. They refuse to recognize that Donald Trump's misogyny and the misogyny of Evangelical pastors whose abuse has been outed by #ChurchToo is the same misogyny women all around the world face each day. That misogyny is one and the same, and it is enabled and protected by patriarchy. We must make those connections so that our defiance, disobedience, and disruption of patriarchy can be as global as patriarchy.

Words like "feminism" and "resistance" are being drained of their meaning when we offer them up as band-aids that offer temporary relief to women and girls against the vagaries of patriarchy. I have had enough of giving women and girls ways simply to survive rather than tools to fight back. The danger and fear that should emanate from feminism and resistance must not be stamped out. Feminism should terrify the patriarchy. It should put patriarchy on notice that we demand nothing short of its destruction. We need fewer road maps toward a peace treaty with patriarchy and more manifestos on how to destroy it. *The Seven Necessary Sins for Women and Girls* is my manifesto.

CHAPTER 1

Anger

i will raise my voice / & scream & holler / & break things & race
the engine / & tell all yr secrets bout yrself to yr face.

—NTOZAKE SHANGE, *for colored girls who have
considered suicide / when the rainbow is enuf*[1]

ONE DAY WHEN I was four years old, a man stopped his car on the street under my family's balcony in Cairo, pulled his penis out of his pants and
beckoned for me to come down. He did the same to my friend who had
been talking to me from her family's balcony across the street. I was so
small that I needed a stool to see my friend from above the balcony railing.

I was enraged at that man, even though I was a child. How dare he ruin
our reverie; two little girls, happy, oblivious to the street below, which was
mostly quiet and therefore perfect for our cross-balcony afternoon conversations. It was our time together. How dare he interrupt us?

I waved my slipper at him to frighten him away. I believed I could shoo
him away with just my anger. I absolutely believed in my rage, convinced
that it could frighten away a grown man who had decided to stop his car
underneath my balcony and wave his penis at two little girls. Who does
that? In what world is that acceptable?

I honor that angry four-year-old girl. I honor her belief that she deserved to be free of molestation, free of interruption, free of a man who
believed he deserved her time and attention. She was born with a pilot
light of anger, tenacious and sure of its right to flare whenever treated
unjustly. I believe all girls are born with that pilot light of anger. What
happens to it as they grow into women?

What would the world look like if girls were taught they were volcanoes, whose eruptions were a thing of beauty, a power to behold and a force not to be trifled with? What if instead of breaking their wildness like a rancher tames a bronco, we taught girls the importance and power of being dangerous?

What if we nurtured and encouraged the expression of anger in girls the same way we encourage reading skills: as necessary for their navigation of the world? What if we believed that, just as reading and writing help a girl to understand the world around her and to express herself within it, expressing her anger was also a necessary tool for a girl making her way through life. Imagine a girl justifiably enraged at her mistreatment. Imagine if we acknowledged her justifiable anger so that a girl understood she would be heard if anyone abused her and that her anger was just as important a trait as honesty. And imagine if we taught a girl that injustice anywhere and against anyone was also worthy of anger, so that she developed a keen sense of compassion and justice and understood that injustice, whether personal or affecting others, was wrong?

What kind of woman would such a girl grow up to be?

We must teach girls that their anger is a valuable weapon in defying, disobeying, and disrupting patriarchy, which pummels and kills the anger out of girls. It socializes them to acquiesce and to be compliant, because obedient girls grow up to become obedient foot-soldiers *of* the patriarchy. They grow up to internalize its rules, which are used to police other women who disobey. We should not let patriarchy hammer girls into passivity. Well-behaved, quiet, acquiescent, and calm: no more.

From a very young age, girls are socialized, taught, and have it hammered into their consciousness that men and boys have a right to our attention, our affection, our time, and more. The child who demands her mother's or an adult's attention, barging into their conversations and turning the adults' heads to see the child, is taught not to interrupt the grown-ups. But the courtesy is rarely returned, especially to girls. I was as angry at that man's interruption of my time with my friend as I was at his exhibitionism.

One of the reasons I loved to stand on my stool and look out over the balcony was to see a grown-up who lived in my little friend's building across our quiet street. The woman's name was Mona (an adult who had the same name as mine!). My mother reminds me that every day a jeep would arrive to take Mona to her administrative job with the military at a nearby facility. I would watch Mona in her meticulous beige uniform in awe. My awe for military garb began and ended with adult Mona, because as an adult myself I am antimilitarism, but for four-year-old me, Mona the adult across the street was a woman with the same name as mine who looked like the most important person in the world. A jeep came to pick her up for goodness' sake! I imagined that no one interrupted her as rudely and in such a predatory way as that man flashing his penis had to us girls. Just as I would grow up to understand the danger of military garb of any kind, I would also grow out of the naivete that had me imagining that the world afforded women an uninterrupted and assault-free life.

I was still very young and unaware that whether women are young or grown-up, patriarchy and the misogyny it enables and protects spares no one.

Looking back now, that afternoon became a template for so much to come. The joy, camaraderie, and awe that I associated with my little perch on our balcony overlooking the street were tainted by that man, penis on full display, beckoning for my friend and me to go downstairs and meet him. My anger at that man was a most natural and justifiable reaction, untainted and uncensored. My moral compass was finely tuned to the true north of Mona and her well-being. I knew I deserved better. Many years later, when I included that incident in an essay I published (in Arabic, in an Egyptian paper) about the many times I've been sexually assaulted by men, a man emailed to ask me, "What was so special about you at four that anyone would expose themselves to you?" As if having a penis flashed at you was a compliment. As if a four-year-old girl could, under any circumstances, be "special" enough to warrant having a man expose himself to her.

If women and girls were free, being a girl or a woman anywhere living under patriarchy would ensure us access to an infinite supply of rage that would terrify men such as my "What was so special about you at four that anyone would expose themselves to you?" correspondent, and it would terrify the man who *did* expose himself to me when I was four. Instead, patriarchy keeps *us* terrified, demanding from us an endless supply of patience, passivity, and obedience, as it pathologizes and snuffs out our justifiable rage.

As I grew into my own adult Mona, over the next several decades, I would learn the many ways that men interrupt and violate. If I were to use paint to mark which parts of my body men have groped, pinched, or otherwise touched without my consent, my breasts, my crotch, and my backside would be covered. But I am enraged the most, still, at that man who exposed himself to me and my friend.

I often wonder what happens to the anger of girls as I try to trace the line between the four-year-old enraged that her conversation with her friend was interrupted by a man exposing his penis to them, and the fifteen-year-old twice assaulted at hajj. Instead of the immediate rage of the four-year-old, my fifteen-year-old self was choked with tears and shame. I am not victim-blaming myself. I understand that we respond to trauma and assault differently and that freezing is one of many responses. I am instead wondering where my rage went—and why.

From early on, girls around the world are told that they are vulnerable and weak. Parents, friends, and teachers decimate their power, snuff out that pilot light of anger, so much so that research shows that by the age of ten, girls believe they are indeed vulnerable and weak. That finding is from the Global Early Adolescent Study, which looked at gender expectations around the world by gathering data on ten- to fourteen-year-olds in Belgium, Bolivia, Burkina Faso, China, the Democratic Republic of Congo, Ecuador, Egypt, India, Kenya, Malawi, Nigeria, Scotland, South Africa, the US, and Vietnam.[2] I have listed all fifteen countries because it is imperative that we recognize that whether in Columbus, Cairo, or Calcutta, whether "over here" or "over there," patriarchy is universally crushing girls into submission. As different as those countries are when it comes to wealth, religious belief or practice, and other variables, the findings of the six-year study were depressingly uniform.

"We found children at a very early age—from the most conservative to the most liberal societies—quickly internalize this myth that girls are vulnerable and boys are strong and independent," Robert Blum, a professor at Johns Hopkins University and the director of the Global Early Adolescent Study, told *Time* magazine.[3]

While boys are fed the stereotype that they are strong and independent, and are encouraged to go outside and have adventures, girls are told to stay at home and do chores. Girls are socialized to understand—again at the shockingly young age of ten—that their primary asset is their appearance. But who needs a study to tell you that when you can trace the short trajectory from the girl who believes she is a superhero to the girl stuck in an endless rut of sorrys, who starts every sentence with "Sorry but . . . ," and who would apologize for breathing if she could but apologizes instead for taking up space that boys are only too happy to claim?

I had no words for the sexual assault I experienced as a teen. No one I knew had ever shared a similar horror. My family had just moved to Saudi Arabia, and it was the first time in my life that I was covered from head to toe in the white clothing required of female pilgrims at hajj. That such a violation was happening to me as we performed the fifth pillar of our religion at Islam's holiest site was unthinkable to me. Who would believe that something so awful had happened to me at such a sacred place? It was better to stay silent, I decided. The men who assaulted me knew that no one would believe me. Though I had obviously done nothing to be ashamed of, I felt it anyway. Something broke in me, and it took years to acknowledge.

Being covered from head to toe during the hajj had not protected me. Yet, afterward, all I knew was that I wanted to hide my body from men. So I began to wear hijab in earnest.

The Global Early Adolescent Study has shown that girls across the world are taught that their bodies are both an asset and a target. They must cover up and stay away from boys if they want to keep themselves safe from sexual assault, and if they are assaulted it is their fault. I learned to cover up as a tactic for protecting myself. This is not unusual. In Egypt, girls as young as six wear hijab as part of their school uniform, and in the US, girls are sent home from school if their skirt is too short or their clothes are deemed "distracting" to boys and male teachers. In neither the US nor Egypt—nor anywhere, actually—is that constraint turned on boys. Why are girls taught that their safety is their burden to bear, that what they wear or don't wear is the reason they're assaulted? Surely the burden must be on boys instead? Surely we should be teaching boys from a very young age not to assault girls so that they grow up to become men who don't assault women regardless of how they're dressed.

This book is not the place where you will hear the reasonable argument that patriarchy is bad for men and boys too. It is indeed. There are plenty of other books that make that argument and urge men that it is in their own interest to join forces with women to dismantle patriarchy. I refuse to focus on and will not plead with those who benefit from my oppression to join a fight against a centuries-long systemic oppression that not only hurts women and girls and all who deviate from the template of heterosexual, conservative, and, mostly, rich men, but kills them. But as the global study found, the freedom that boys are raised to believe is the birthright that awaits them as men can lead to recklessness, such as substance abuse and dangerous driving. Still, girls are more endangered by patriarchal socialization: they are twice as likely to experience depression by the age of sixteen (according to the *Journal of Psychiatry and Neuroscience*),[4] more likely to enter into marriage when they're children (according to Human Rights Watch),[5] and HIV rates for women are higher than for men (according to UNAIDS, the joint United Nations Programme on HIV and AIDS).[6]

It is exactly that constraint and fear, the double nursemaids of patriarchy, that drum anger out of girls as they grow up. While girls learn to retreat to protect themselves, boys are taught the opposite. We teach girls to capitulate, ostensibly for their own good, but drumming the concept of subservience into their heads comes with "a very heavy price," in the words of the researchers. What chance does a little girl's rage stand when she faces, in every country where the study was carried out, the "hegemonic myth" that girls are vulnerable and weak and boys are strong and independent? These are not biological differences, the researchers stress. These are social norms. This is patriarchy.

Boys are rarely sent home from school because of what they are wearing. They are not socialized into thinking their appearance is their most important asset, nor are they taught it is their fault if someone sexually assaults them for the way they look. They are not held responsible for "distracting" girls or women teachers. And how heterosexually biased are such teachings? Whose gaze are we centering, and whose gaze is the one around which schools set their wardrobe and attire policies?

It would take a few more years and feminism—and multiple more times when my body was groped, pinched, and touched without my permission during the nine years that I wore hijab—to know unwaveringly that sexual assault has nothing to do with how you're dressed. It has everything to do with the predator who assaults you.

What is particularly cruel is that, especially in the West, society increasingly feeds girls "you can do anything" and "girl power" lies while the patriarchy remains intact. They can't. And they have to know why: patriarchy. As long as patriarchy exists, we can feed girls all the slogans we want, but they will not have power and they will not be able to do whatever they want. As the Global Early Adolescent Study makes abundantly clear, it is no use pretending that girls in Western societies are free of the patriarchal social norms that girls in non-Western societies are taught. That is a comfortable delusion that serves only to keep at arm's length and out of sight just how pervasive patriarchy is, everywhere. It is shit for girls everywhere, not just "over there."

In societies that are usually described as "traditional" or "conservative," it is also cruel to hide behind the cover of religion and culture to try to justify the blows of patriarchal conditioning. It is cruel to abandon women and girls to a culture they had no say in ratifying and to a religion they had no say in interpreting, and which in many cases practically demands they worship men: from a male god to their fathers to their husbands—the literal patriarchs.

If we are to save girls, wherever they live in the world, if we are to nurture the pilot light of anger that guides them to their true north, feminism must be as universal and commonplace as patriarchy. But it must be a feminism that terrifies patriarchy, a feminism fueled by rage as foundational to its strength. Anger is that bridge that carries feminism from idea to being, from the thought "How the fuck is this happening?" to "This must fucking stop."

We must teach girls to be free. We must teach girls that they have the right to live without fear of being interrupted, assaulted, insulted, or otherwise abused. We must teach girls to seek adventures and to be independent. And we must teach boys constraint. I hate that word, and I hate the idea of stamping out anybody's freedom, but if the freedom that boys are taught is that their right comes at the expense of girls—which it does—then we are raising boys with the wrong lessons. We must teach boys that girls do not owe them time, attention, affection, or more; that the bodies of girls belong to girls, and that assaulting or abusing girls is wrong. Full stop.

A feminism that must respect "culture" and "religion" is a feminism that is shackled to respecting two basic pillars of patriarchy, pillars that were erected to keep women, girls, nonbinary and queer people in our "place," which is, of course, subservient to heterosexual men. We need a feminism that is robust, aggressive, and unapologetic; a feminism that defies, disobeys, and disrupts that patriarchy, not one that collaborates with, coddles, and complies with it.

We must recognize women's universal rights and by extension a universal feminism in the same way that we have a Universal Declaration of Human Rights, an international document that states basic rights and fundamental freedoms to which all human beings are entitled. The Universal Declaration of Human Rights was adopted by the UN General Assembly December 10, 1948, and marked the first time that countries agreed on a comprehensive statement of inalienable human rights. Universally, patriarchy crushes girls. But depending on where you live, your racial and ethnic background, and your sexual orientation, misogyny is not the only oppression you must fight. While girls everywhere face the brunt of patriarchy, when patriarchy marries with other forms of oppression, it becomes particularly brutal. The more marginalized you are, the sharper the blows of patriarchy and its attendant oppressions. In the US, gendered racism means that, for example, the victims who have accused the singer R. Kelly of sexual assault were mostly ignored because they were Black women. Unlike the famous and privileged white women who accused the movie producer Harvey Weinstein of sexual assault, who were interviewed and invited to write opinion pieces—all those things take courage, and I salute those women who spoke out—the victims of R. Kelly, many of whom were teenage girls, were rarely sought out by the media. There are many grassroots activists who have been working to advance the rights of women and girls of color, such as Tarana Burke, who first used #MeToo in 2006 and has become better known in the wake of the Weinstein scandal and appropriation of the hashtag she started. But gendered racism is often ignored.

According to a study published in 2017 by Georgetown Law's Center on Poverty and Inequality, as early as age five, young Black girls in the

United States of America are viewed less as children and more like adults when it comes to discipline in schools.[7] All girls are punished for behavior considered "unfeminine," but a racist society that neglects and mistreats Black girls and which denies them their girlhood also punishes them when they react with justifiable anger at their mistreatment.

"If our public systems, such as schools and the juvenile justice system, view black girls as older and less innocent, they may be targeted for unfair treatment in ways that effectively erase their childhood," Rebecca Epstein, lead author of the report and executive director of the Center on Poverty and Inequality, told CNN.[8]

How else to react but with anger when you are dealt the double blow of racism and misogyny? In her essay "A Lot to Be Mad About: Advocating for the Legitimacy of a Black Woman's Anger," which appeared in the anthology *Feminism Is: South Africans Speak Their Truth*, businesswoman, writer, and public speaker Owethu Makhatini explains the bind that Black women find themselves in when they live in racist and misogynist societies.[9]

"I fought long and hard not to be the angry Black woman, and yet here I am. I am livid. I have denied my anger. I have been ashamed of my anger. I have felt like a monster and scrambled to find ways to disguise my fangs. I have held my anger deep in the pit of my stomach and let it eat me up. I have had furrowed brows and tears of pure, animalistic anger well up my eyes and burn my cheeks."[10]

But that anger is important and is liberating, she insists.

"I am angry because I care. I am angry because I want to be and feel free. I care about how the world is invested in breaking my people and me. I want to fuck it all up. Set everything on fire and start all over," Makhatini writes.

As patriarchy wraps its tentacles around more and more forms of oppression, the space for girls' rage shrinks. The justified and righteous reaction to injustice thus becomes a privilege. Imagine being a Muslim girl in the United States: on one side are Islamophobes and racists who are certainly not feminist and who do not care about the well-being of Muslim women and girls. On the other is your community, so eager to defend its men that it too easily overlooks the misogyny that does exist. All that either side wants to talk about—and if you are lucky, might allow you to talk about it too—is what is or is not on your head. If Muslim women are portrayed as voiceless and always covered in black veils, Muslim girls are rarely if ever acknowledged. Black girls from the age of five are treated as more mature and older than they actually are and are punished more harshly than white girls for the same behavior. Know that Muslim girls are not expected to have a voice at all, let alone misbehave, act out, or display unfeminine behavior. They must be silent and submissive. Privilege is stacked: being male, white, American, etc. Lack of privilege is too. Black Muslim girls are caught in a trifecta of oppressions: misogyny, racism, Islamophobia. To whom do they express their rage that they are unseen and unheard, or their rage at being caught between a rock and a hard place?

If you take that measure, if you walk away from the center of power, or what is considered the default identity in every country, be sure that the person most marginalized will be the girl. And, in turn, the less privilege a girl has—be it for her race, class, sexuality, religion, ability—the less license she has to be angry.

To illustrate: in my country of birth, Egypt, the most marginalized girl would be a poor girl belonging to the Christian community, which is estimated to number about 10 percent of the population and is a target of both state and social discrimination, as well as attacks, many deadly, by armed Islamic militants.

In India, look for the most marginalized community and you will find the country's Muslim minority and the Dalit community, the lowest caste of the country's Hindu majority. And know that girls of both those communities do not have the luxury of anger or of raging against injustice.

One of the biggest indictments of just how worthless girls and their words are came during the trial for sexual assault of former USA Gymnastics and Michigan State University doctor Larry Nassar, when more than 150 women and girls came forward to accuse the doctor of abuse, beginning in 2015. One of the most moving witness testimonies came from Kyle Stephens.

When Kyle told her parents at age twelve that Nassar had been abusing her since she was six, they not only did not believe her, but they made her apologize to her predator who had persuaded them that Kyle was lying, the *Washington Post* reported.[11] Stephens believes that her father's suicide in

2016 was motivated in part because of guilt at not believing his daughter. Again and again, news reports told us that parents believed Nassar the predator over their own daughters.

Imagine the damage done to those girls' sense of truth and justice, and to their sense of trust. Imagine their sense of betrayal that the people closest to them, those very same people who are supposed to protect them, were the very same people who believed the predator over their daughters.

Confronting Nassar as adults, the women gave heart-smashing testimonies, often with their parents crying in the courtroom with them. The anger and the sense of betrayal that their parents had sided with their abuser against them reminded me of Egyptian feminist Nawal El Saadawi's description of her genital cutting at the age of six—the age Kyle Stephens was when Nassar began sexually abusing her. "I just wept, and called out to my mother for help. But the worst shock of all was when I looked around and found her standing by my side . . . right in the midst of these strangers, talking to them and smiling at them, as though they had not participated in slaughtering her daughter just a few moments ago," El Saadawi writes.[12]

Witness the variety of ways patriarchy enlists parents in different forms of "slaughter" of girls.

A judge sentenced Nassar to 40 to 175 years in prison for sexual assault. But who will hold accountable the patriarchy that not only enables and protects a predator for years but also persuades parents to believe a predator over their own daughters? How does a girl recover and heal from such betrayal? Who will hold accountable a racist patriarchy that pays no attention to the years of abuse of teenage girls by a famous and powerful man because the girls are Black and because the gendered racism of American society reserves its most forceful cruelty for Black girls? Who will hold accountable a patriarchy that insists on cutting off completely healthy body parts of hundreds of thousands of girls around the world in the name of "culture," sometimes in the name of religion, but always with the goal of controlling female sexuality?

"Perhaps you have figured it out by now, but little girls don't stay little forever," Kyle Stephens told Larry Nassar. "They grow into strong women that return to destroy your world."[13]

I want a world where little girls are believed by their parents. I want a world where little girls don't have to wait until they are women to destroy their predator's world. What would that world look like?

During the days of witness testimonies at Nassar's sentencing, as women gave voice to years of trauma and betrayal, the feminist and author Ursula K. Le Guin died. Her commencement speech at the women's college Bryn Mawr in 1986 gives us a road map to what that world would look like when girls are believed, in which girls believe they have the power to destroy their predators.

"We are volcanoes. When we women offer our experience as our truth, as human truth, all the maps change. There are new mountains. That's what I want—to hear you erupting. You young Mount St. Helenses who don't know the power in you—I want to hear you," Le Guin told the young women preparing to graduate.[14]

Instead of teachings girls they are weak and vulnerable, we must teach them to know the power in them. Instead of teaching them to withdraw from the world for their own safety, we must teach them instead to be as loud, as visible, as troublesome, as unruly, as angry as they want so that the world knows to ignore their voices at its peril. We must teach them to erupt! Girls are born with plenty of rage already, but we squash it. They are taught to be polite, to be well-behaved, and to not make a scene. We tell them not to raise their voice and not to speak too much. We send them to ballet class and not often enough to martial arts class. And if, after all of that, they still manage to simply say they wish to be free of sexual abuse, a worse silencing happens: their own parents don't believe them, or their parents partake in the mutilation of their own daughters, ostensibly to protect them from sexual desire.

I want to bottle-feed rage to every baby girl so that it fortifies her bones and muscles. I want her to flex and feel the power growing inside her as she herself grows from a child into a young woman.

To beat the patriarchy, we have to start early. We need curricula that include lessons on the importance of rage, the various ways to express and use it. We must show girls as wide a range of examples of women and queer people who are angry, who express rage, who are not polite or compliant, and who proudly make a scene. What would a curriculum on "Rage for Girls" look like?

My curriculum would include June Jordan's "Poem About My Rights,"
in which she brilliantly and beautifully explains how sexual violence must
be connected to state violence and power, which in turn must be connected to the violence and power of the family.[15] In her poem Jordan
moves seamlessly from misogyny to racism to colorism to colonialism, occupation, and war, showing how systems of oppression work together and
must be connected when we analyze their harm so that we understand that
patriarchy and the various oppressions it enlists do not exist in isolation or
their own separate compartments.

The poem is a masterclass in connecting the personal with the political,
the body with the world, the injustices of the family to the injustices of
society to the injustices of the state. It is the perfect poem to explain what
I call the Trifecta of Misogyny. Just as I insist that we connect the victims
of R. Kelly's sexual abuse, the victims of Larry Nassar's sexual abuse, and
the victims of female genital mutilation (FGM) together so that we can
see patriarchy in action and how it wraps its tentacles around racism as it
neglects Black girls, and around culture and religion to justify the FGM
of girls around the world—Muslim and Christian in my country of birth,
Egypt—so too must we connect the way the state, the street (society), and
the home (the family) together oppress women and girls around the world.
That is the Trifecta of Misogyny.

Near the end of the poem, June Jordan puts everyone—state, street,
and home—on notice:

I am not wrong. Wrong is not my name

We must teach girls that their anger at their mistreatment, abuse, or
diminishment is not wrong. We must show them what a woman who is
sure that her anger is justified sounds like. Jordan, a Black, bisexual poet,
feminist, and activist, was a woman whose pilot light of anger burned
brightly and wondrously. She understood and insisted that we, too, understood the ways that race, gender, and sexuality connect. Her poetry,
as well as her columns and essays, force us to see how the systems of oppression that affect us individually are connected to the communal—the
personal to the political—through class, state, and imperial oppression.
That is universal feminism. It is exactly the feminism that we must raise

girls with: a feminism that connects our rage at the injustices we suffer personally—and our right to that rage—to the rage at the injustices others suffer because of the actions of governments—ours or theirs. The state, the street, and the home: connect the oppressions that take place everywhere, June Jordan tells us.

Much like Ursula K. Le Guin's rousing commencement speech, a keynote presentation that June Jordan gave at another women's college, Barnard, is a reminder of the importance of older women who model anger, who emphasize the power of rage, and who present anger and rage as legitimate feminist behavior for younger women in complicated and powerful ways that continue to guide and shake us today. Where Le Guin reminded her audience of young women that breaking silence was subversive and urged them to recognize their own power—erupt!—Jordan urges her audience to connect the oppressions of the state, street, and home as the tools of power that work to silence us all, and to direct our anger at all those interconnected injustices.

> That confrontation with heavyweight intolerance carried me through our Civil Rights Revolution and into our resistance to the War Against Vietnam and then into the realm of gender and sexual and sexuality politics. And those strivings, in aggregate, carried me from Brooklyn to Mississippi, to South Africa, to Nicaragua, to Israel, to Palestine, to Lebanon and to Northern Ireland, and every single one of those embattled baptisms clarified pivotal connections among otherwise apparently disparate victories, or among apparently disparate events of suffering, and loss.[16]

In connecting the ways to resist interconnected injustices, Jordan tells her audience, she was forced to analyze the "world-wide absurdity of endangered female existence," and to ask, Where is the feminist revolution?

"I mean why is that our universal situation? And when will we revolt against our marginalized, pseudo-maverick status and assert our majority, our indispensable-to-the-species' power—and I do mean power: our verifiable ability to change things inside our own lives and in the lives of other folks, as well."

Jordan was calling—like Le Guin did—on young women to recognize the power they have. She was calling for a universal feminist revolution against universal patriarchy: that's the message we must give to girls and young women. And in so doing, we model for them how to maintain the pilot light of anger that patriarchy is determined to extinguish.

"I have evolved from an observer to a victim to an activist passionately formulating methods of resistance against tyranny of any kind," Jordan says.

And at the heart of "resistance against tyranny of any kind" is rage. Jordan said so in a 1989 column she wrote for the *Progressive*: "I do not believe that we can restore and expand the freedoms that our lives require unless and until we embrace the justice of our rage."[17] That is exactly what we must teach girls—the justice of their rage. It is the fuel of our feminist revolution.

I devote so much of this chapter to the importance of nurturing anger in girls because I am frustrated at the question "Why aren't women more angry?" or "What is stopping women from being angry?" We should be asking instead "What happens to the anger that girls are born with? How can we nurture it?" How much harder it is to start "teaching" women how to be angry than it would be to support girls in expressing the anger they are born with and which they have every right to express against the ravages of patriarchy that surround them at every aspect of their lives. Patriarchy and its teachings extinguishes so much, including anger.

Anger is important in girls because waiting for patriarchy to self-correct, to do the right thing, to do the moral thing, has got us not very far. Anger is a first step to putting patriarchy on notice that we are done waiting.

We will never upend the norms that we force onto girls that teach them constraint and fear, and which extinguish their pilot light of anger, if we continue to advocate a slowly-slowly feminism that does not scare men or that respects "culture" and "tradition." A feminism that doesn't want to scare men is a feminism that will never challenge patriarchy. Men have nothing to fear unless they are invested in upholding patriarchy and the various oppressions it subjects onto women. If the idea that we must end such systemic oppression frightens men, let them be frightened! But it is telling that they are frightened. They are frightened of losing privilege, entitlement, and their right to continue to hurt and diminish women and girls.

Something interesting and revealing happens when you emphasize the importance of nurturing anger in girls. Suddenly, people—mostly men— start to worry that you are encouraging violence, that you are telling girls to imitate boys, and so forth. "Anger is destructive," they insist. "Teach girls to be kind. There is too much anger in the world. Don't add to it." It is almost as if they think that boys have a copyright to anger and that anger always expresses itself violently. It is almost as if they are saying, "Yes, let boys be invincible. Teach girls to be invisible." It is definitely an indication of just how much patriarchy fears the power of anger in girls. And that is exactly what I want us to teach girls: that their anger terrifies patriarchy. In that case, let it be terrified!

Patriarchy worries when you talk about encouraging and nurturing anger in girls because it wants to deny girls a necessary response to injustice. Patriarchy knows that when we nurture anger in girls, they will hold patriarchy accountable and that those girls will grow up to be women who demand a reckoning. It does not want that reckoning, and we must demand it.

Patriarchy prefers instead that girls perform a self-reckoning, one in which girls learn to turn anger not outwards where it belongs and can target injustice, but inwards. The result is that instead of using anger to destroy patriarchy and its injustices, anger instead destroys girls. Instead of turning their rage at being diminished and abused outwards at patriarchy, girls learn to turn it inwards as sadness and shame, which debilitate and consume girls. In other words: girls become too consumed with that inner fighting against themselves to fight patriarchy externally. Girls grow up consumed with self-hatred and trauma, with little energy left to terrify anyone, let alone patriarchy. Sadness, not anger, becomes the currency of girls. Sadness does not terrify patriarchy.

A Rage for Girls curriculum must be subtitled "How to Terrify the Patriarchy." Its anthem must be "Fucking fear me," not "Woe is me."

After the 2017 iteration of #MeToo, after every revelation that yet another famous or powerful man had assaulted or abused women, hundreds and thousands of women shared searing personal stories on social media.

It takes courage to share those stories, and it takes resilience to read them because they are often triggering and retraumatizing. Yet I wish the stories came with more anger than sadness and shame. Again and again, it is as if women cut open a vein to bleed out the most gut-wrenching stories, which are often questioned by men who mock or doubt or otherwise offer opinions no one asked for instead of just listening. I wish more of the testimonies expressed a rage that more than just worried patriarchy. I wish the testimonies expressed less sadness and shame and more anger toward it.

At a concert in the summer of 2018, I felt the power of young women turning their anger outwards and putting patriarchy on notice, telling it, "I am fucking done." Leading them in that unadulterated anger was the singer Halsey, one of the few female stars who has used her platform to openly express sexual desire for both women and men. For example, she recorded a duet with another openly bisexual female singer about a relationship between two women.

Concerts, much like congregational prayer or pilgrimage, allow us to lose ourselves in the communal. Teenage girls are a major source of fandom and money for the music industry. They are often portrayed as hysterical or out of control. All things girl-related are mocked—from the colors they like, to the music they listen to, to the books they love. Patriarchy keeps boys in line by taunting them with proximity to girlhood: you run like a girl, stop crying like a girl, and so on. To that end, power is rarely associated with girls. Consider instead the power behind the passion girls have for music. For the girls who fainted during Beatlemania or at any other megastars, in place of "hysteria" and "screaming" and "shrieking," which is how the male-dominated music media usually report on teenage girls and music, replace those pejoratives with "rage" and "power." That is what Halsey led during her song "Hurricane" in the concert that I attended. She essentially acted as a conductor for the rage and power of young women. And it was glorious.

Halsey has said the lyrics about the young woman in "Hurricane," which she cowrote when she was nineteen, "mean that she [the young woman] will not be victimized. She belongs to no one but herself."[18] At the concert, Halsey led the audience in a refrain from the song, "I'm a hurricane"—to which she added "Fuck."

The force of hundreds of girls and gender-queer pre-teens (Halsey draws a young and queer audience) chanting, "I'm a fucking hurricane! I'm a fucking hurricane!" over and over is revolutionary! The walls shook with the reverberation. The collective power and rage in that concert hall could have gone out that night and torn the patriarchy to bits. Girls know their power. They are born knowing it. Which is why patriarchy socializes it out of them, and why it extinguishes the pilot light of their anger.

Thirty-seven years before Halsey released "Hurricane," a punk band called X-Ray Spex, fronted by nineteen-year-old Poly Styrene, who, like Halsey, was biracial, released their first song. And what a revolution it was. As she sang: "Some people think little girls should be seen and not heard."

Listen to "Oh Bondage! Up Yours!" in its entirety and tell me you aren't ready to destroy the patriarchy. The power and rage in that song can indeed tear it to bits. If you think its opening lines are a tongue-in-cheek play on the "sugar and spice and all things nice" stereotypes that were once used to entrap girls in the straitjacket of femininity, but which are now outdated and belong in some faraway past, then you are woefully unaware of how dire it still is to be a girl today. Everywhere.

I discovered that music could be mine when I was nine years old in 1976 in London, thanks to a small yellow transistor radio that I would stick to my ear for hours. It might have been tiny, but there was no masking the rage-in-three-and-a-half-minute jolts otherwise known as punk that it pumped into my ears. I had it tuned to the radio station that played the latest hits, which in the late 1970s were a mix of disco, rock, and, more and more, punk music. The fury and ferocity of punk thrilled me. That raw, primal rage against so many things—be it the monarchy, parents, rival bands, whatever the lead singer was yelling about—mesmerized me. I was too young to go to any clubs or concerts, but I understood the power of that rage that poured into my ears.

But most of the voices yelling in my ears were men. Their yells and growls were an early lesson in who had the right to be angry. Worse, they were an early lesson that even in spaces that are anti-establishment, even in spaces that rail against power structures, it was men who did the railing, and they railed just enough to get power for themselves; they did not rail against patriarchy. That was not unique to punk, of course. A similar pattern existed and continues in anti-racist movements that fight white supremacy but do not challenge the supremacy of patriarchy, among activists who fight an authoritarian regime and yet do not challenge the authoritarianism of patriarchy, and so on. A similar dynamic exists in hip hop and other musical forms. The punks of my pre-adolescence gave me an early lesson that men challenged other men for power in order to secure a share of that power for themselves, not for equality and justice for all. They rarely if ever fought the patriarchy because they recognized how it benefited them.

Because they were significantly fewer than their male counterparts, the women punks who did yell into my ear remain icons and heroes. Every musical genre has had a paucity of women. Every generation of women has found too few women who penned and sang the anthems of their childhood or youth. This despite the fact that teenage girls are a massive market that helps keep the music industry alive. Consumers, yes. Creators, not so much. The female punks of my childhood are a reminder of who nurtures the pilot light of anger for girls. The songs they wrote, the way they dressed, the way they sang took aim at the patriarchy, capitalism, racism, and consumerism and most defiantly rejected demands that they be pretty, polite, and well-behaved. They demolished doors and challenged the male musical establishment and the sneering and dismissing music media. I know that for every generation there are female musical icons that model rage and rebellion. I celebrate them all. But how do I love Poly Styrene, born Marianne Joan Elliott-Said, born to a Scottish-Irish mother and a Somali father, ten years before me, in 1957.

The Rage for Girls curriculum must show girls that their anger has every right to exist. It must keep their pilot light of anger burning strong and bright. It must be filled with women who have raged and won. Girls must see that anger is a most natural and justified force. It is the fuel necessary to defy patriarchy and the tangled web of oppressions it weaves to ensnare us in marginalization that goes further than just misogyny. It is the backbone of our defiance. It is the energy we need and, in many instances, crave.

I return often to the Black lesbian poet and feminist intellectual Audre Lorde's essay "Uses of Anger: Women Responding to Racism," in which she declares, "Every woman has a well-stocked arsenal of anger potentially useful against those oppressors, personal and institutional, which brought that anger into being. Focused with precision it can become a powerful source of energy serving progress and change."[19]

I have written this book for a global audience of feminist revolutionaries. The United States is not the center of the feminist universe. But the US behaves like it is the center of all universes, and the world pays it a lot of attention. And having lived in the United States since 2000, I have learned the denial that many white Americans succumb to when it comes to gender issues. Many white Americans will confidently tell you that "it's shit over there" for women—meaning anywhere but the US but too often concentrating on Muslim-majority countries—and in the same breath "be thankful that you live over here." Such denial only serves to strengthen patriarchy and to hurt those most affected by patriarchy and the myriad oppressions it allies with: women of color, working-class and poor women, disabled women, and queer and trans women. There is an unjustified overconfidence among white American women, especially about the achievements of feminism and what it has shielded them from. Few women around the world share the delusions of white American women about the achievements of feminism. Such overconfidence is one of the reasons that white American women finally began to be angry after Trump was elected. Where have they been? The fact that it took Trump to finally ignite white women's rage—not including the 47 percent[20] who voted for him—and not the decades of misogyny, racism, bigotry, and other forms of discrimination that led to it, is a reminder of how privileged and sheltered white American women have been from the injustices that ignite rage in Black women and girls, and for which they are punished and stereotyped. Those white women have allowed their race to trump their gender, believing that their docility, compliance, and allegiance to white supremacy will protect them from the ravages of patriarchy that the rest of us experience. They are what I call foot soldiers of the patriarchy. White women have the most privilege of expressing anger and are the last to express it, because they are sheltered from so much that ignites anger in the rest of us. Then, when white women finally find their anger, it is considered a revolution, when in reality they are finally catching up to the revolution of rage that swept up the rest of us.

When Black women warn us—from Anita Hill, whose 1991 testimony that US Supreme Court nominee Clarence Thomas sexually harassed her was not believed, to Tarana Burke, who since 2006 has been insisting we must say #MeToo to support women and girls with the least amount of power to fight patriarchy—America does not listen, because white supremacy is in power. When white American women finally feel the damage of patriarchy, they pay attention. It is time—it is way beyond time—for white American women to recognize that no amount of acquiescence will protect them from patriarchy.

For too long, men have called us names designed to insult, but also designed to imply we are too angry to be taken seriously: Feminazi. Ballbreaker. Crazy feminist. Bitch. Witch. Yes, I am those things, we must say. Yes, I am an angry woman. And angry women are free women.

CHAPTER 2

Attention

Unsolicited masculine sexual attention and the drive to control feminine bodies goes hand in hand.

—VIRGIE TOVAR, *You Have the Right to Remain Fat*[1]

WHO DO YOU THINK YOU ARE?
Ah, those words! Not so much music to my ears but the cue for my symphony for *your* ears. When I hear them now, they serve like the conductor's tap-tap-tap on her stand, sheet music in front of her, as she prepares her orchestra to fill a hall with its notes, harmonies, solos, and crescendos. There was a time when those words reeled me in, as the lasso of patriarchy they are designed to be. But now, instead of constraining me as the tools of shame and weapons of patriarchy meant to serve as gatekeepers of my ego and ability, they unleash the symphony of ME, MYSELF, AND I, which I have become a virtuoso at performing, which I know I deserve to stage, and which I perform so well that I compel you to listen.

What does my symphony of ME, MYSELF, AND I sound like? It sounds like me taking up space, filling up an entire hall. It sounds like me saying I have earned that space and you will listen. It sounds like me shouting: I deserve this! And it sounds like me saying I am important, what I have to say is important.

The most subversive thing a woman can do is talk about her life as if it really matters. It does. If anger is the first "sin" that defiantly tells patriarchy we are done waiting for it to self-correct, and if anger is loaded with energy, as Audre Lorde says, then when we use anger with focus and precision, it can create progress and change, then attention—demanding it, commanding it, seizing it—defies patriarchy by declaring "I count."

It is revolutionary to say "I count" when patriarchy demands that you must be "modest" and "humble." It is revolutionary to declare "I count" when according to patriarchy's twenty-four-hour cycle of attention, twenty-three hours and fifty-five minutes are the natural property of men. Women can forget about our fifteen minutes of fame—that's far too generous! Woe is the woman who demands more than her allotted five minutes.

Attention is power. When you command attention, you command power, and so patriarchy has muddied the waters around attention with the word "whore." A word intended to shame is used to convince women that to want attention is to want something shameful. Much like sex.

Attention, unlike sex, is something that the heteronormative patriarchy tells men they usually give and women usually take. Men take pleasure, while women give it. And so, when a woman gives sex away too "easily," she's labeled a "whore"; when she takes "too much" attention, she's also a whore—an "attention whore." Always a whore. Like sex, attention will always be used against you. Maybe it's because you want the "wrong" kind, or maybe it's because everything you do is "just for attention." Always a whore.

If it weren't for attention, and my command of it, I might not be alive.

Once upon a time I was arrested twice in less than a year in two different countries for essentially the same thing. That's because I am an enemy to patriarchy, everywhere. My feminist fight against patriarchy is one that I carry within me, like a portable revolution. It fuels every minute of each of my days, and it is a revolution that targets many things. Along with misogyny, I fight authoritarianism, racism, bigotry, and a host of other oppressions and injustices that prop up patriarchy. Think of patriarchy as an octopus, with each of its tentacles representing the oppressions it utilizes to move through our world. We must be reciprocally nimble and multifaceted in our fight against it.

Patriarchy does not exist in a vacuum. It does not operate on a Monday and a Thursday and then take a break, handing over the reins to the other oppressions until it is ready to strangle us with as many of its tentacles as it can again. Patriarchy utilizes several oppressions that we must target together if we want to be free.

During my two arrests, I was targeting several of those tentacles. The first time I was arrested—in Cairo in November 2011—I was not supposed to be there. I had been in Morocco speaking at a conference, after which I was booked to fly to Brussels to address the European parliament about women and revolutions. Instead, I bought a ticket to Cairo to be a woman in a revolution. While I was in Morocco, a protest had broken out on Mohamed Mahmoud Street, near Tahrir Square in Cairo. As I had since the January 25 revolution broke out earlier that year, I followed events in Egypt closely on social media such as Twitter and on news sites. I learned that the protest where I would eventually be arrested had begun after soldiers and police set fire to the tents of a peaceful sit-in by families who had lost loved ones during the January 25 revolution that had drawn millions of Egyptians to the streets earlier that year. The mass uprising forced the country's dictator, Hosni Mubarak, to step down on February 11 after thirty years in power. A military junta comprised of nineteen generals took over until elections were held. It had done little to hold accountable anyone from the regime—Mubarak officials or police—for the more than eight hundred Egyptians who were killed during the revolution (between January 25 and February 11).

Reading about snipers taking aim at the eyes of protesters and seeing photographs of the corpses of protesters being thrown into piles of trash by security forces enraged me. But I knew I had to join the protest when I read that boys as young as twelve were taking part, with their mothers' telephone numbers written in marker on their forearms so that if they were killed, the morgue knew who to call. I cried when I read a tweet by a woman who said an elderly man in the protest turned to her and urged her to return to Tahrir Square, telling her, "You look educated. I am old and will die soon and Egypt will need you and your skills. Don't put yourself in danger."

So in Cairo, after an activist friend of mine and I made it to the front line of the protest and were entrapped by plainclothes security people until riot police came to beat and arrest us, I was exactly where I should have been, because I believed in that protest and had joined it to honor the courage of those who had fallen and been hurt.

The riot police who surrounded me—three or four of them—beat me with their night sticks and then dragged me to a no-man's land that lay between a makeshift barrier that marked our front line and the security forces' front line. In the no-man's land, they sexually assaulted me, called me a whore, and then dragged me to their supervising officer who threatened me with gang rape. I was detained by the Interior Ministry for about six hours and then was taken to military intelligence, which held me for another six hours, during which they blindfolded me and interrogated me. During the twelve hours of my detention, I was denied the medical attention I had demanded for the injuries from my beating. When I was finally released and had returned to my hotel near Tahrir Square, a woman who followed me on Twitter offered to take me to the hospital. There, X-rays showed that the beating from the riot police had broken my left forearm and my right hand.

A cast was put on each of my arms from my wrist up to my shoulder, which I was told I needed to keep on for six weeks to give my fractures time to heal. After my time at the emergency room, some friends took me out for a meal and had to feed me and help me drink from a glass because my two arms in a cast rendered me unable to perform the simplest of tasks.

But I was lucky. I was alive—albeit with broken bones and a sexual assault—and I was free. Neither would have been the case were I not who I am. While riot police were beating me, I lost my smartphone, which meant that I effectively dropped off the radar for several hours. During my detention at the Interior Ministry, an activist I did not know had come to negotiate a truce with the police. I asked him to get me onto Twitter, where I had a following of about five thousand followers at the time. I tweeted "beaten, arrested, interior ministry." Almost immediately after, the activist's phone battery died. I found out later that soon after my tweet, the *Guardian* newspaper and *Al Jazeera* had reported about me and my tweet, the State Department had tweeted back to let me know they heard and would look for me, and that within fifteen minutes, #FreeMona was trending globally.

My fame saved me. If I were an unknown woman, I might well have been gang-raped or killed. Soon after I was treated for my injuries, I appeared—with both arms in casts and along with X-rays of my injuries—on one of the most popular television shows in Egypt to expose what the police had done to me by way of showing what they were doing to protesters. I also spoke to media from around the world. I emphasized that being a well-known writer had likely saved me from the even worse fate meted out to protesters who are not as well known.

Enter the Attention Detection Brigade.

I was accused by some of "throwing myself at police" so that they could hurt me so that I could appear on television. That was particularly stunning to hear, because I have appeared on television many times to share my expertise on a host of issues. During the eighteen days of the Egyptian revolution I had been on an array of television and radio shows to comment and analyze on events in Egypt. Prior to 2011 I had appeared on media outlets to talk about being Muslim in Europe and the US, women's rights in Saudi Arabia, and had commented on news such as the arrest of Saddam Hussein by US forces during the war in Iraq, the ban on face veils in France, and the role of freedom of expression in the aftermath of the publication of cartoons of the Prophet Mohammad in a Danish newspaper. I did not need to endure the pain of a broken arm that needed surgery and a hand fractured in two places so that I could appear on television. Perhaps worse, I was chided, *You are monopolizing your injuries for fame.* That was particularly infuriating because it was a reminder that you're damned if you do and damned if you don't. Women often don't report sexual assault because of shame or taboo or because police across the world do not take our reports seriously, and even if they do, the rate at which rape and sexual assault cases are tried in court, prosecuted, or end in conviction is low. Then we are condemned for not speaking out or for waiting too long to speak out. A feminist organization in Cairo told me that at least twelve other women were sexually assaulted in an almost identical manner during the protest where I had been beaten, assaulted, and detained, but that none of them had spoken about what had happened to them because they were ashamed or had been silenced by their families. And yet when I appeared on media to expose what the Egyptian regime's police did to me and reminded the audience that women with less privilege and less "fame" than I have fare much worse—I said in many interviews that if I were an unknown, working-class or poor Egyptian woman, I am not sure I would have survived—I was accused of "monopolizing my injuries for fame."

The second time I was arrested was in the New York City subway in September 2012, after I spray-painted over a pro-Israel advertisement I considered racist and Islamophobic. The ad read: "In any war between the civilized man and the savage, support the civilized man. Support Israel. Defeat jihad."[2] I was enraged that it portrayed support for Israel as the "civilized" option and opposition to Israel as being "savage." I was jailed overnight; arraigned before a judge; offered a plea deal, which I rejected; and set to stand trial until, two years later, the presiding judge dropped the charges in the interest of justice. My protest was a form of civil disobedience that I believe is necessary to make racism socially unacceptable. My protest was also a reminder that it is possible to leverage your fame, platform, and the attention you garner to fight against those tentacles that patriarchy entraps us with.

In the days before I spray-painted over the advertisement in the New York City subway, I learned that the ad was paid for by a group listed as an Islamophobic and racist hate group by the Southern Poverty Law Center. I learned that each ad cost $6,000 and that although the transportation authority had not wanted to post the ads in subway stations, a judge had ruled they were protected speech.

Some people had created alternative ads on social media such as Twitter, while others had considered protesting next to the ads while holding alternative messages. Here's where my thinking came in. I do not have $6,000 disposable income that I can devote to a counter-ad campaign. Racist groups have deep pockets! What I do have—my "wealth," so to speak—is the attention that I can garner, which, I feel, obliges me to fight harder than those who have less privilege. For example, I am a US citizen, which means that if I get arrested during a protest or at any other time, I have more rights than someone who is a resident or is undocumented. In the case of this ad, I wanted to leverage that privilege. Also, because I considered the bigotry behind the ad, sponsored, remember, by an anti-Muslim hate group, a form of bullying of Muslims, and because I am of Muslim descent, I wanted to be seen publicly fighting back: as a feminist especially, because so much media coverage of Muslims protesting offense is of angry Muslim men. I protested that ad because I was furious that in its wording, Israel and jihad were given as the two choices, and I choose neither, and because the use of "savage" juxtaposed with the word "civilized" was an old racist dog whistle that has been used against indigenous people, Black people, and all people whom white supremacists want to dehumanize to justify violence against them.

But I did not want to make my protest by merely standing next to the ad holding up an alternative. That would have been too polite. Racism and bigotry are not polite, and I refuse to be polite in my fight against them. Also, I chose to spray the word "racist" over the ad with hot-pink spray paint to play with the symbolism of pink, a color maligned because it's associated with girls, a color considered nonthreatening and which I wanted to use as part of my nonviolent civil disobedience. In the end I only managed to spray blobs of color because, as I realized as soon as I started to spray-paint, it is hard to control a can of that stuff!

I was charged with criminal mischief, making graffiti, and possession of a graffiti instrument. I was accused of being a "vandal." A racist and bigoted ad was deemed protected speech and my protest, which I consider also to be protected speech, was deemed vandalism. I am proud of my protest, and I would do it again. Since the election of Donald Trump as president, it has become obvious that the cries of "freedom of speech" that condemned my protest and those of others who had also protested and defaced the ad were cries that refused to recognize how white supremacists and Islamophobes were manipulating and weaponizing the importance of freedom of speech to fuel their hate and bigotry. Protecting freedom of speech is important, but for them it had become conflated with protecting their right to be racist and bigoted. And that must be protested and made socially unacceptable.

The patriarchy did not wait long to respond when I was released after twenty-two hours.

I was accused of "wanting" to get arrested for attention. It is true I wanted to get arrested. I wanted to highlight the importance of protesting racism as a way to make it socially unacceptable. But when I was accused of "staging" my spray-painting for publicity, I had to laugh. Again, I do not need to get arrested to be on television. I am often interviewed on various media outlets, and the journalists and editors who follow what I say in my columns and on social media pick up on issues that I highlight through my words or actions. Just as I do not need to have my arm and hand broken by the police to get attention or fame, I don't need an arrest for that either.

A newspaper's video team was coincidentally at the station where I spray-painted over the ad. They filmed my arrest, and the footage went viral. Part of the reason that happened is because I *am* already famous. I'm glad about that. I wanted opposition to the racist and bigoted ad to be known all over the world. I was not the only person who was arrested that day protesting the ad. Others were briefly detained for tearing the ads down or otherwise defacing them (several of the ads appeared throughout the subway system). When I heard from people across the US and from other parts of the world expressing solidarity and telling me that my protest and arrest had inspired them to be more vocal and public in their opposition to racism, I was glad that I "did it for attention."

Just as the attention that I garner helped save my life when I was assaulted in Cairo and helped kick into action a campaign to release me, attention helped me when I was arrested in New York City. A lawyer, Stanley Cohen, believed in my protest and represented me pro bono for two years until the charges were dismissed. Cohen told me when he came to represent me at my arraignment that activists from the Occupy Movement, who had learned via Twitter that I had been arrested, had alerted him of my arrest and asked him to help me. I am grateful for his help and for so generously donating his time in defense of my right to protest racism and bigotry. Cohen is a veteran activist who also understands the importance of attention for the various causes we fight for.

So it was no surprise that after I launched #MosqueMeToo I was yet again accused of "doing it for attention." I don't dispute that. Why would I? My ideas are important and they deserve attention.

I will take more than my allotted five minutes. Attention does not sully my message—it *enables* it. Attention is in fact necessary for my message to reach as big an audience as possible. As a writer and activist, I need attention for my words and the causes I fight for. Attention helped save my life in Cairo—how about that for irony, patriarchy? And attention helped me get legal representation in New York City. Take that, patriarchy.

Attention is a reward, a burden, a taunt, a taint, an accusation. Attention is a bone that patriarchy dangles in front of women: if we want it too much, we're whores; if we don't want attention when it determines we should have it, it stalks and beats us with it. We can't win.

And so we should refuse to play. We should defy and subvert patriarchy's rules on attention instead. Whether you are a female politician or a female model or a female novelist or a female cashier or a female anything, women are too often assumed to wake up with a single thing on our minds: how can I draw attention to myself? Thus, one of the quickest and most pernicious ways to diminish a woman who is too _____ (fill in the blank: loud, challenging, defiant, disruptive) is to accuse her of "doing it for attention."

Witness how in 2017, when Democratic US representative Frederica Wilson of Florida, said that President Donald Trump told the widow of a soldier killed in action in Niger that "he knew what he signed up for, but I guess it still hurt," the rinse-and-repeat cycle of the Attention Detecting Brigade—i.e., patriarchy—went into full swing. Trump accused Wilson of being a liar.[3] Conservative media outlets painted Wilson as "desperately seeking attention." Fox News.com published an opinion piece in which the author, a psychologist, accused Wilson repeatedly of being an attention seeker.[4]

This treatment is meant to achieve several goals. First, it aims to punish women who speak out, especially if our "attention seeking" directly challenges the patriarchy. In this case, Wilson had exposed the callousness of the president. Second, it is meant to undermine our original point: shaming us for speaking, then diminishing our intellectual authority. Third, because Wilson is a Black woman, she is judged more harshly. The queer Black feminist Moya Bailey has coined the term "misogynoir" to describe the double burden of misogyny and racism that Black women are subjected to.[5] Representative Wilson was not only challenging the patriarchy; she was also challenging white supremacy, both of which are embodied in the person of Donald Trump.

When reality TV star and model Amber Rose posted a photograph on Twitter in 2017 of herself in sunglasses, a bikini top, a coat, and nothing else to promote her annual Amber Rose SlutWalk Festival to raise awareness of gender inequality and sexual violence, British TV personality Piers Morgan was the most predictable Attention Detection Agent ever. He slut-shamed Rose: "'The only way for a woman to succeed in life is to post nude photos of themselves to millions of strangers'—said no true feminist ever," Morgan tweeted. And mansplained feminism to her: "This isn't feminism. It's attentionseekingism."[6]

Again: a white man took it upon himself to put a Black woman in her place, believing he was entitled to punish her by shaming her because she dared to command attention in a way she saw fit, in a way that defied what he, and, by extension, the patriarchy, disapproved of. Morgan's response was also a reminder of why SlutWalks began and why attention that does not acquiesce to patriarchy's dictates is attention women must be punished for receiving. In 2011 the *Toronto Star* reported that a Toronto police officer said that "women should avoid dressing like sluts in order not to be victimized."[7]

The bar that is set to judge women and find them guilty of "doing (x, y, z behavior) for attention" is so low because women are deemed worthy of just those metaphorical five minutes of the twenty-four-hour news cycle.

As evidence, examine how little we hear from women.

A 2017 Women's Media Center (WMC) report found that female journalists continue to report less of the news than do male journalists for twenty top news outlet shows in the US.[8] The "Divided 2017" statistics, which were released in conjunction with the WMC's annual *The Status of Women in the U.S. Media* report, found the gender gap was especially glaring in television: at ABC, CBS, and NBC, men report three times as much of the news as women do. The WMC, which monitored news outlets for three months of 2016, found that work by women anchors, field reporters, and correspondents actually declined from the previous year, falling to 25.2 percent of reports in 2016 from 32 percent, when the organization published its previous report in 2015. That gender gap also exists in traditional newspapers, online news, and wire services, the WMC report said.

It makes for depressing reading.

BROADCAST: Overall, men report 74.8 percent of the broadcast news; women report 25.2 percent.

NEWSPAPERS: Overall, men report 61.9 percent of the news in print; women report 38.1 percent. None of the print outlets achieves gender parity.

ONLINE NEWS: Men receive 53.9 percent of bylines.

WIRES: Men report 62.4 percent of the stories generated by the two main wire services. Women report 37.6 percent.

I was not joking about our allotted five minutes!

The gender gap is equally grim when it comes to movies, either appearing in them or making them. A study by the University of Southern California's Annenberg School for Communication and Journalism into the 1,100 highest grossing films from 2007 to 2017 found that women, minorities, and members of the LGBTQ and disabled communities are rarely heard or seen on the big screen.[9] Even worse, as *Variety* reported, "Men are two times more likely to have a speaking role in a movie than women and the number of female speaking roles in films has actually slipped from where it was in 2008 and 2009."[10]

Of the 48,757 characters in the films surveyed in the Annenberg study, just 30.6 percent were female speaking characters, which is a reminder of how patriarchy assigns importance to men over women generally. But look what happens to that allotted five minutes for women when you factor race, ability, and sexuality: of the 30.6 percent allotted to female speaking characters, just 29.3 percent of those characters were from underrepresented racial/ethnic groups, 2.5 percent had disabilities, and less than 1 percent were members of the LGBTQ community.

It is imperative, always, to understand that patriarchy intertwines with other systems of oppression to create a hierarchy of favor and marginalization. In the top one hundred films of 2017, forty-three films had no Black or African American female characters, sixty-five were lacking Asian or Asian American female characters, and sixty-four films had not even a single Latinx woman character.[11] Seventy-eight films depicted no female character with a disability, and ninety-four films did not have a single female lesbian, bisexual, or transgender character. In the hierarchy of attention, the transgender community is the most marginalized and rendered invisible: in four hundred films from 2014 to 2017, there was only one trans character, according to the Annenberg study.

Part of the reason that films fail to reflect the diversity of our reality can be explained by the lack of diversity of those who make those films. The Annenberg study of the 1,100 highest-grossing films from 2007 to 2017 found that of the 1,223 directors surveyed, just 4.3 percent were female, just 5.2 percent were Black or African American, and just 3.1 percent were Asian or Asian American. But I believe there is more to the lack of parity than those statistics might indicate.

Patriarchy uses attention as a reward for those it anoints as worthy: The white. The thin. The cisgender. The feminine. The able-bodied. When we say "pay attention," we should be cognizant of the aspect of reward at play. Patriarchy pays attention to those who fall within its conventional notions of beauty. Those conventions depend on where you live, but in many parts of the world, for example, due to the legacies of white European colonial power and the more contemporary prevalence of Hollywood-produced films (as discussed in the Annenberg study) in which white supremacy has promoted whiteness as the default, the Eurocentric notion of white feminine beauty is paramount.

The converse is also true. By withholding attention, by not "paying" it, patriarchy punishes. Attention is withheld from fat women. Attention is paid to femininity in women. For transgender women, attention can be both a reward and life threatening. There is pressure on transgender women to conform to femininity—to pass, to conform to conventional notions of beauty, so that they are rewarded with the "right" kind of attention that admires rather than the wrong kind that is suspicious and violent and punishes their inability to conform. Trans women of color in the United States have an average lifespan of thirty-five years.[12] The less a trans woman "passes," the more violence she is subjected to. The further one is from whiteness and thinness, the further from "beautiful," according to the patriarchy and its cisgender standards, the less deserving of attention. Attention is both reward and punishment. It is how patriarchy regulates us.

What would the world look like if we did not wait to be anointed worthy of attention according to patriarchy's standards? What if we commanded, seized, and created attention instead of waited to be "paid" attention?

Again, the most subversive thing a woman can do is to talk about her life as if it really matters, because it does. It is in the name of that subversion, for the sake of defying the patriarchy, that we must declare, "I deserve attention," "I demand attention," and "My life is important, my views are important, and they deserve attention." We must understand the importance and power of being "attention whores."

How revolutionary is seizing attention with our stories? The power of commanding attention was a primary driver in the revolution of Irish women who, in 2018, galvanized their compatriots to overwhelmingly repeal by referendum the Eighth Amendment of the Irish constitution. The successful vote made possible the reform of abortion laws in Ireland, which were so prohibitive that a stream of women who could afford it made their way to England every year to get a medical procedure they were denied in their own country, and some of those who could not were forced to carry to term a pregnancy they did not want, while others died because they were denied a procedure that was necessary to save their life. By voting to repeal the Eighth Amendment, the people of Ireland were repealing a clause that had been inserted into their constitution in 1983 and gave the "unborn" a right to life equal to that of a pregnant woman. In an exit poll conducted by Irish state broadcaster RTE, in answer to "What had the biggest impact on your vote?"

- 43 percent cited personal stories of women in the media.
- 34 percent said it was the experiences of people they knew.
- 10 percent said it was posters and campaigns leaflets.
- 7 percent cited direct contact with campaigners.
- 24 percent said "other factors."[13]

In other words, attention won the day: the belief that women's stories were important and deserving of attention, that the experiences of Irish women were worth the attention of their country. Put simply: women count.

The revolutionary power of saying "I count" has been especially poignant for me as an Egyptian. My country of birth has been under military rule since 1952. No revolution happens overnight, and January 25, 2011, was no exception. One of the many factors that led to that revolution, I believe, was the increasing ability—facilitated by blogs and social media—of young people to say "I count." In a country where you are barred from having any say in politics, culture, or the economy; where expression and assembly are severely curtailed; where old people—read: old men—whether in military garb or in civilian dress run and control everything, there is a revolutionary thrill to saying "I count." I am not saying that blogs or social media caused the revolution or that it was a "Facebook revolution," as some have erroneously called it. Revolutions require courage and risk and feet on the ground. Oppressed people have a need to recognize their right to exist, to protest injustice, and to revolt against tyranny, and they have a need to recognize that they are capable of and have a right to say "I count. I deserve better." By saying those things on blogs and on social media, and also by finding kindred spirits—others saying "I count" and "I deserve better"—young Egyptians especially understood their individual power in a milieu that often favored the group over the individual. They also discovered the collective power of several people saying "I count" and "I deserve better." The revolution announces itself when the individual and the collective connect and become ready to risk putting their feet on the ground for an uprising.

That is how I see the individual and collective power of women demanding and seizing attention. Conversely, that is why women are shamed for "doing it for attention." Patriarchy recognizes the potential power of saying "I count" and "I deserve attention." And patriarchy recognizes, much as Egypt's military dictatorship does, the collective power of women seeing and learning from and showing solidarity with each other's "I count."

When I started #MosqueMeToo to encourage fellow Muslim women to share experiences of sexual harassment and assault during the pilgrimage, or hajj, and at other sacred places such as mosques, the Attention Detection Brigade was ever vigilant. I was told both that I didn't "deserve" attention—as if being sexually assaulted was a compliment—and I was told that I was talking about the sexual assaults I'd been subjected to because I wanted attention. The distance from *You're an ugly lying whore. Who would want to sexually assault you?* to *You just want attention* is classic patriarchy.

Regardless of where and how a woman exposes sexual harassment and assault, regardless of who she is, what she was wearing, and whether she was sexually assaulted in a sacred place or a secular one, she is more than likely going to be told she is just angling for attention. As if recounting trauma brought us multi-film deals and eternal fame and fortune, instead of what we actually endure: suspicion, condemnation, judgement, and vitriol.

It helps to see patriarchy as oppressive as military rule has been in Egypt, in order to appreciate the revolutionary potential of social media, as alternatives to mainstream media/traditional media. Social media can serve as a platform for women, nonbinary people, and the queer community, collectively and individually, to say "I count" and "I deserve attention," and it can carve spaces where women and nonbinary people can find each other in ways that were previously not possible. A cursory glance at women who have seized attention online makes it clear how threatening such defiance is to the patriarchy and its ability to wield attention as a bone to reward or to punish us. Such women who have imposed a discourse that was not there before, who show us the importance of saying "Look at me on my own terms," are quickly derided as narcissists or, worse, are punished for daring to say "I count."

In the space of six weeks in 2018, four prominent Iraqi women were murdered or died in mysterious circumstances—Instagram star Tara Fares, women's rights activist Su'ad al-Ali, prominent beautician Rasha al-Hassan, and plastic surgeon Rafif al-Yassiri. Note the common denominator: attention and beauty.[14]

After Fares was shot dead in her car, her friend Israa al-Obaidi, the model and Instagrammer, left Iraq. Obaidi herself had received death threats for "daring to be visible in a conservative country," according to *Deutsche Welle*.[15]

"The Iraqi woman is targeted because of freedom," Obaidi told *DW*. "There are some people that do not want women to have freedom to speak, wear what she wants and work, because we now have an important role and our voices are being heard."

Iraq has not recovered from the ruinous US invasion in 2003 and the subsequent war, but whether in times of war or in times of peace, regardless of political system or religious belief, one thing is clear: patriarchy is everywhere. The misogyny it enables and protects is especially vicious in wartime, when the bodies of women become proxy battlegrounds where rape and sexual violence are used as weapons and when women are often the most affected by draconian measures of "law and order," established to control the chaos unleashed by war and conflicts. Those four prominent Iraqi women were targeted and punished for daring to command attention, for believing "I count," and as an example to other women of what awaits them if they similarly dare. Their killings are a reminder of how threatening it is to patriarchy when a woman commands attention.

The murder of Fares, especially, echoed the killing of Pakistani social media star Qandeel Baloch in 2016. The brother of the twenty-six-year-old celebrity publicly confessed to being "proud" that he had drugged and then strangled Baloch.[16] Apparently, he did not like the attention her popularity had garnered, although ironically he was fine with all the media attention he garnered when he confessed to killing his sister. There is attention, and there is attention.

In a poignant tribute to Qandeel, Issam Ahmed, the Pakistan corre-spondent for the Agence France Presse news service, captured the subver-siveness and the danger of Qandeel's high profile when he wrote, "We could see that what Qandeel was doing was different: she wasn't seeking the spotlight, she was seizing it, and turning its full glare on Pakistan."[17]

That is the revolutionary power of seizing attention. It can get you killed, yes, because it deeply threatens patriarchy's ability to control you. Despite whatever progress Pakistan had made in women's rights, including having a female prime minister in Benazir Bhutto, who was assassinated—again the price a woman pays for commanding attention—wrote Ahmed: "this seeming progress toward gender equality belies *the everyday struggles that women are forced to endure at the hands of men who seek complete control over everything, from how they dress and speak to their access to public and pro-fessional space* (emphasis added)." Ahmed's words are an almost direct echo of those of Israa al-Obaidi when she talks about the targeting of prominent women in Iraq. What does seizing attention and then turning its full glare on Pakistan or Iraq or anywhere mean? It means exposing the hypocrisy of patriarchy in the way that it determines who can and who can't demand attention.

Why are women who seize attention like Qandeel so revolutionary, even as some of their cohorts and seemingly natural allies criticize and diminish their importance? Ahmed notes that some Pakistani liberals dis-missed Qandeel as an "attention-seeking diva" because they considered her "so far removed from the norm that her antics would not serve any cause but her own." What does that actually mean, when Qandeel would often say that she heard from other young women in Pakistan saying that she emboldened them? Why must a woman be firmly within the accepted norms of her society in order to be considered worthy of whatever at-tention she garners? Surely those "liberals" were spouting the patriarchal line that divvies out attention like a reward to those women it deems worthy of it.

I agree with Ahmed when he writes, "In Pakistan's reality, [Qandeel's] willingness to embrace her sexuality and defy societal norms was a bold, deeply political statement." Surely, I believe, if your "community" is ready for you, you are too late! The revolutionary potential of Qandeel was, as Ahmed writes, this simple: "a loud, proud, in-your-face feminism that sought approval from no one." That is what made her a threat, and it was that threat that her brother strangled, so proudly.

Qandeel Baloch embodied the importance and the danger of attention in the fight against patriarchy. For the longest time, and still the case in so many places, men spoke and we listened with no ability and no platform on which to talk back. Now we are talking back and we have platforms on which to talk back. Qandeel Baloch's brother murdered her soon after his sister posted selfies with a senior Islamic cleric in Pakistan, which spurred a media frenzy that caused the cleric to lose his government job. According to Issam Ahmed, the selfies that Qandeel posted of herself donning the cleric's hat were her way of "poking fun not only at the hypocrisy of the cleric but Pakistan's clergy in general."

"He is a blot on the name of Islam. Who is he to claim to be a guardian of the faith?" Qandeel had told Ahmed of the cleric.

According to CNN, Qandeel's brother called that particular controversy over the selfies, which had outraged their conservative rural community, "the end of it," saying, "I planned this after her scandal with the mufti and was waiting for the right time."[18] The frenzy led to Qandeel Baloch's real name being revealed and to demands by her family's community that her brother do something about it; in other words, to silence her.

It is dangerous to say "I count," and it is dangerous to poke fun at the self-importance of the appointed guardians of the patriarchy. Qandeel "didn't realise she was crossing the line," Shehryar Mufti, front man of the Pakistani rock group Bumbu Sauce, told the *Guardian*. "It is one thing to challenge an abstract notion like society or patriarchy. It is another thing entirely to call a state-endorsed cleric out on being a complete sleaze."[19]

What is that "line" and who draws it? In the competition Woman vs. Community, attention is used against the woman to maintain the power of the community. If she seizes too much, she must be brought back into line. If she says things that the community deems "wrong" or "dangerous," she must be reeled in. What is that "community" and whose interests does it represent?

Too often, "community" is synonymous with men and the privileges of patriarchy, and too often, self-appointed male leaders of the "community" are the ones who determine what sort of behavior is "too far." The word and the concept "community" are much like the word and concept "culture." They are a popular way to rein in people—read: "women"—and tell them that they must not oppose a behavior or way of being because it is part of the "culture" or what the "community" wants. Who determined that it was culture and who speaks for the community? Men and men. That is the simple answer. The more complicated answer is men and men *and* a social construct, a system—patriarchy—that enables and protects them at the same time it socializes women to internalize the dictates of patriarchy and accept them as culture and as community. If women created culture and community, we would not be accused of "going too far."

We must protect the perceived outliers of the community because it is on the margins, where the community has consigned them, that the revolution begins. The revolution does not begin in the middle. The middle is too comfortable and too invested in the status quo. The middle is in the stranglehold of patriarchy and the tentacles of oppressions patriarchy uses to bolster its hold. And that is why attention is important for those on the margins, the outliers, and we must resist the urges of the "community" to bring us all into line. By demanding that Qandeel be taught a lesson, patriarchy was reaffirming its right to punish those it deems unworthy of attention. Qandeel Baloch's death was a terrible reminder of the price paid by those who dare to seize attention. To honor her, we must keep seizing attention and consider it part of our revolutionary arsenal against patriarchy. We have been taught a false humility. We must defiantly declare that we deserve attention. We must understand that patriarchy uses false scarcity to pit us against each other. Women who have a platform must signal-boost those who have less. We must understand that patriarchy pits us against each other, and we must resist its prodding to tear down "attention whores." We must all become attention whores.

Self-expression is important for those marginalized by patriarchy: Fat women, trans women, disabled women, nonbinary people, and the queer community, who are too often punished by invisibility. All women deemed unworthy by patriarchy of attention.

In her book *You Have the Right to Remain Fat*, Virgie Tovar reminds us that patriarchy's prevailing beauty standards control women's body size as a way of controlling their lives. It rewards those it deems "beautiful" with attention, at the same time punishing those it deems unworthy for any attention they garner.[20]

"The years I spent being taught fatphobia by my peers growing up, and then by media destroyed my sense of self," Tovar writes.

> All that was left in the wake of my dazzling and silly personality was a desire to never feel like an outsider again. Being weird and bossy and theatrical and curious had always been the best things about me. But those qualities attracted attention, and attention was emotionally dangerous. All that was left was a traumatized approval-seeking girl with no sense of her own magic. It was disproportionately at the hands of boys my age that I was taught that I was worthless. The justification was that they didn't find me desirable and this was a punishable offense to them.

Ask who you don't see and understand why you don't see them and understand how important attention is for them. We can use attention as a way to arm ourselves against the invisibility that patriarchy wants to impose on us. Social media has become a platform for that fight, from accounts that document the experiences of trans women and men to accounts of fat activists who not only espouse body positivity as a tool against pressures on women especially to succumb to thinness but also to fight the ways patriarchy rewards some bodies and punishes others. A popular refrain is "effyourbeautystandards" (fuck your beauty standards). What does it mean to snatch attention like that? To say "Look at me," when patriarchy does not think you should be seen? It means rendering patriarchy's power moot. We do not need the blessing of patriarchy. We are worthy of attention as we are. We deserve attention.

After Egyptian riot police broke my left arm and right hand, I dyed my hair red because I wanted to be seen. I wanted to say, "Fuck you, you didn't kill me. I am still here. I am not scared. I am not hiding. You can't miss this red hair." And I moved back to Cairo from New York City. A friend suggested I revert to black hair so that I wouldn't stick out in Cairo, but that's exactly what I wanted: to stick out.

At the age of sixteen, I vowed I would become a journalist because I wanted to be free. My family had moved to Saudi Arabia from the UK in 1982 and I felt like I had been put on trial, found guilty of being a teenage girl and sentenced to life in prison. Being a journalist would be my way out, I was convinced. It would be expansive, and it would be the antithesis of the suffocation of my life in Jeddah.

I kept that vow to myself. I did indeed become a journalist. Over a ten-year period, I reported from Egypt, Libya, Syria, Saudi Arabia, Israel, Palestine, and China. I am proud of the reporting I did for a number of media outlets. But when I moved to the US in 2000, reporting no longer felt as expansive as it did when I was sixteen. After the attacks on September 11, 2001, when Muslims were spoken about and spoken over, and few if any Muslim women were speaking for themselves, I was less interested in reporting the views of others and wanted to tell the world my views—I wanted to use "I." And so I vowed I would become an opinion writer.

I kept that vow to myself. Very soon after I began to say "I" in my opinion columns, I was put on yet another (symbolic) trial, charged with the double crime of being audacious enough to think that my "I" counted and that I deserved an opinion. I was found guilty of being a woman writer and given the life sentence of that easiest of epithets for women: an attention seeker. When the Attention Detection Brigade that presides over the trials of women is in a particularly poetic mood, the epithet became "attention whore."

Saying "I" in my weekly columns meant I had to be punished. I used to dread the online comments posted to the newspaper's website. They would often accuse me of having my column dictated/written by a "boyfriend," because who could imagine a woman saying "I count"?

You need a robust ego to be a feminist. You need a massive amount of faith in yourself and your right to be seen and heard in order to be a warrior against patriarchy—because it is war. And one of the most effective ways that patriarchy disarms us, and leaves us insufficiently prepared for that war, is by stripping us of our right to attention. Seize it. Demand it. Command it. Patriarchy scares us into a false humility by calling us "attention whores" just as it scares us of the word "whore." I am a whore. There. I said it. Say it. And seize attention.

CHAPTER 3

Profanity

Uncle Sam, I want to know what you're doing with my fucking tax money. . . . Because I'm from New York, and the streets is always dirty. We was voted the dirtiest city in America. There are still rats on the damn trains. I know you're not spending it in no damn prison because y'all be giving n****s like two underwears, one jumpsuit for like five months. . . . What is y'all doing with my fucking money? . . . I want to know. I want receipts. I want everything.

—CARDI B[1]

MY NAME IS Mona Eltahawy and this is my declaration of faith: Fuck the patriarchy.

Whenever I stand at a podium to give a lecture, I begin with that declaration of faith. Whether I am speaking on a panel on feminism in front of an audience of one thousand in Lahore, Pakistan; at a summit for activists and politicians working to end violence against women and children in Dublin, Ireland; on a stage as part of an evening of multigenerational African feminists in Johannesburg, South Africa; or at a lunch for medical students in New York City, USA, my declaration never changes.

I could say, "Dismantle the patriarchy." Or, "Smash the patriarchy." Or use any number of verbs that signal urgency, but I don't. I am a writer, and I understand how language works. I understand how audiences—and readers—react to the language I use. I know exactly what I am doing. And I say, "Fuck the patriarchy," because I am a woman, a woman of color, a Muslim woman. And I am not supposed to say "fuck."

In my experience, almost nothing can match the power of profanity delivered by a woman at a podium, unapologetically. Because how many women—not to mention women of color or Muslim women or working-class women, or, or, or . . . —are ever even invited to the podium? And of those, how many, when they get on stage, still speak as if they are asking for permission to speak? I have lost count of the number of times that I have heard women on a panel preface every contribution as if our right to speak is an imposition, as if our contribution is a burden, as if our thoughts are secondary or tertiary even to the discussion at hand. How many times do you hear a woman dismiss or diminish her right to comment on an issue by saying, "I am not an expert, but . . ."? How many times are women interrupted, spoken over, and spoken for?

We must recognize that the ubiquitous ways patriarchy has socialized women to shrink themselves—physically and intellectually—extend also into language, into what we can and cannot say. It is not just a fight for airtime. It is not just a policing of women's egos. It polices women's very language.

At the heart of that policing, standing guard over our language like a baton ready to strike, is a concept that seems deceptively simple: civility.

When Donald Trump was elected, many truths that white Americans were oblivious to—willingly or naively—were forced onto their consciousness. It was impossible to deny that racism was a driving force behind his election, and yet analysts and pundits insisted it was the "suffering working class" (read: white working class) and "economic anxiety," as if people of color who were working class were immune from suffering or economic anxiety. Many white Americans exclaimed, "This is not the America I know," precisely because they had refused to or had never had to come face to face with that racism, and Trump's shameless expression of racism and bigotry finally forced some of them to see that America. Those of us who are not white and who have experienced that racism all too well have long known that America. Denial and gaslighting—the latter, a form of psychological abuse that aims to make someone doubt their own thoughts, beliefs, and perceptions—went on full throttle as talking heads, politicians, media, and others went out of their way to blame everything but racism for Trump's success at the polls. Moreover, those of us who insisted on calling racism what it was rather than by a series of euphemisms were urged not to call a racist a racist, and we were instructed to be civil when arguing with Trump supporters. For the sake of unity, free speech, and healing, civility was held up as paramount. The obsession with civility, no matter what, was at times bipartisan, as when both Congresswoman Nancy Pelosi, a Democrat, and Congressman Steve Scalise, a Republican—both of whom are white—criticized Maxine Waters, a Black Democratic congresswoman, for encouraging her supporters to protest Trump administration officials in public wherever they saw them.[2]

But paramount to whom? Who does civility serve?

Racism is not civil. Racism is not polite. And yet here were all those people lined up to insist that we be civil when talking about Trump and his supporters. Those people lined up to insist on civility were, of course, white. For white Americans who have no experience of racism, it is a concept, a theory, an idea to be debated, and not a lived reality to be endured or survived. Fuck that.

Those who insist on civility in the face of its very opposite are those least affected by the incivility that Trump represents. They have more power and privilege than most of us. It is imperative to recognize that we are not playing on a level playing field. I refuse to be civil with someone who refuses to acknowledge my humanity fully.

It is often easier to point out the incivility of racism than it is to point out the incivility of patriarchy. But just as civility is a luxury that only those unaffected by the bold racism of the Trump era can afford, I believe civility is similarly a luxury afforded by those unaffected by patriarchy. I will not be civil to anything or anyone that refuses to acknowledge the full humanity of women and girls. This is a battle. To that end, the shock and the offense profanity causes are necessary and important.

Filthy. Disgraceful. Indecent. Vulgar. That is what the powerful and their enablers will call you if you dare poke them in the eye—even when you are invited to do it.

Take comedian Michelle Wolf who, in April 2018, let loose a bipartisan evisceration of Beltway politicians and media in her role as host/performer at the White House Correspondents' Dinner. (Tellingly, the notoriously thin-skinned President Donald Trump did not attend.) After peppering her speech with several swear words, as well as references to sex acts and genitalia, Wolf was criticized by an uneasy alliance of both supposedly free-speech obsessed conservatives and supposedly free-speech obsessed journalists. The hypocrisy was hard to miss.

"I think sometimes they look at a woman and they think, 'Oh, she'll be nice,' and if you've seen any of my comedy, you know that I don't—I'm not," Wolf told National Public Radio (NPR) after the event.[3] "I think they still have preconceived notions of how women will present themselves, and I don't fit in that box."

It is instructive that in the era of Trump—a man who has torpedoed the notion of civility—women are still expected to be polite and demure. One criticism of her performance was that she did not cater to the room: "She knew that the speech—at least in parts—was likely to go over like a lead balloon in the room. And that it would stir huge amounts of controversy in its wake. THAT WAS THE POINT," wrote CNN editor-at-large Chris Cilliza.[4]

At a time when the word "resistance" has been sanitized and neutered, a "vulgar" Wolf understood the power of words and used them to deliver a knockout punch to a crowd more accustomed to being comfortable. As Cillizza put it: "She wanted to napalm the room and she did. Unapologetically."

That is the power of profanity—and why it is important for women to not shy away from it.

Trump has boasted that his celebrity lets him "grab [women] by the pussy." He has used a host of epithets to describe women, whether they're journalists, political opponents, or TV hosts. He has gone out of his way to be the antithesis of civil toward Black women, displaying blatant misogynoir in a country where Black women are disproportionately affected by violence and where medical negligence leaves them especially vulnerable.[5] It is stunning that women are still expected to cater to the room.

Profanity is an essential tool in disrupting patriarchy and its rules. It is the verbal equivalent of civil disobedience. Fewer people are as expert at disrupting patriarchal authority with the power of her words than the Ugandan scholar and feminist Stella Nyanzi, an epidemiologist at Makerere University who holds a PhD in sexuality and queer studies. She understands the agility of words and their ability to disturb the powerful and their networks of wealth and privilege. She describes herself as a "queer laughist" and defends LGBTQ rights in a country where homosexuality is illegal and where, the *Guardian* reports, the first lady—known as Mama Janet—"has been accused of working with extremist US evangelical

Christians to spread homophobia in Uganda [and] said she serves only because she was appointed by God."[6]

Nyanzi is an activist who goes to schools to teach girls and boys how menstrual health products are used in a country where it is estimated that at least 30 percent of teenage girls miss school when they start their period, according to the nongovernmental organization (NGO) Build Africa.[7] Sanitary pads are imported in Uganda and too expensive for many families. Of the girls that Build Africa spoke to, 90 percent said they used rags in place of pads during their period.

Nyanzi is a feminist who has stripped naked at her university to protest the closure of her office and who talks openly about sex in a country where women are expected to be "gentle and quiet" and, as journalist Barbara Among told Canada's *Globe and Mail*, discuss sex and menstruation only in private with a mother or aunt.[8]

In other words, Nyanzi is a force who strategically uses profanity to take aim at patriarchy on behalf of those most harmed by it. When Uganda president Yoweri Museveni—who has been in power since 1986—reneged on an election promise to provide Ugandan schoolgirls with sanitary napkins, Nyanzi took to Facebook, writing, "That is what buttocks do. They shake, jiggle, shit and fart. Museveni is just another pair of buttocks. . . . Ugandans should be shocked that we allowed these buttocks to continue leading our country."[9]

That has been described as the least expletive-laden of the insults she had flung at Museveni by then, and yet she was detained in a maximum security prison for five weeks in 2017, ostensibly over that post. Many suspect however that her detention was more likely connected to her criticism of "Mama Janet," the first lady, Janet Kataaha Museveni, who told parliament in her capacity as education minister—a position she was given by her husband—that there was no money for menstrual health products.

"What malice plays in the heart of a woman who sleeps with a man who finds money for millions of bullets, billions of bribes, and uncountable ballots to stuff into boxes but she cannot ask him to prioritise sanitary pads for poor schoolgirls?" Nyanzi asked on Facebook.[10]

Nyanzi is a hero. Her insistence on violating patriarchy's rules by talking explicitly about taboo subjects—be they the president's buttocks, sex, sexuality, queerness—should be studied everywhere as a masterclass in the power of refusing to obey the rules of "politeness." Who made those rules?

"Uganda was colonized and Christianized by the British. . . . We were brought up to be good girls, to be decent, to be polite, to speak nicely to authority. Women here are not to be heard, they shut up, they don't speak, they're to be seen as beautiful," Nyanzi told the *Globe and Mail* in 2017, explaining perfectly the origins of "civility" and why profanity is a powerful tool to upend that civility, which is foundational to patriarchy.[11]

Under the British and other empires, white, Christian values were imposed on colonized people—a narrow set of values, of what is and is not "decent" and "respectable." It was against that set of values that "radical rudeness" was used by activists in colonial Uganda.

In an article in the *Journal of Social History* historian Carol Summers explains that activists in 1940s colonial Uganda, especially in the kingdom of Buganda, defied, disobeyed, and disrupted power—both of the British colonizers and of the colonizers' local allies—via "a rude, publicly celebrated strategy of insults, scandal mongering, disruption, and disorderliness that broke conventions of colonial friendship, partnership, and mutual benefit."[12]

Who determines what is "civil" and what is "rude"? Who benefits from upholding those social codes? In the 1940s it was British colonizers—the patriarchs of their day—and the networks of power they facilitated.

To place Nyanzi's deliberate profanity within the historical Ugandan context—and to understand the disruptive power of rudeness then and now—it is instructive to note that what made the rudeness of the "disorderly, intemperate and obnoxious" Buganda rebels "more than just adolescent immaturity . . . was that it was rooted in an understanding of the significance of social rituals, constituted a strategy to disrupt them, and was tied to an effort to build new sorts of public sociability to replace the older elite private networks."

In other words, it is imperative to understand how civility, decorum, manners, and the like are used to uphold authority—patriarchy, whiteness, other forms of privilege—and that we are urged to acquiesce as a form of maintaining that authority. Whether we are urged to be civil to racists or polite to patriarchy, the goal is the same: to maintain the power of the racist, to maintain the power of patriarchy.

Pause for a minute and reflect: how does one woman and her Facebook posts threaten a man who has ruled for over three decades?

It is rare that a formidable opponent to power focuses so much of their opposition on the well-being of that most neglected of demographics: girls, and especially poor girls. Poor girls around the world who menstruate miss school days. Further, the United Nations children's agency UNICEF estimates that around 60 percent of girls miss school in Uganda because their schools lack separate toilets and washing facilities to help girls manage their periods, and the aid agency Plan International says hundreds of girls in Uganda are susceptible to child marriages after parents pull them from school after their periods start.[13] This is obviously not an exclusively Ugandan problem, but Nyanzi is starting her fight where she is.

The *Guardian* reported that when Nyanzi was first summoned to the criminal investigation directorate over her Facebook posts, she asked supporters to go with her and bring with them sanitary pads that would be delivered to Ugandan girls.[14] And there, in front of the offices of investigators, out of that act of defiance in a country where menstruation is supposed to be whispered about, Nyanzi launched Pads4GirlsUG, a crowdfunding campaign to raise enough money to provide pads for one million girls. Two weeks later that goal was reached thanks to donations from people inside and outside Uganda. Nyanzi was arrested and detained at the end of a fund-raiser for the cause, in April 2017, more than two months after she put the "pair of buttocks" post on Facebook. Perhaps Nyanzi was also being punished for acting to fill a void left by the state. Authoritarians insist on being the only providers for their impoverished populace, even when they claim they do not have enough money to provide what they had promised, even when those authoritarians enjoy wealth accumulated over three decades, and even when they refuse to allow anyone else to provide an alternative, either politically or financially. In any case, it strongly appeared that Nyanzi was being chastised for the "rudeness" of her words and actions.

According to Maria Burnett, associate director of the Africa division of Human Rights Watch, Museveni wanted to punish Nyanzi and by extension also threaten her supporters, already beleaguered by his homophobia and authoritarianism. "There is no doubt that the way in which she was arrested was about seeking to intimidate and terrify her and her family and her community of supporters who are largely drawn from Uganda's human rights, women's and LGBTI movements."[15]

Nyanzi was charged under the 2011 Computer Misuse Act with "offensive communication" and "cyber harassment" of the president. She pleaded not guilty but was denied bail and detained in a maximum security prison for five weeks.

Ever the radical and ever rude, Nyanzi was adamant that the judge and the court understand her words and actions. Her friend, the prominent Ugandan LGBT activist Kasha Jacqueline Nabagesera, wrote on Facebook that Nyanzi told the judge: "Offensive communication? Who is offended? How long are Ugandans going to be silent because of fear? . . . I am an academic, poet. A writer. I use my writing metaphorically. I have called the president impotent, a rapist, a pathetic pair of buttocks. He lied to voters that he would provide pads and Ugandans are offended that he is such a dishonorable man. It is we who are offended, not him."[16]

After she was released on bail following her arrest in 2017, Ugandan prosecutors demanded that Nyanzi be subjected to a psychiatric evaluation under the terms of a rarely used colonial-era law—because, of course, only a crazy woman would dare insult the president in this way. "They just want to declare her an idiot so they delegitimize a legitimate form of expression, and send her away to a mental health hospital," said Nyanzi's lawyer Nicholas Opiyo, who is also director of the civil liberties NGO Chapter Four Uganda.[17]

What is it that threatens Museveni so? Why do the Facebook posts of Nyanzi and her needling of Mama Janet so bother the Musevenis?

"In the past, Museveni's major opponents have either been a sitting government, gun-toting rebels, or social media activists hiding behind pseudonyms, and fellow politicians who have challenged him in elections," wrote Haggai Matsiko.[18] "Most have been men and they have used weapons that Museveni has always found ways to outmatch given his firm grip on state resources."

Enter Nyanzi, who told the *Globe and Mail* that language was her "soft ammunition" in a nonviolent struggle.

"What other avenues do we have left to us?" Nyanzi asked "We don't have guns or money. But I can still write and think and insult and abuse."[19]

Dictators, authoritarians, and patriarchs demand obedience, despise disruption, and are especially angered by disrespect. In fact, they consider any demand for accountability a form of disrespect. How dare we question them? How dare we expect justice? How dare we dare to be anything but quivering and fearful? How dare we tell them to fuck off, for any reason at all? We are not obligated to show respect to those in power. How dare Nyanzi highlight the hollow promise of a dictator who co-opts poverty for electioneering? How dare Nyanzi demand accountability from a dictator who himself demands and is used to getting acquiescence?

And yet calling the president a "pair of buttocks" is offensive! And yet talking about periods—blood, something that comes out of vaginas!—is offensive! In Uganda, as in too many countries around the world, menstruation remains taboo. Not only are girls unable to afford sanitary products, not only do their schools fail to provide them with sufficient and separate washrooms to help them manage their periods, not only is the president of their country monopolizing period poverty for hollow election promises, but girls and women are also expected to shut up about it, because talking about periods is considered rude and makes people uncomfortable. Heaven forbid we talk about blood! Remember: commercials for sanitary products use a blue liquid as a stand-in for menstrual blood. God forbid we make men uncomfortable!

What is more offensive—that Nyanzi called the president of her country a "pair of buttocks" or that girls are missing out on and dropping out of school? Surely such misogyny is more offensive than words. Consider that the same president targeted by Nyanzi's profanity has himself assumed the right to be profane, warning his enemies that they would be "touching the anus of a leopard" (playing with fire) if they dared cross him.[20] But of course the patriarch gives himself rights he denies others, especially pesky, troublesome women who dare hold him accountable.

Surely poverty is more violent than insults lobbed at any nation's president? Surely we should be more offended that girls are being pressured into having sex by boys who offer to buy them sanitary items than by a university professor who dares smash taboos of talking openly about menstruation and sex?

Feminism terrifies authoritarians. It is especially thrilling to see a feminist emerge as one of the most formidable challengers to the fourth longest-serving leader on the continent of Africa, whose rule has been marred by corruption and human rights violations. Nyanzi employs profanity to disobey the father, the patriarch in the form of the president, and to defy the "mother of the nation," in the form of Mama Janet, his wife. Nyanzi wrong-foots patriarchy by disrupting its business as usual with a feminism that advocates for poor girls, for queer Ugandans, and against the violence that women are socialized to accept as their destiny. In June 2018 she helped organize and led the first-ever protest of its kind in Uganda against rising violence against women, including murder, rape, and kidnapping for ransom.[21]

Nyanzi takes aim at an intersection of powers with her profanity and her actions. She works with an alliance that she has built to disturb an intersection of oppressions. The Ugandan women's march, which was organized by the Women's Protest Working Group, took place on the last day of Pride month and was joined by members of the LGBTQ and sex-worker communities.

"On the night of the march, a member of the [Women's Protest] Working Group, Lydia Namubiru, was asked in a television interview why LGBTQ persons were allowed to participate and given a platform to speak," writes journalist Jacky Kemigisa. "Namubiru calmly responded that she had actually been invited to join the protest group by a sex worker and an openly gay Ugandan. She stated that these marginalized groups are at the forefront of fighting for women's rights."[22]

Homosexuality and sex work are criminalized in Uganda, with the former punishable by life imprisonment and the latter by seven years. Although there was some homophobic backlash after the march, Kemigisa says the Ugandan feminist movement's ability to draw together diverse groups and to garner attention both online and offline for the unsolved murders and mutilations of women must be considered a victory so far. What is more offensive? That women are not safe and neither the government nor the police care? Or that queer people and sex workers joined a march that said "Enough"?

"This march's intersectional makeup and celebration of difference should therefore be celebrated, as should the Ugandan women's movement's turn from basic activism to radical feminism," Kemigisa writes.[23]

It is that radicalism that Stella Nyanzi has galvanized. It was no surprise that in September 2018, just three months after the women's march she coorganized and led to demand police action over rising violence against women, Nyanzi took another profane swipe at President Museveni—and his late mother—that landed her back in prison.

Coinciding with the day that Museveni chose as his official birthday—September 15—Nyanzi published a six-stanza poem on Facebook in which she wishes that the birth canal of Museveni's mother—whom Nyanzi mentions by name, which in and of itself is a taboo—had poisoned him during birth. "You should have died at birth, you dirty delinquent dictator," Nyanzi ends her poem. She posted directions to her house and invited Museveni to arrest and beat her.

"This poem surpasses anything she has done in the past in her war of attrition with Yoweri Museveni," writes essayist Mary Serumaga in an article that looks at events in Uganda that took place between the women's march at the end of June 2018 and September of that year, when Nyanzi posted her poem wishing that her country's dictator had died at birth.[24]

Feminism does not operate on a separate sphere of existence. Nyanzi is part of an increasingly vocal and visible opposition to Museveni's rule. This opposition includes members of the Uganda parliament who were tortured so badly by Museveni's security forces that one of them was left fighting for his life and another had the skin on his hands and ears peeled off.

That is the kind of violence that society at large understands. That is the kind of violence that captures headlines and media attention. The struggle for us as feminists has always been to force our societies to recognize violence against women and girls as outrageous and worthy of our rage as having the flesh on your hands and ears peeled off. Nyanzi joined protests against the violence of Museveni's regime and has supported activists and members of parliament singled out by his security thugs. The challenge will always be this: will activists who are not part of the "feminist movement" turn out for Nyanzi and other Ugandan women when they march against violence against women? The women's march was inclusive of LGTBQ and sex-worker communities because Nyanzi and her fellow feminists in the movement are determined to fuck patriarchy by joining forces with as many of patriarchy's victims as possible. Across the world, the challenge will always be this: will the politicians and activists who are considered to have a solely "political" agenda include gender

equality in that agenda? Will they turn out to support women in the way
that women turn out to support them? Too often, men fighting other men
for a bigger share of the political pie is considered the "bigger" struggle
while the feminist struggle against patriarchy is considered a "domestic"
and "private" one. The reason, of course, is patriarchy. Those men are
fighting other men over the patriarchy pie. Nyanzi's feminist struggle,
which includes LGBTQ and sex-worker communities, is upending that
patriarchal pie.

Stella Nyanzi is particularly important in the fight for women's rights
because she forces Ugandans to see that the path to liberation is created by
queer women of color. That is true for the whole world. I am sure there
are many Stella Nyanzis elsewhere whom you do not hear about because
so much news is devoted to men fighting men for more power. The revolution lives on the margins. When the history of Uganda is written,
Nyanzi's bold and deliberate profanity must be remembered as politically
important as the "radical rudeness" deliberately employed by 1940s anticolonial activists in Uganda. They were defying, disobeying, and disrupting the British occupation. Nyanzi is defying, disobeying, and disrupting
an occupation force that persists: patriarchy.

Nyanzi was put on trial for her poem. Who will put on trial Museveni
and his torturers? That impunity is what should be considered profane.
Torture is more offensive than words in a poem. Having the flesh of your
hands and ears peeled off is the greater insult! The rape and murder of
women and the ensuing police apathy are more offensive than a poem
calling the ruler of your country a "delinquent dictator." Patriarchy punishes women for profanity because it wants us to forever remain within the
straitjacket of niceness and politeness, despite the violence it subjects us to.

Again, as in 2017, Nyanzi was charged with "offensive communication" and "cyber harassing" the president and, this time, his late mother.
She faced a one-year prison sentence if convicted. She turned down bail,
choosing instead to remain in jail during her trial so that she could teach
inmates how to use Facebook. Nyanzi's trial began on March 1, 2019, and
was underway at the time of writing.

"Vaginas," "cunts," and "pussies." As women, we must endure hearing
those parts of our bodies used as the most salacious profanity and yet, as
women, we are chastised if we dare to curse or simply utter those words

given to our genitalia. Patriarchy insists on controlling women's mouths and vaginas and, by extension, everything that enters and exits those orifices. Patriarchy insists that it and it alone can police those orifices. Patriarchy reserves for itself the power to offend, the power to be obscene, the power to name bits of our bodies when it wants and to determine their gender, to use them against us, and to punish us for daring to think that those parts of our bodies are ours, whether by name or in fact.

This is not to exclude the transgender or nonbinary and gender-nonconforming communities. I recognize that not all women have vaginas and that vaginas are not exclusively female. I connect them to femaleness here because patriarchy does insist that we follow the dictates of a strict gender binary in which vaginas are inherently female. It is within that strictly cisgender, heteronormative and heterosexual world that vaginas must be both controlled and used as the foundation of so much that is considered profane, including the language of cursing. It is cis-heteropatriarchy that insists on the right to use vaginas to insult and also insist on prohibiting women from cursing, even though our body parts are being used to fuel profanity. It is a world in which "vaginas," "pussies," and "cunts" are words that are deemed inherently female and at the same time inherently profane.

I claim my vagina, my pussy, and my cunt. I am uncivil. I reject decorum. I insist we tell that cis-heteropatriarchy to fuck off.

I often remind audiences when I speak that patriarchs around the world, especially religious conservatives of all faith backgrounds, are obsessed with our vaginas. My message to them all—be they the Muslim Brotherhood in Egypt or what I call the Christian Brotherhood (usually referred to as Evangelicals) in the United States, or any other brotherhood that controls religion with the zeal of bouncers in charge of the most exclusive velvet rope—is to stay out of my vagina unless I want them in there.

Stella Nyanzi's use of profanity as a direct challenge to patriarchy is clear and deliberate. She intends to insult and to offend. And patriarchy swoops in to punish her for such daring. But patriarchy's policing of women's language is not just limited to deliberate use of profanity. Patriarchy also insists that it and it alone determines when something is offensive. Patriarchy's stranglehold over what is and is not offensive can manifest most absurdly, as it did in June 2012. Lisa Brown, a Democratic state representative in Michigan, was banned from addressing her colleagues after it was ruled she had "violated the decorum of the house" when she used the word "vagina" during a debate over a controversial anti-abortion bill.[25] The bill was part of a package of proposed legislation pushed by Republicans always eager to limit or entirely curb a cis-woman's ability to control her reproduction, and in this instance, even limit what a woman can say about a part of her body as her bodily integrity is put up for debate and a vote.

And exactly how did Lisa Brown "violate the decorum of the house"? "Mr. Speaker, I'm flattered that you're all so interested in my vagina, but 'no' means 'no,'" said Brown, a mother of three who opposed the bill because it ran contrary to her Jewish beliefs. For daring to use the word "vagina" during a discussion among lawmakers about a proposed law that would essentially control vaginas, a woman in possession of a vagina was found to be guilty of violating the "decorum" of the house. And that is exactly why I say fuck civility. Decorum rules, remember, were created by men and for men to control a place that they imagined would always be for and about men. And then the girls ruined it all.

That is why I say, "Fuck the patriarchy."

A Republican state lawmaker who complained about Brown's language wonderfully encapsulated the absurdity.

"What she said was offensive," complained state representative Mike Callton, a Republican. "It was so offensive I don't even want to say it in front of women. I would not say that in mixed company."

Patriarchy wants to control vaginas, but it also wants to control who has the right to even say the word "vagina." Not only that, patriarchy screams "decorum" when we dare to fight back. And exactly what was "so offensive" that Callton could not repeat it in mixed company? The word "vagina"? Or that an owner of a vagina was telling men trying to establish control over vaginas that she was fighting back? Was it the "no" of autonomy and agency that so offended? How dare a woman declare autonomy! How dare a woman demand agency over her own body! Or was it the suggestion of sex implicit in Brown's "Mr. Speaker, I'm flattered that you're all so interested in my vagina, but 'no' means 'no'"? Is sex profane?

Why is it profane? Or was it that by her allusion to sex, Lisa Brown was reminding everyone that the conservative opposition to abortion has less to do with a professed concern over fetuses and more to do with controlling and punishing women's desire and sexual agency?

It is all of the above. And that's why I insist on saying, "Fuck the patriarchy."

And all of the above was at play in the clusterfuck—for there is no more apt a way to put it—that ensued when the Russian feminist collective and rock group Pussy Riot performed a "punk prayer" inside Moscow's Cathedral of Christ the Saviour in February 2012, while dressed in bright dresses and balaclavas as they mock-prostrated before the altar. The song eviscerated a host of patriarchs and their excesses, including but not limited to Patriarch Kirill I of the Orthodox Church and President Vladimir Putin and his authoritarian regime. After Pussy Riot's "punk prayer," three of the performers were sentenced to two years in a penal colony for "hooliganism motivated by religious hatred."[26] One band member was freed after her sentence was overturned on appeal.

One of the two members who were imprisoned, Pussy Riot cofounder Nadya Tolokonnikova, explains in her book *Read & Riot: A Pussy Riot Guide to Activism* that their action in the cathedral garnered the disapproval of both secular and religious patriarchs.

"The next day, Putin and the patriarch [Kirill I] get on the phone. The presidential administration called the right people. The main question in the Pussy Riot case was, Who was more offended by the Punk Prayer, Vladimir Putin or the patriarchy? 'Church and state are separated under the Russian Constitution, but in our hearts, in our thoughts, they are always together,' according to Putin," Tolokonnikova writes.[27]

The performance lasted only forty seconds before Pussy Riot left the cathedral and eluded the guards who tried to capture them. The trial and prison sentences handed to two band members for just forty seconds of daring to challenge patriarchy with a profanity-laden "punk prayer" was a reminder that feminists terrify authoritarians, secular and religious.

"It was just a prayer. A very special prayer," Tolokonnikova writes. "The most important dictator, Putin, is really afraid of people," as Pussy Riot member Squirrel says. "More specifically, he's afraid of Pussy Riot.

Afraid of a bunch of young, positive, optimistic women unafraid to speak their minds."

In her unabashedly profane book—one chapter is entitled "Make Your Government Shit in Its Pants"—Tolokonnikova reprints the lyrics to the full song, called "A Punk Prayer: Mother of God, Drive Putin Away." The lyrics, too, are unabashedly profane, lashing out at all patriarchs of Russia and condemning homophobia. Like Stella Nyanzi's alliance of communities, Pussy Riot recognizes that those patriarchs are enemies of feminist and LGBTQ rights.

In a documentary made about the Pussy Riot collective and their renegade performance, several men interviewed made clear that the "offense" was not just profane lyrics that "insulted" Putin and the patriarch of the Russian Orthodox Church, but also the word "pussy" itself in the name of the collective. Reading Tolokonnikova's book, with its liberal and comfortable sprinkling of profanity, is a reminder of how freedom from patriarchy's shackles of decorum is important. Freedom is astonishing and breathtaking. Freedom is terrifying when those who insist on that freedom are those whose submission you have been socialized into believing is your bequeathed right. How dare women connect the patriarchy of their country's authoritarian president to the authoritarianism of the patriarchs of the Russian Orthodox Church who support him; how dare they use a word that calls to mind vaginas *and* chaos? How dare they use a word that forces men to imagine not only a vagina but a vagina that rises up against patriarchy?! How dare women use a word that belongs to patriarchy—because, of course, pussies belong to patriarchy—as part of the name of their punk feminist collective that demands freedom for the pussy from patriarchy?!

What sweet revenge for that pussy that, as Tolokonnikova says in *Read & Riot*, "People don't call it the Cathedral of Christ the Savior anymore, but rather the Pussy Riot church."

I will always remember that once in New York City, when both my arms were still in casts after Egyptian riot police broke my left arm and right hand, a Muslim woman who, to be fair, had invited me to events and conferences she had once organized, told me something like, "Many people in our community support you, but they would support you more if you didn't say 'fuck' so much."

And then there was the time when the editor whose publication has frequently published my work asked me to stop saying "fuck" on social media. He was especially troubled by my use of "I don't give a flying fuck" on Twitter. Not that I need a reason to say "fuck," and I never pass up a chance to fling out a "flying fuck," but that particular week we met when I was on Twitter yelling "flying fucks" was the week when I launched #MosqueMeToo. I had been bombarded with "You're too ugly to be sexually assaulted" and a compendium of hate aimed at shaming and gaslighting me for speaking out against sexual assault.

Surely, my arms in casts and the violence that put them in those casts are bigger issues for "our community"? Surely, the misogyny I receive daily is more offensive than my saying, "I don't give a flying fuck"? I do not want to be a part of a community that believes it has a right to police my language and which makes its acceptance and support of me conditional on self-censorship. Similarly, I do not want to write for a publication that demands I self-censor, even when I am not a full-time employee of that publication.

After the editor asked me to stop saying "fuck" on social media, I took to Twitter to discuss, under #WhyISayFuck, which I created, my love of and insistence on profanity. I was stunned that I was expected to be "polite" even as I'm accused of lying about being sexually assaulted. I was supposed to be "polite" when I'm called an "ugly lying whore." And by saying "fuck" I had apparently lost my "moral standing." I described how often after I have said "fuck the patriarchy" and other profanities while speaking on a stage, women in the audience tell me how much they love how free I am in my language—their words—and how important it is for them to see a woman so openly and unashamedly swear. I asked women on Twitter what profanity meant to them.

"One of my favorite childhood memories is that I came home and witnessed my mom pounding a pan on the counter and screaming 'Fuck . . . !' When she noticed me she looked me in the eye and said 'Sometimes you just gotta say Fuck!'" one woman wrote.[28]

"And people HATE when women say it. There is power in the word," wrote another woman.[29]

"For me a reaction to being expected to be quiet and ladylike," added another woman.[30]

One woman told me, "Being a professional from a working class background I struggle with saying 'fuck.'"[31] It was a reminder of how the intersection of class, gender, and race and other forms of oppression are all used to police women's language. The less power a woman has, the less freedom she has to curse. The more a woman is caught in the intersections of oppressions, the more her language is policed.

Enter Cardi B, a woman who, according to every code of "civility" and "decorum," was not supposed to thrive let alone succeed but whose mere existence is a wrecking ball to that intersection of oppressions: misogyny, racism, and class prejudice.

Cardi B was born Belcalis Almanzar to a Dominican and Trinidadian family. She made history in April 2018 when her song "Bodak Yellow" topped the *Billboard* Hot 100 chart, making her the first female rapper to have a number-one single as a solo artist since Lauryn Hill in 1998. A former stripper whose income from dancing helped her leave an abusive relationship and put her through community college, Cardi B reached that milestone by dislodging Taylor Swift—poster girl of white and blond "respectable" femininity—from the top of the charts. This goes some way to explain why so many of us love the woman who calls herself the "regula, degula, schmegula girl from the Bronx."[32]

She amassed a massive audience on Instagram and the-now defunct Vine in a reminder of how social media have become platforms for voices too often barred from the "mainstream," be it media, politics, or culture, because they were too much—too profane, too sexual, too loud, too everything. Those voices are often the voices of marginalized women—women of color, working-class women, queer women, disabled women, women who are not white and blond poster girls of "respectable" femininity.

Cardi landed a role in the VH1 reality show *Love & Hip Hop* and from there went on to a musical career that quickly brought her nominations and awards, and had some of the biggest names in the industry acknowledging her power by featuring her in their singles and lining up to be guest vocalists on her debut album. If some mocked her—for being "ratchet," for her accent, for her voice, for her anything—Cardi B's success laughed right back in the face of any detractors. If some criticized her profanity, as they did when she visited her former high school and cursed while talking to the students—Cardi disarmed them with her candor.

To the Instagram user who complained, "The cursing was so unnecessary. She is such a ratchet that she forgot that she was speaking to students regarding their education," Cardi clapped right back.[33]

"When I speak my ideas to these ceo who want to give me equality and checks for their brands they understand me clearly . . . where is your perfect English have taken you?"[34] Unfiltered. Unspellchecked. Ungrammared.

She went on:

"When I talk to people I speak straight from the heart and with passion with passion come cursing and realness. This is a highschool I'm going to talk to these kids not like a president but like a friend they can relate to!"

Patriarchy works hard to censor that "realness" via the "politics of respectability," a concept coined by the Harvard professor of Afro-American studies Evelyn Brooks Higginbotham.[35] It refers to ways members of marginalized groups police each other in an attempt to replicate mainstream values as a way to achieve acceptance. It is an especially sharp tool used against women of marginalized groups.

Soon after she gave birth to her first child, Cardi's husband, the rapper Offset of the rap trio Migos, posted a naked picture on Instagram of the new mother. When some on the social media site criticized her—one user called her a "hoe" for appearing naked—Cardi B defended her right to be a "nasty ass, freak ass bitch" who could not be shamed.[36]

"Let me be free," Cardi told her critics in a live video broadcast on Instagram. "If I wanna be half-ass naked, why not? A bitch used to be a whole motherfucking stripper. If I wanna feel sexy, if I want y'all to see my motherfucking body, why the fuck not?"

Cardi goes on to give a masterclass in the futility of trying to reconfigure herself in accordance to the dictates of those politics of respectability—read: patriarchy—which she admits she had briefly obeyed.

Let me tell you . . . how I been trying to like clean my image up, right?
I don't know if you all noticed, but for a hot minute, even before I was
pregnant I wasn't doing scandalous outfits. I was trying to show as much
less skin as possible. When I perform, I would wear like leotards and shit
but not extremely revealing. Like I really [didn't] want to be too sexy
and everything because I felt like I needed a more cleaner image. And

then it's just like, for what? For what? Like yesterday, when I posted myself half naked and everything, it's just like, why should I act like I'm a fucking angel? I'm not a motherfucking angel. I'm a motherfucking nasty ass freak ass bitch. Why should I clean my image up? Why should I act like I'm a saint? Why should I wear skirts that are to my ankles every single day? Y'all still gonna call me a ho. Y'all still gonna call me a motherfucking stripper. Y'all still gonna call me all that shit.

You can't win for trying when you're a woman like me, Cardi is saying. And women like her are not supposed to talk back. And if they do, they are not supposed to be heard by millions. Cardi B has more than forty-one million followers on Instagram. Having looked patriarchy in the eye and blinked for just a second, it must not be lost on us that after Cardi B explains that she no longer gives a fuck about "cleaning up her image," she ends that video with a profanity-laden demand to know where her tax money goes. Demanding accountability from the government, rejecting a politics of respectability that wants to shame her for her agency over her body, and refusing to be anything but a "nasty ass freak ass bitch"—Cardi B's very presence, as well as her chosen forms of expression, demolish the power of "respectability," which, like "civility," is foundational to the power of patriarchy. Her language, her body, and her refusal to shrink challenge multiple oppressions aimed at debilitating women like her. Cardi B will not be diminished.

The politics of respectability makes examples of women as warnings to other women: caution, this is not the kind of woman you should admire. Michelle Wolf is a comedian with her own TV show. Stella Nyanzi is a university professor. Lisa Brown is a lawmaker. Nadya Tolokonnikova is a punk feminist activist. Cardi B is a trend-setting musician. A young Muslim woman wrote to me to tell me she had reviewed my first book, *Headscarves and Hymens*, which was published in 2015.[37] I clicked on the link she sent and read that for a long time she had been scared to read my writing because she had heard that "Mona Eltahawy is too loud, swears too much and goes too far." I understood that those descriptors had all been meant as insults. I knew that they were meant as warnings intended to scare readers away. And I knew that for many people they worked, but I took them as compliments. Women are supposed to be "less than," not "too much." Women are meant to be quiet, modest, humble, polite, nice, well-behaved, aware of the red lines. They are supposed to tread softly and within their limits. I am proud to be described as "too loud, swears too much, and goes too far." When a woman is "too much," she is essentially uncontrollable and unashamed. That makes her dangerous. I am especially proud that those attributes are used to describe my writing.

One of my literary heroes is the queer Chicana poet, writer, and feminist theorist Gloria Anzaldúa. In her 1981 essay "Speaking in Tongues: A Letter to 3rd World Women Writers," Anzaldúa explains the importance of writing:

"Writing is dangerous because we are afraid of what the writing reveals: the fears, the angers, the strengths of a woman under a triple or quadruple oppression. Yet in that very act lies our survival because a woman who writes has power. And a woman with power is feared."[38]

We must make patriarchy fear us. We must reject politeness; there is nothing polite about patriarchy. We must reject civility; there is nothing civil about racism or misogyny or transphobia. Warnings precede profanity, to protect the sensibility of the reader; where are the warnings that precede patriarchy to protect the lives of women and girls? Curse words are bleeped out of television and radio broadcasts; how do we bleep out patriarchy?

What would the world look like if the energy spent policing language, especially female language, was invested instead into policing the very real harm of patriarchal—and the often connected racist—violence?

Once while standing in line at Denver airport security, a white man— another passenger waiting to go through—demanded I "prove" I was a US citizen. "Fuck you!" was my immediate response. Another white man immediately and predictably chimed in: "Language! Language!" But what is really more offensive here: the first man's xenophobic prejudice or my language?

Actress Helen Mirren, who is child free, has said that if she had had a daughter the first words she would have taught her would have been "fuck off," because girls are raised with the expectation of politeness and sometimes politeness is the wrong response. Let's teach all our girls to say "fuck," loudly, proudly, and be unfiltered and uncensored.[39]

We need more nongendered swear words. In my determination to re-ject profanity that diminishes and insults femininity, body parts associated in a misogynist and trans-exclusionary way with cis-women, and which compares a man with that most helpless and therefore most reviled of creatures, the girl—e.g., "stop crying like a girl"—I have started using the epithet "Fuck off, kitten." Kittens are cute, the word itself is gender neu-tral, and, because they are infants, I use the word to diminish the mostly adult men at whom I yell it on social media.

There are several studies that show that people who use profanity are more intelligent than those who are "polite." But I don't swear because I want extra gold stars for my IQ. I swear because I insist that my language be as free as I want to be. I say "fuck" because I will own that word when I want. I own my body, and I own my language. Patriarchy insists it controls our mouths just as it insists it controls our pussies and our cunts.

Fuck the patriarchy.

CHAPTER 4

Ambition

People's reaction to me is sometimes "Uch, I just don't like her. I hate how she thinks she is so great." But it's not that I think I'm so great. I just don't hate myself. I do idiotic things all the time and I say crazy stuff I regret, but I don't let everything traumatize me. And the scary thing I have noticed is that some people really feel uncomfortable around women who don't hate themselves. So that's why you need to be a little bit brave.

—MINDY KALING, *Why Not Me?*[1]

JANUARY 20, 2050

Three women are about to be inaugurated.

The women got to know each other in 2015 on a social media app called Twitter after a feminist they followed posted a series of tweets on *Born in Flames*, an underground queer anarchist feminist film in which women use direct action to fight for women's rights.

Donya Zaki is sixty and is about to become Egypt's first woman president.

Areej Mohamed, fifty-five, is about to become Saudi Arabia's first woman mufti.

Octavia Hernandez, fifty-three, is about to become the third consecutive woman president of the United States of America, having just beaten Chelsea Clinton in a primary. Americans were fed up with political dynasties, and as a reminder of patriarchy's long shelf life, a seventy-year-old woman was considered too old to be president.

Donya, Areej, and Octavia had all determined that their inaugurations would occur on the same day to honor the solidarity that had kept them going since they first met on Twitter.

Not only was Donya about to become Egypt's first woman president; she was also openly bisexual and a poet, the perfect antidote to decades of hypermasculine Egyptian politics. Donya had enthusiastically joined the 2011 revolution but was quickly frustrated with how male-centric it had become. She watched in horror as it turned into a game of political musical chairs between the military and the political Islamists of the Muslim Brotherhood.

In 2018 she joined an underground anarcho-feminist movement called Sekhmet's Sisters. Sekhmet was an ancient Egyptian goddess of retribution and sex. As Donya described her: "First she'd kick your head in, then she'd fuck your brains out."

Her first presidential decree was to build monuments in every Egyptian city to the Revolutionary Sisters, to honor the courage of women who had exposed the so-called virginity tests the military had subjected them to in March 2011.

Areej was an atheist but had agreed to accept the post of first woman mufti of Saudi Arabia because she still believed in change from within. When she was seven, one of her cousins, Maha, died in a fire after "morality police" refused to let her and her schoolmates out of their burning school building because the girls weren't wearing veils. Nobody would tell Areej what happened to Maha, but by 2018 she had figured it out and joined Khadija's Daughters Brigades, an underground radical feminist movement, which social media helped her find and connect with.

In 2018 membership in the underground brigade soared after the favorite son of the new king ordered the detention and torture of women's rights activists just before he lifted the world's only ban on women driving. Feminists had long campaigned for the end of not just the driving ban but more importantly the guardianship system, the very foundation of patriarchy in Saudi Arabia by which women are rendered perpetual minors who require the signature of a male guardian to do many basic things.

For years Khadijah's Daughters Brigades had been underground and obscure, and were reconciled to forever remaining that way because who cared about women's rights when the kingdom sat on the world's largest oil reserves and spent billions on arms from the most powerful country in the world? And then a male journalist who was mildly critical of the Saudi regime after having once been a royal insider was murdered and dismembered at the order of the crown prince, it was believed. And finally the world paid attention.

It was not lost on Areej and her comrades in Khadijah's Daughters Brigade that it took the murder of a man and not fifteen schoolgirls to get the world's attention.

The brigade took advantage of the subsequent royal family's caution and defensiveness to launch determined and increasingly audacious civil disobedience. Within a few years, Khadijah's Daughters Brigades had overthrown the Saudi royal family and the zealous clerics who helped bolster them. A parliamentary democracy was established in the kingdom, and the coalition government asked Areej to become mufti because they understood that once Saudi Arabia turned feminist, it would turn every Muslim-majority country upside down.

One of Areej's first fatwas was to allow women to have multiple spouses—feminism and polyamory at once—not bad.

Octavia's lessons in front-line feminism blossomed thanks both to her friendship with Donya and Areej, through whom she understood how her country's successive administrations had helped prop up authoritarian regimes, and to what was happening at home.

Why so many women presidents in the US? Thank you, Donald Trump and the racist religious zealots who had elected him in 2016. While Donya fought the Muslim Brotherhood in Egypt, Octavia fought the white Christian Brotherhood in the US, which considered women walking incubators whose wombs were more regulated than guns. She was enraged that 47% of white women voters voted for Trump. How could so many women vote for a man who had been accused of sexual assault by more than a dozen women? Mona Eltahawy, the feminist who Octavia, Donya, and Areej followed, called such women foot soldiers of the patriarchy. When she was asked, "Why do women fight feminism?" Octavia would quote Octavia Butler, the author of speculative fiction she was named after: "Drowning people sometimes die fighting their rescuers."[2]

In 2018 Octavia's American Muslim friends told her their mosque had been firebombed by a white supremacist. They were lucky—they had left the building just hours earlier. And then Trump banned Muslims from six countries from entering the US.

And then Octavia's cousins and friends and schoolmates started disappearing because Immigration and Customs Enforcement (ICE) agents picked them up work, at clinics, at schools, and even in courtrooms where they were testifying against abusive spouses. Octavia understood that for women of color, misogyny often intersects with race and class to make life even harder. When she heard that a seven-year-old girl from Guatemala had died of dehydration and shock after she was detained by agents while crossing the border in 2018, Octavia joined a movement to dismantle the fascist service ICE.

She vowed to become president and to abolish prisons and borders, and make the United States of America a sanctuary country for refugees. Her heroes—the three Black, queer women who had formed Black Lives Matter to fight for the recognition of the full humanity of Black Americans against police brutality—had taught her the importance of revolutions that intersect race, class, and gender.

One of Octavia's first decrees was to make public the Harriet Tubman Underground Feminist Railroad. The three friends had launched the network in 2020 to offer feminist aid—be it to whisk away girls in danger of forced marriage or to help those in need of a safe abortion or those who needed shelter from both ICE and abusive men.

Some were surprised at the triple inauguration of Donya, Areej, and Octavia, calling it too radical. But revolutions—like the revolutionary worlds in the futurist writing of Octavia Butler—demand that we imagine a world that does not yet exist. And, really, how radical can a movement demanding the end of misogyny, racism, and bigotry be in 2050?

At the end of their inaugurations, the three women shouted the same declaration: Fuck the global patriarchy!

■   ■   ■   ■

AMBITION IS A SIN because patriarchy wants women to be *less* than; having ambition means being *more* than. In 2015 I was one of ten writers invited to speak at the opening night celebration of the week-long PEN America World Voices Festival. We were asked to imagine the future we wanted to see, and I wrote the 2050 inauguration scenarios above as my contribution. I wanted to see women in the future as *more than*. It was not necessarily just about women in power but rather about imagining women doing things we rarely see them do. And it was not just about women occupying positions in which we rarely see them but also about women dismantling structures that determine which positions women should and should not occupy, could and could not occupy, and, just as importantly, what women should and should not want. Being ambitious discombobulates patriarchy because ambition smashes those restrictions. Having ambition is believing that you will not be contained by should/should not, could/could not. Ambition is being more than.

You cannot be *more than* when patriarchy crushes you into being *less than*. We learn early. "Bossy." "Bitch." "Show-off." "Selfish." "Pushy." The list of epithets that serve as synonyms for women who are perceived to be ambitious is a reminder of that sin of ambition. Those epithets are about being liked: patriarchy socializes women and girls to want to be liked. I do not want to be liked; I want to be free. And to that end, my ambition is to destroy patriarchy.

Who or what determines what women are supposed to be, want, and do? Primarily, of course, patriarchy. But patriarchy works in tandem with other forms of oppression. That is especially the case for women of color and women from marginalized groups. Working in tandem, patriarchy, racism, and capitalism delineate where women should be. Those three constructs squeeze women into being less than. They work so seamlessly together that ambition is rarely seen outside the borders of those constructs. A popular portrayal of ambition presumes one's goal is to become a CEO, to have a corner office, or to become rich. It is by and large written about and for the middle- and upper-middle-class white woman's experience. The tenacious ethos of "having it all" never seems to disappear. What is "all"? How freely can women choose from among the various things that comprise that "all"—work, family, both, none? Surely such freedom depends on where you were born, to what privilege, and how complicated is the Venn diagram of oppressions that color your life.

What is ambition liberated from all of that? What is ambition when you are a woman of color? What is ambition for a woman whose goal is not to become a CEO? What does ambition look like for a woman whose goal is not to become rich? What is ambition liberated from corporate success? What is ambition for a woman who is poor? Answers to all those questions invariably lead to more questions. What is work? What is the definition of success? And those questions in turn lead to the options or "choices" that women are told are theirs. Where along the atlas of options does the shoreline of "work" begin and the landmass of "family" end?

It is impossible to answer those questions without recognizing the impact of patriarchy, racism, and classism on the lives of so many women. What is ambition liberated from all of those oppressions?

I am the eldest daughter of the eldest daughter of her mother. When I trace that maternal line, I trace the cartography of ambition that I have inherited and to which I have added my own mountains, forests, and waterfalls. My maternal grandmother got married after she finished high school. During her life, she was pregnant fourteen times. Eleven of the pregnancies went to term and brought into this world my mother and her ten siblings. My mother went to medical school in Cairo, Egypt, where she met my father, a fellow medical student whom she married after they graduated. I am the eldest of my parents' three children. My mother and father earned master's degrees in medicine (in Egypt, medical school does not require a pre-med degree as in the United States) around the same time as each other, and they were both awarded Egyptian government scholarships to go to London to earn PhDs in medicine.

What should your goals be when your mother has done it "all"? To follow? To replicate? Or to upend it all and do something completely different? The space between my mother and her mother, the space between my mother and me: those are the borders on the Map of Ambition that we each have drawn. My mother wanted me to become a physician like her and my father, but my ambition from the age of sixteen was to become a journalist, because journalism for me was freedom. I became that journalist, and I am also a feminist who is recognized by readers and followers of her work across the world. My mother's PhD is a tangible marker of ambition pursued and fulfilled. When a young man visiting a mosque in Lahore, Pakistan, with his brother and sister approached me as I was taking pictures of the heritage site to ask if I was "the Egyptian feminist I saw on *Al Jazeera*," is that ambition pursued and fulfilled? I am the proud inheritor of my mother's Map of Ambition.

When I trace the lines of that Map of Ambition we have drawn, I am determined to pencil in how racism and capitalism have impacted our stories. During my school years in the UK, where we lived from 1975 to 1982, my teachers—mostly white women—would always ask me, "What does your father do?" when asking about the reasons my Egyptian family were first in London and then Glasgow. It was the height of second-wave feminism and yet women who were working outside the home assumed my mother did not. My teachers assumed we were all just following my father around. I was too young to understand at the time what was at play, but I see it now: the racism of lower expectations. My teachers could not imagine that an Egyptian Muslim woman could be in the UK for any other reason than to follow her husband there. They could not imagine that an Egyptian Muslim woman could be in the UK for any other reason than to be someone's wife and someone's mother, and not instead to study for her own PhD. Or that she could be all three things at once.

The blueprint of my own Map of Ambition has been a work in process, the ink so fresh, that I wonder when I survey it if I have drawn success. In a notebook entry in April 2018, which I entitled "Freedom," I wrote:

"I have $300 in my bank. Am I free? I try to own as little as possible. I refuse to own a home because I believe it is a privilege closed to too many. Financial independence is touted as a key to freedom. But what is exchanged? What are the work obligations?"

Am I considered successful if I have $300 in my account? I know that I am supposed to feel embarrassed to have such a small amount of money, especially at my age, but why? Must I be wealthy for my ambition to be considered worthy of all the years I have poured into it? It has never been my goal to be wealthy. Does that mean I am less ambitious than I thought?

When I ask those questions of myself and when I remember with the hindsight of an adult the questions my teachers asked me about what my father did that brought us to the UK, I am reminded of why we must liberate ambition not just from patriarchy but also from capitalism and racism. My teachers' inability to imagine my mother's agency and ambition leads me to wonder what further limits existed on their imaginations when it came to the lives and possibilities of other students of color. Although the mid-1970s were the height of second-wave feminism, I am sure my teachers' inability to imagine agency and ambition for my mother can also be attributed to that great grim reaper of female agency and ambition: patriarchy, I see you! That double whammy—the racism of lower expectations and the acquiescence to patriarchy is a reminder of the threat, then and now, posed to fledgling ambitions by the constipated imaginations of those entrusted with their education. How does an imagination limited by racism and capitalism affect students of color, and in turn what messages do students from working-class backgrounds receive about what is possible for them?

"Ms. High School Teacher, as a white teacher who was employed in a low-income and predominantly Latino community, you should be the last person advising students to discourage us," wrote Desiree Martinez, a native of South Central Los Angeles and the first person in her family to go to university. Her open letter was addressed to a white high school teacher who upon hearing that it was Desiree's ambition to enroll in UCLA advised her not to aim so high and to consider instead community college.[3]

"We needed you to support us, I needed you to encourage me to apply to an institution that I honestly didn't believe I had a chance at getting into. I was lucky enough to find another teacher to provide me with that support, but what about those students who didn't?" Desiree wrote in a published letter called "Dear High School Teacher Who Tried to Discourage Me from Applying to UCLA, I'm a BRUIN Now!"

That other teacher who gave Desiree the support she needed was a teacher of color who reminded Desiree that she was capable of meeting that challenge of attending UCLA. She thanks him for "pushing me when I needed it the most" and says he is "the example of the kind of educator I strive to be." The website La Comadre, where Desiree Martinez's letter is posted, says that "upon experiencing the lack of representation of students of color at UCLA, she began to advocate for education reform in order to fight for the empty seats in higher education that her classmates didn't have the opportunity to fill," and that she is "heavily involved in combating educational inequity in her community" with the goal of working for the California Department of Education.[4]

Patriarchy, racism, and a host of other isms do not bid farewell to a teacher at the door to a classroom, sitting politely outside waiting for the teacher to finish educating impressionable minds before re-inhabiting them again for the world at large. Teachers take into the classroom the same biases and prejudices they carry within them outside of school. If my teachers could not or would not imagine ambition and agency for my mother, my siblings and I had the privilege of having our mother model-ing at home for us the behavior of an ambitious woman. We had parents who were each other's intellectual and professional equals, who promoted knowledge as the most important thing in the world. My younger sister as a toddler would sit on the dinner table with our father as he pre-pared slides for the medical students he was teaching, preparing her own "lecture" comprised of scribbles and drawings on the transparent sheets that were once used with overhead projectors. One day, to her dismay, our father mistakenly threw her transparency in the trash. "My lecture! My lecture!" she complained until our father dug it out of the garbage, brushed it down, and returned it to Professor Toddler. That same sister grew up with the ambition of becoming an academic and has since earned her own PhD.

It is hard to be what you can't see—which is why teachers of color are important in countries like the United States and others, where racism is known to work in tandem with patriarchy to hold back students of color at schools. It is why, no matter what country, it is imperative to have teachers from marginalized communities, because representation matters, be it ethnicity, religious, ability, gender, or sexuality. The teacher who discouraged Desiree Martinez's ambition was a white woman. The teacher who encouraged her was a man and, like Desiree, Latinx. Women of color fight not just sexual discrimination but racial and, in the case of Desiree, economic discrimination, too, as a working-class woman of color.

"Our analysis suggests that teacher expectations do not merely forecast student outcomes, but that they also influence outcomes by becoming self-fulfilling prophecies," write Seth Gershenson, associate professor of public policy at American University, and Nicholas Papageorge, assistant professor of economics at Johns Hopkins University, authors of a study released in 2017 on the impact of racial attitudes of teachers on their stu-dents' college attainment.[5]

As reported in the *Chronicle of Higher Education*, the study features data on the academic ability of six thousand students who were in the tenth grade in 2002, their socioeconomic status, and the expectations of two teachers on whether these students would graduate from college. The data was from a longitudinal database of the US Department of Education's National Center for Education Statistics.[6]

The researchers wanted to examine the gaps in the expectations of Black and white teachers of the same Black and white students. The database they used for analysis portrayed the views of two teachers for every student and gave demographic data on the teachers as well as the students. The study found that teachers expect 58 percent of the white students and only 37 percent of the Black students to go on to obtain a four-year college degree (and then perhaps a graduate education).

"When teachers of different races evaluated the same black student, white teachers were nine percentage points less likely than their black colleagues to expect that student to earn a college degree. This gap was more pronounced for black male students than for black female students," the *Chronicle of Higher Education* said.

Were the white teachers being more realistic?

"The study found that all teachers are a bit on the optimistic side regarding students' chances of later success. But the gap between optimism and reality is far greater for white teachers and white students than for other teachers and black students, meaning white teachers' high expectations of white students could be giving them an edge," the *Chronicle* said.

Those expectations and that optimism—that belief in the student, the encouragement of their ambition—matter.

"White or black, students with similar preparation are more likely to graduate from college if their high school teachers believe that they will. This is why teacher expectations, and any racial bias, matter so much," the *Chronicle of Higher Education* concludes.

The authors of the study are clear: "We find that the nature of white teachers' expectations places black students at a disadvantage. For a student with a given objective probability of college completion, white teachers are less optimistic when the student in question is black."

It is important, they say, to increase the numbers of teachers of color and to teach the teachers the role and impact of bias and high expectations. The authors include in their study the story of Desiree Martinez, the Latinx student whose white teacher dampened her ambition of attending UCLA. Her open letter to that teacher is a perfect exposition on the power of expectations.

"Low-income students don't need educators who discourage them from pursuing their dreams, the media already does a tremendous job of doing that. We need people who are willing to believe in us and realize that we're not broken. As students from low-income communities, we are powerful, intelligent, and worthy of educators who support our wildest endeavors," writes Martinez.[7]

When I think of my mother going to medical school in Cairo in the 1960s, I think about her ambition and her belief in that ambition. I think about how when my mother was nine years old, a group of army officers, backed by a popular revolution, overthrew the monarchy and ended British occupation of Egypt. The head of those army officers, Gamal Abdel-Nasser, established a form of military-backed dictatorship that has gripped Egypt ever since. Military rule has been disastrous for Egypt. In early 2019, human rights groups estimate there are sixty thousand political prisoners in Egypt and that my country of birth is the third-biggest jailer of journalists in the world. One of the few beneficial things that Nasser did in Egypt was to make education free, opening it up to millions of Egyptians. Under British occupation, previously free secular public schools began to charge fees. Nasser made education free for all Egyptians, starting with schools and later including higher education.[8] Some Egyptians enjoyed political freedom under the monarchy, but no country is free under foreign occupation, and poverty and social inequality trapped millions of Egyptians. For a few years after the 1952 coup/revolution, free education helped many to get a previously unattainable advantage that enabled them to enter the workforce. "Free" is relative, of course, because even if there are no fees or tuition to pay, there are still the expenses of books and supplies to take into account. My parents, who were both born in 1943 to families from a middle class that has since significantly been reduced in Egypt, were part of that first generation to grow up in the era of free education.

As with many newly independent, postcolonial countries, eager to tap into local talent and build a country free of occupation, the sciences, medicine, and engineering were considered the top fields in Egypt at the time. As a result, the majority of my aunts and uncles competed for spots in degree programs in those fields. It is a reminder of how ambition can be socially engineered.

And in a reminder of how politics impact ambition, it is instructive to recognize that after Egypt kicked out the British occupiers, the military moved in with its own form of occupation that has continued to this day. It is no better to be occupied by your own armed forces. The ambitions and the hopes of millions of Egyptians have been crushed by authoritarianism and corruption. The majority of the population of the Middle East and North Africa, the region that includes Egypt, is younger than thirty years of age, and yet it is a part of the world ruled by old men. Many of the young people who took part in the revolutions and uprisings that began in Tunisia in 2010 and have come to be known as the Arab Spring joined the protests because they recognized that political repression was suffocating their ambition. The authoritarianism in the region has excluded young people not just from political opportunities but also from opportunities in the arts, the media, and the economy. And this repression is even worse for women who must contend with social and sexual oppression, in addition to the political oppression that men face. The situation is even worse for poor women and women from marginalized groups in the region. Our military-backed regimes in Egypt, which have ruled us since 1952, can be directly blamed for killing the ambition of millions of people. Poverty and social inequality have worsened in Egypt, and the goal of the January 25, 2011, revolution—"The people demand the fall of the regime"—remains unfulfilled. We got rid of one representative of that regime—Hosni Mubarak, who ruled Egypt for more than three decades—but are still fighting to be rid of the regime itself, of military rule.

Many things can ensnare women's ambition, catch at its sharp edges until they are blunted, tarnish its shiny parts until they are dulled, chip away at its peaks until they are flattened. It is all done with the insistence that women and girls must be less than: racism insists that women and girls of color be less than their white counterparts; patriarchy insists that women and girls be less than men and boys. Sometimes we see an especially blatant example of just how patriarchy does that.

In the summer of 2018 Tokyo Medical University (TMU) was forced to admit it had "systematically lowered the scores of female applicants to keep the number of women in the student body at around 30 percent," Agence France Presse reported.[9] An independent probe later found that the school had rejected about a quarter of female applicants who took the 2017 and 2018 exam and who had achieved scores that should have qualified them for admission. The news agency reported that a group of twenty-four women had demanded 100,000 yen ($880) each in compensation from the school, citing "mental anguish," as well as requesting a refund of exam and travel fees.

Unsurprisingly, the university blamed women for getting in their own way. The determination to limit to 30 percent the number of women admitted to the medical school, said an unnamed source to the newspaper *Yomiuri Shimbun*, was due to "concerns female graduates were not going on to practice medicine in employment."[10] The university claimed that Japan would be left with a shortage of doctors because women would take long periods of leave after marriage. "Many female students who graduate end up leaving the actual medical practice to give birth and raise children," the source said.

Translation: women cannot win. They might think they can qualify for medical school—and in fact their entrance exam scores proved as much—but their ambition will be stamped upon, suffocated, and discarded, because how dare the owners of wombs (and again this misogyny is directed at cis-women) think they can be doctors *and* mothers—the chutzpah of my mother who was both!

Patriarchy socializes women to believe their primary role is to become mothers whose most noble role in life is to raise children. If women dare think they can be something *more than* just a mother, if women dare think they deserve time to fulfill what patriarchy constantly tells them is their primary role in their life, they will be reminded that they are taking up what is rightfully a man's position—being a doctor. And if women refuse to willingly pack up their ambition and go home and play Mummy and Nanny, then the powers that be will erect barriers to women's ambition and deny them their rightful place in a medical school for which they had qualified.

Why aren't male medical students leaving medical practices to help raise the children they brought into this world? Why isn't Japan a kinder and more supportive country to women who want to be medical doctors and mothers? Why is it only women's ambition for which patriarchy must act as a gatekeeper?

If you suffered the delusion that patriarchy plays fair, note this: it gets worse. Pushed by TMU's admission that it had deliberately barred the entrance of qualified women, the Japanese government launched an investigation. A report said that female applicants were discriminated against at four of the eighty-one schools the government studied.[11]

Three of them—Tokyo Medical University, Juntendo University, Kitasato University—admitted the issue and apologized, while the St. Marianna University of Medicine denied the claims.[12]

If you thought women were being punished for daring to have both wombs and ambitions; if you thought patriarchy punished women for daring to think they could take places that rightfully belong to men in medical school, Juntendo University took such patriarchal gatekeeping even further. Admitting that it had rigged entrance exam scores, Juntendo University wrongly turned down 121 women between 2016 and 2018, the Australian Broadcasting Corporation reported. How and why they did that is astounding. Contending that women "have higher communication skills" and were therefore at an advantage in the face-to-face interview portion of their medical school applications, the university made those interviews harder for women by making the pass mark for women 0.5 points higher than for men.[13]

"The idea was to rescue those boys and based on this idea, we compensated," university president Hajime Arai said.[14]

Patriarchy "rescuing" boys! Imagine that. As if that it is not the raison d'être of patriarchy. Instead of a form of positive discrimination or affirmative action that recognizes the obstacles patriarchy places in the way of women and the ways it privileges men and boys, Juntendo University instead wanted to "rescue those boys."

"Women mentally mature faster than men and at the time they take the university examination, women tend to have a higher communication ability," said Hiroyuki Daida, dean of Juntendo's Faculty of Medicine. "We were thinking of compensating the gap between male and female to secure fairness in the judgement."[15]

We should pay attention when patriarchy so starkly defines "fairness." We should be grateful when patriarchy tells us what we have suspected all along but which we are subjected to gaslighting for exposing. I literally had to read twice those excuses given by the university's president and that dean of its medical school, which were, incidentally, supposed to be apologies. It is instructive that "fairness" meant rigging the results to "rescue those boys."

The moral of the story from the medical school rigging controversy in Japan is that cis-women are punished for refusing to sacrifice themselves absolutely on the altar of biological determinism, and that women are punished for being more skilled at a trait that patriarchy nurtures in them but discourages in men—communication skills. How dare women think they can be *more than*. Our lot is to be *less than*. And patriarchy will work to ensure that. That is why ambition is a sin.

Why should we play when the game is designed so that we lose? Countless articles implore women to aim higher, to be more confident, more ambitious. When those women who worked and studied hard to fulfill their ambition of becoming medical doctors did just that, they found the goalposts had been moved to "rescue those boys." In the name of "fairness," the system was rigged to advantage men. That is exactly what patriarchy is: a social construct that privileges male dominance. Aim higher, women are told! Be more confident! Be more ambitious! And yet, a survey by the Boston Consulting Group, a global management consultancy, that looked at 200,000 employees, including 141,000 women from 189 countries, found that women did not lack ambition or confidence but patriarchy killed their ambition and confidence, just as the Japan medical school controversy exposed.[16] In the survey, aimed at dispelling the myth of a gender ambition gap, women were found to be just as ambitious as men at the start of their careers and that *companies* were at fault for stamping out women's ambition, not family status or motherhood.[17]

Researchers also found that women's ambition eroded faster than men's at companies lacking gender diversity. At such companies, the ambition gap between women and men aged thirty to forty was 17 percent, and at these firms only 66 percent of women sought promotion, compared with 83 percent of men. At firms where employees felt gender diversity was improving, there was almost no ambition gap between women and men aged thirty to forty, and 85 percent of women sought promotion, compared with 87 percent of men.

Companies are a microcosm of patriarchy. The latter protects and enables misogyny, so unless companies actively mitigate against that, what other outcome besides the destruction of women's ambition is to be expected? So much research is carried out to tell us what we already know: patriarchy protects and enables men; it benefits men; it ensures that structures built by men and for men continue to be as hostile as possible to women. Telling women to aim higher, to be more confident, to _____ (insert verb) _____ (insert adverb) as patriarchy remains intact is to insist that an individual take on a system by herself and then blame her when her individual efforts fail to dent that system. It is sadistic. It is unfair. It is the system that fails women, not women who fail themselves.

What is ambition liberated from a corporate paradigm? Does ambition exist without "work"? And who determines what work is worthy of ambition? It is instructive to remember the following from the book *Feminism Unfinished*:

> We cannot expect poor women feeding their families on food stamps to have the same priorities as female lawyers hoping to become partners in law firms. We cannot expect working-class women concerned with getting sick leave to have the same priorities as college professors. We cannot expect women who face both sex and race discrimination to develop the same priorities as women who face only sex discrimination. This diversity shows, for example, that it is a mistake to characterize feminism as a movement of career women. Some feminists prioritized women's right to take employment on an equal basis with men, while others asked for greater respect and support for women's unpaid domestic labor—not to mention the majority of feminists who wanted both. There has never been a single, unified feminist agenda.[18]

What ambitions is a working-class woman allowed to have? Is a girl of color in a racist society allowed to have ambition at all? Where does ambition end and where does exploitation begin when a woman from the Philippines takes a job as a domestic worker in Kuwait, where she will make ten times what any job in her home country will pay her? In capitalist societies where neoliberal policies privilege a free market over working conditions that are the antithesis of freedom, is work the end result of ambition or the place where ambition goes to die? When workers are exploited and humiliated as they make our devices—from smartphones to tablets to laptops—and are exploited and humiliated as they prepare our purchases for delivery in the warehouses of an online retailer whose owner is the wealthiest man in human history, surely dignity and a right to a basic income should be ambitions we all strive for. Patriarchy, racism, and capitalist exploitation cannot be solved on a per individual basis by celebrating exceptional cases who survive and thrive despite those systemic oppressions.

In an essay in the anthology *Double Bind: Women on Ambition*, the poet and author Erika L. Sanchez writes searingly about the difference between her own ambition and her working-class Mexican immigrant parents' ambition for her.[19] She reminds us of the pressures on the children, particularly the daughters, of immigrants to conform to and fulfill dreams of parents they know sacrificed and risked so much for the sake of their children's success. But what is success? Sanchez explains that for her working-class parents and family, "success meant sitting at a desk; it meant you had air-conditioning in the brutal summer months; it meant your boss didn't talk down to you because you didn't speak English; it meant you didn't hear *la migra* would depot your ass while you were minding your own business trying to make a living."

Sanchez, who knew as a child that she wanted to be a writer, says that while everyone in her family was hardworking, "nobody, *nobody*, had the kind of life I wanted, particularly the women." After completing her master's degree and experiencing a fulfilling but financially precarious few years of freelance writing, Sanchez seemed to have arrived at success when she was offered a full-time office job writing about reproductive rights for a public relations firm. It paid well, but the office culture and working conditions—which a friend of Sanchez's described as "a sweatshop of the mind"—triggered severe anxiety in Sanchez, who eventually quit. "I had never felt so devalued and disrespected in my entire adult life," she writes. A week after she left the job, which she understood had triggered her anxiety because it demanded conformity in the way that her family did when she was a child, Sanchez got a consulting job that gave her the opportunity to travel and also write about feminist topics.

"I was mobile and independent, privileged to make choices my mother could never even fathom. When she crossed that border thirty-eight years ago, she was giving me permission to cross my own," Sanchez writes.

Sanchez's essay moved me because, despite the differences in our families' backgrounds, we are both daughters of immigrants who resisted what our respective cultures wanted for us as girls. We both grew up navigating the world of our parents and the world they took us to. We both wanted to be what we could not see—writers—and made it up as we went along.

"I was convinced the world would never allow me to be who I was," Sanchez writes.

Ambition is defiance. It is a middle finger to patriarchy's insistence that we shrink ourselves. Attention and ambition are cousins. The former defies patriarchy through the belief that "I deserve attention" and the latter by declaring "I am more than." A similar arrogance fuels both attention and ambition. I am a big fan of female arrogance. The "who do you think you are" that punishes the "sin" of attention also pushes back against the "sin" of ambition. Who do I think I am? Someone who I believe is more than what she is told she could be. I believe I am one of the most important feminists in the world today and that is why I wrote the book you are reading. It has been my ambition to be an author who is read around the world and whose work is influential and a source of power, for women especially. It is my ambition to be known for work that defies, disobeys, and disrupts patriarchy. It is my ambition to be a radical and relevant voice against patriarchy, racism, classism, homophobia, transphobia, and all forms of bigotry. And I believe I am succeeding. That is who I think I am. Am I arrogant in believing that? Who cares? I have fucking earned it.

You can see how upsetting female ambition is to the patriarchy via a cursory look at popular culture: from the tantrums thrown by male fans of the *Dr. Who* television show at the news that a woman would play the eponymous character, to the tantrums thrown by male fans of the film *Ghostbusters* to news that it would be remade with an all-female cast, to a host of other instances of men raging at women daring to think they have the right to be leading actors in positions patriarchy had promised were the copyright of the boys' club.[20] Remember: the "boys" need "rescuing."

Heaven forbid other women see—i.e., get ideas—that we too can be the star, not just of a hit television show or a movie franchise but simply of our own lives. When men are not throwing a tantrum at the offense of women's ambition spilling out into places they were promised belonged to them, and only them, they are actively working to destroy women's ambition and to make an example of the few who dare to step out of their boxes. Take the British sports journalist Vicki Sparks, the first woman to commentate on a live World Cup match for British television, whose history-making feat was not uniformly celebrated.

"I prefer to hear a male voice when watching football," Jason Cundy, who once played for English soccer teams Chelsea and Tottenham, told *Good Morning Britain*.[21] Why is a male voice necessary to describe, analyze, and opine on twenty-two men kicking around a football on a pitch? Cundy's reason says as much about patriarchy's gatekeeping of women's ambition as it does about what it allows in men, because, remember, patriarchy hurts men too. Said Cundy, "Ninety minutes of hearing a high-pitched tone isn't really what I like to hear. And when there's a moment of drama, as there often is in football, that moment needs to be done with a slightly lower voice."

Beyond the naked misogyny, I doubt that Cundy paused for a second to consider that male voices register on various points of the scale determined by patriarchy as appropriately "lower"—read: manly, masculine, acceptable.

There is a photograph that I kept next to me as I wrote this chapter because it is a perfect embodiment of "can you be what you cannot see?" It is of a group of Indian women wearing saris, some with flowers in their hair, smiling, laughing, and hugging each other. They look like they are exactly where they need to be. They belong. They look to be celebrating, holding each other in joy and pride.

The women are Indian Space Research Organization scientists and engineers celebrating at the Spacecraft Control Center, on September 24, 2014, after India's Mars orbiter *Mangalyaan*, meaning Mars craft in Hindi, successfully entered the planet's orbit.[22] How often do we see female space scientists and engineers? How often do we see space scientists and engineers who are not white men? How often do we see women celebrating in a work environment who are not white women or dressed in Western corporate uniforms of "success"? India had just become the only country to complete a probe trip to Mars on its first attempt, and it joined the United States, Russia, and Europe in successfully sending probes to orbit or land on Mars. The mission also made India the first Asian country to reach Mars, after an attempted launch by regional rival China failed to leave Earth's orbit in 2011.

Ambition is fueled by more belief than is needed to send a probe to Mars. You can calculate how much fuel you need to get to Mars and you can finesse your calculations to guarantee that landing. Ambition— particularly when it is liberated from patriarchy and from the wealth that is so often used as a marker of ambition's "landing"—can be much harder to launch and its success more elusive to measure.

The Swedish artist Hilma af Klint is a particularly relevant example. What besides levels of ambition worthy of a Mars mission could fuel an artist's belief in her mission and her art such that she essentially invented abstraction, years before the male giants who are usually acknowledged with launching that movement, in her studio in Sweden, away from public validation, and in the knowledge that the world was not yet ready for her art? As I was writing this chapter, I visited the first American large-scale exhibition of af Klint's art at the Guggenheim Museum in New York City. In 1906, when she was in her early forties, af Klint began a series of non-figurative paintings that preceded by years the work of Vasily Kandinsky, Piet Mondrian, and other modernists. To her contemporaries, af Klint was known for conventional figurative art. But between 1906 and 1915, af Klint created 193 works known as *The Paintings for the Temple* after re-ceiving what she called a commission from an unseen spiritual guide, part of the "High Masters," with whom af Klint and a small female collective had been communicating via a psychograph, a device designed to enable psychic communication.

Af Klint showed only a few examples of her abstract paintings publicly during her lifetime, curator Tracey Bashkoff explains in the notes accom-panying the exhibit *Hilma af Klint: Paintings for the Future*:

> At the beginning of a notebook from 1932, af Klint wrote that her spir-itually informed works, including *The Paintings for the Temple*, should not be exhibited until twenty years after her death. Nonetheless she did not keep her works entirely secret. With *The Blue Books* [notebooks in which af Klint catalogued her most important body of work], af Klint created a tool that would allow her to selectively share her paintings. . . . These volumes would have enabled af Klint to show trusted viewers the forms, colors, and symbolism of her works. This gesture and others

make apparent that af Klint's priority was not to keep the paintings secret but to ensure that the conditions were correct for their proper re-
ception. Af Klint's lack of confidence in her contemporaries may have
been well founded. At the time she made these works, the art world was
generally dismissive of work made by women, while many critics did
not take abstraction seriously.[23]

Patriarchy robbed a talented artist of recognition during her lifetime.
It did not crush her ambition—she knew she was more than patriarchy
allowed women to be—but it denied her of a rightful place in what we call
history. It denied other female artists of a role model, and it denied the rest
of us who revel in a history that is not written by men and about men of a
woman whose ambition buoyed her and assured her she was creating her
own history. Af Klint created art not within that world's then capitals of
Paris and Vienna but in Stockholm, despite a lack of recognition and validation. She knew the world was not ready for her. What an utterly familiar
story. It is not that af Klint did not believe in her work. On the contrary,
she knew its worth. But she did not have faith in the public at large.

Although it was popular among other pioneers of abstract art of af
Klint's time, the spiritualism that informed much of her work gave Hilma
a way to survive and to circumnavigate that great gatekeeper of female
ambition: patriarchy.

"Spiritualism would eventually help af Klint make the major artistic
breakthrough represented by *The Paintings for the Temple*. In employing
spiritualism as a way to break from the constraints of the past, the artist was not alone. The majority of spiritual mediums during the period
were women, and many used channeling as a way to overcome society's
marginalization of their voices by claiming direct access to an absolute
authority," Bashkoff writes.

"We are the granddaughters of the witches that you could not burn,"
says one of Egyptian artist Ghada Amer's paintings.[24]

Until we divorce patriarchy from ambition and ambition from patriarchy, we will forever force women and girls to shrink their ambition to fit
that asinine phrase "women can do whatever men can."

I don't want to do anything a man can. I want to be free.

Here is how we pass the baton of ambition from woman to girl.

When one of my nieces was eight years old, she told me she had been looking up pictures of our family online.

"I saw one of you . . ." She paused. "Never mind."

I thought she had wanted to say she had seen a picture of me with my arms in casts after Egyptian riot police assaulted me and that she had paused mid-sentence because she was worried she would upset me with a bad memory. After a bit of cajoling by her mother, she finally told me that she meant she had seen a picture of me getting arrested in a Times Square subway station in New York City after I spray-painted over a racist advertisement in 2012. My darling niece thought I would be upset that she had seen a picture of me getting arrested for doing something I had vowed to do. I was proud of my civil disobedience, for which I was jailed overnight and charged with criminal mischief, making graffiti, and possession of a graffiti instrument. A judge eventually dropped the charges in the interest of justice.

I told my niece that I was proud of getting arrested. We had a good chat about why I spray-painted over the ad and why protesting was important. And then, together, we looked at the pictures of me getting arrested. And our conversation continued:

NIECE: I know why you got tattoos (pointing to my forearms).
ME: Why?
NIECE: Because they broke those arms and you wanted to say "I'm free and awesome."(Pause) Why did they break your arms?
ME: They wanted to scare me and make me go home and stop protesting.
NIECE: Did you go home?
ME: No.
NIECE: Good!

Let us always tell girls they can be *more than*.

CHAPTER 5

Power

Like a LOT of Black women, I have always had to invent the power my freedom requires: All my life I've been studying revolution. I've been looking for it, pushing at the possibilities and waiting for that moment, when there's no room for rhetoric, for research or reason: when there's only my life or death to act upon. Here in the United States you do get weary, after a while; you could spend your best energies forever writing letters to the *New York Times*. But you know, in your gut, that writing back is not the same as fighting back.

—JUNE JORDAN, *On Call: Political Essays*, 1985[1]

WHAT IS A POWERFUL WOMAN?

In 2014, my father and I went to a Cairo cafe to watch the final match of the men's World Cup, which is held every four years and that year was being hosted by Brazil. The match ended with Germany beating Argentina to once again clinch the cup. Despite our national team's failure to qualify for that year's tournament, the cafe was full because Egypt is a country that loves football, or, as you may know it, soccer. The men's World Cup is the most-watched sporting tournament in the world, and by the time the final match was on, because of the time difference between Egypt and Brazil, Muslims who observe the holy month of Ramadan, which coincided with the 2014 tournament, had ended their fast and had flocked to cafes for coffee, tea, and water pipes.

During the ceremony to hand out the cup to the winners, a boy sitting with his family at the table next to ours pointed at the television screen where a woman was standing at a podium, awaiting the players.

"Who is that woman, Baba?" the boy asked.

"That is the president of Brazil," his father replied.

"A woman can be president?" the boy asked.

I could not have orchestrated the moment better myself. I live for moments like that—when, for a brief moment, what seems impossible is right there in front of you. And after the World Cup final, when the entire world had tuned in to watch the most popular sporting event. I turned to the boy and launched into my teaching moment.

"The World Cup this year is hosted by Brazil, which has a woman president. The two teams who just played in the final—Germany and Argentina—also have women leaders. Look, see that second woman on the stage? That's the woman who is the leader of Germany," I said, pointing to German chancellor Angela Merkel, who stood next to then Brazilian president Dilma Rousseff as the players shook hands and hugged the leaders who awarded them medals. Only then Argentinian president Cristina Fernández de Kirchner was absent. "One of these days, Egypt will have a president who is a woman," I said. Who knew that a men's sporting event would provide me with one of my feminist moments in my hometown!

I wanted the boy and the two girls sitting with his family to know that women could be presidents and leaders. You need to see what you want to become. There was a time when women were powerful in Egypt. We had a god-king called Hatshepsut, who gained power during Dynasty 18 (1550–1295 BC) and for more than twenty years was the most powerful person in the ancient world.[2] But in our modern era? I wanted to be able to point to someone who was still alive as a reminder to those three children that women could be powerful.

If we had had more time than just the trophy ceremony of the World Cup, I would have told those children that power is more complicated than who serves as presidents and chancellors. Power lives in more places than the presidential office, and there are other ways besides politics to be powerful. I would have launched into a longer feminist teaching moment in which I insist we must differentiate between power that dismantles patriarchy from power that is used in the service of patriarchy.

In the intervening years, two of the countries that were led by women during the 2014 World Cup have since served as reminders that when it comes to appreciating the impact of patriarchy on power, we must ask a much bigger and more complicated question than simply "Can a woman be president?" We must ask equally pertinent questions: Is that woman feminist? Is she invested in dismantling patriarchy? Will she use her power to uphold or diminish patriarchy? Both Brazil and Germany have given us complicated answers.

Brazil might have once elected a female president, but it remains solidly patriarchal. Just 15 percent of Brazil's federal and state legislators are women—an all-time high, according to Adriana Carranca in the *Atlantic* magazine.[3] Rousseff, a former Marxist guerrilla who became Brazil's first female president, was impeached by a corruption-tainted senate in 2016 for breaking budget rules.[4] She was succeeded for an interim period by her vice president, a center-right man who named an all-male, all-white cabinet and who lost three ministers accused of corruption in his first month in office. In October 2018, the far-right Jair Bolsonaro, an unabashedly misogynist, racist, and homophobic former army captain defeated the left-wing Workers' Party candidate to become the president of Latin America's largest democracy, which only ended twenty years of military rule in 1985.[5]

To appreciate how patriarchy works, and how it benefits from the very things it claims to fight, witness some of the men who set in motion Rousseff's fall.

"In late 2015, the then-leader of the evangelical bloc and speaker of the lower house, Eduardo Cunha (now serving a 15-year sentence in prison for graft), led impeachment proceedings against Dilma Rousseff, Brazil's first female president; she was removed from office a year later. One of the congressmen who voted to oust her was Bolsonaro. He dedicated his vote to Carlos Alberto Brilhante Ustra, the head of the military dictatorship's torture unit. Rousseff was among those tortured," writes Carranca.

There is a reason Bolsonaro, a character straight out of Misogyny Central, has been dubbed the "Trump of the Tropics." He has used offensive language against women, gay people, Afro-Brazilians, and indigenous people. Chayenne Polimédio writes in *Foreign Affairs* that Bolsonaro "told a female member of congress that he wouldn't rape her because 'she wasn't worthy of it,' explained that his sons would never love black women because his sons were 'properly raised,' and claimed that a particular secretary of women's issues shouldn't have been appointed because 'she was a dyke.'"[6] A father of five, Bolsonaro has said that his only daughter was born due to his wife's "weakness."

If Bolsonaro reminds you of a certain American president, it is no wonder that on the day Bolsonaro was inaugurated, Trump tweeted the new Brazilian president gushing congratulations, telling him "the U.S.A. is with you!" to which Bolsonaro's Twitter account replied: "Dear Mr. President @realDonaldTrump, I truly appreciate your words of encouragement. Together, under God's protection, we shall bring prosperity and progress to our people!"[7]

Similarly, interviews with female supporters of Bolsonaro echo much of the hatred and dismissal of feminism shared by Trump's female supporters. From the idea that Brazilian women don't need feminism because they're not victims to vehement assertions that men and women are equal to boasts that if they could do it—"it" being anything from being wealthy, to juggling work and family, to a host of other privileges—then all women should be able to with enough effort. Nearly always forgotten is that no matter how hard people from disadvantaged or marginalized backgrounds try, a host of inequalities bars them from getting the same opportunities as more privileged people. And much like their American counterparts who support Trump, female Bolsonaro supporters want the right to bear arms rather than the right to dismantle patriarchy—the root of misogynist violence—to protect themselves and their loved ones, the *Guardian* reported.[8]

Brazil is one of the most violent countries in the world for women. In 2017 there were 606 registered domestic violence cases and 164 rapes per day.[9] The numbers could be higher. Those were just the ones that authorities registered.

I call women who vote for unabashedly misogynist candidates like Bolsonaro, especially knowing how dangerous Brazil is for women, foot soldiers of patriarchy. It is especially ironic that patriarchy enables and protects violence against women and yet at the same time presents itself as the great protector of women. That is what Bolsonaro did, presenting himself as a "family values" and "law and order" candidate. The man who told a female member of Brazil's congress—Maria do Rosário—"I would never rape you because you don't deserve it," said during his campaign that he was the only candidate who was truly worried about violence against women because he proposed chemical castration for rapists, the *Guardian* newspaper reported.[10]

When the man elected to lead a country is so openly misogynist, it gives a green light to other men that they too can behave as if women's bodies are fair game. And in a country where violence against women is so high, Bolsonaro is a reminder that when patriarchy offers to "protect you" it comes at a cost. According to the *Guardian*, a recent study found that 58 percent of Brazilians agreed partially or fully with this statement: "If women knew how to behave, there would be less rape."[11] Bolsonaro voted against a 2015 "femicide" law—sponsored by Do Rosário—which gave harsher sentences for homicides motivated by gender. In an interview on International Women's Day in 2017, he said that Brazilian women should "stop whining; stop with this story of femicide," the *Atlantic* reported.[12] According to the BBC, in a 2016 television interview, he said that he wouldn't give a woman employee "the same salary as a man" because women get pregnant.[13]

The *Guardian* reports that in 2013, Bolsonaro coauthored a bill proposing to revoke the right for rape victims to get legal abortions—this in a country remember where 164 rapes were registered every day in 2017.[14] Several days before his election, Bolsonaro signed a "term of commitment" with the Catholic Church, pledging to defend the "right to life, starting from conception." After his election, Bolsonaro said he would abolish Brazil's human rights ministry and named the conservative evangelical pastor Damares Alves to run a newly created ministry of women, family, and human rights, as well indigenous people, estimated to number nine hundred thousand.[15] Alves has said she wants "Brazil without abortion"— it is illegal in Brazil in most cases, anyway—and accused feminists of "making a war between men and women." She "co-founded a group that rescues indigenous children from situations of danger and evangelizes in indigenous communities," the *Guardian* reports, in a reminder of the myriad ways foot soldiers of the patriarchy mirror each other's behavior across the world.[16] She is Exhibit A of the woman elevated by patriarchy, who is given and accepts crumbs in return for a limited form of power.

According to *Foreign Affairs*, women make up more than half of Brazil's total electorate, the number of female-headed households more than doubled between 2001 and 2015, and yet Brazilian women experience higher rates of poverty and unemployment, and lower levels of political partic-ipation, than men.[17] That will not soon change in Brazil or anywhere else as long as patriarchy employs a host of oppressions—represented with alacrity by Bolsonaro and the interests he serves: militarism, capitalism, authoritarian Christian values.

During his time as a lawmaker, Bolsonaro represented the interests of the armed forces, and since his election he has named seven former mili-tary men to head key ministries, the BBC reported.[18] His support base is "what Brazilians call the 'BBB bloc': *do boi, da Bíblia e da bala,* or 'beef, Bible, and bullets,' a reference to rural voters, evangelical Christians, and pro-gun groups. Powerful business groups also voiced support for Bolson-aro," writes Carranca in the *Atlantic*.[19]

Conservatism goes hand in hand with patriarchy, and it must be re-membered that conservatism benefits men while reserving cruelty for women and men who reject its strict codes of conduct. Eighty-two per-cent of Brazilian women are against the legalization of abortion, according to *Foreign Affairs*, and 40 percent are against same-sex marriage. Brazil's evangelical population, which supported Bolsonaro and has proven to be a major pillar of support for Trump, makes up 22 percent of the electorate and is growing.[20]

At the end of September 2018, a month before Brazil's presidential elec-tion, the hashtag #EleNao (Not him) united millions of women horrified at the prospect of a Bolsonaro presidency on social media and inspired hundreds of thousands to take part in the biggest female-led demonstra-tions in Brazil's history. The #EleNao campaigners are part of a wider movement against sexual harassment, sexism, and discrimination. They are the antithesis of Bolsonaro's female constituents.[21]

Few people represented the antithesis of Bolsonaro more than Marielle Franco, a Black, queer woman who was one of Brazil's few Black female politicians. A member of Rio de Janeiro's city council and a human rights advocate against the paramilitary gangs that control poor areas of Rio, Franco was murdered seven months before the presidential election, in March 2018.[22] She was fatally shot in her car, along with her driver, An-derson Gomes, after leaving an event she had hosted to encourage Black women in Rio to participate in politics. Almost a year after her death, two former police officers were arrested in connection with Franco's murder.[23]

That Franco—a young, Black, queer woman who was outspoken in her condemnation of police brutality—was murdered and Bolsonaro—a misogynist, racist, homophobic white man who champions guns and greater police powers—is president, is a shocking reminder of what Brazil is today.

Almost two decades into the twenty-first century, it is clear that Donald Trump is just one of several men who have come to power on an unabashedly patriarchal and authoritarian agenda. The leaders of Russia, China, Egypt, the Philippines, Hungary, Poland, Turkey, Italy, and India especially come to mind.

A 2017 study into right-wing populist voters in Germany, France, Greece, Poland, Sweden, and Hungary by the Friedrich Ebert Foundation (FES), which is affiliated with Germany's center-left Social Democratic Party, found that white women are increasingly drawn to right-wing populist parties and are often more radical than their male peers.[24]

Tellingly, the study found that while many right-wing populist parties have prominent female figures among their leadership, such as Marine Le Pen, who is the leader of France's far-right populist National Rally party; Poland's former prime minister and PiS (which stands for the Law and Justice party) member Beata Szydlo; and AfD (Alternative for Germany) coleader Alice Weidel, women are conspicuous in their absence elsewhere. Most of the right-wing parties' parliamentary representatives are male. In Germany, for example, just ten women are included in the AfD's ninety-two-seat-strong parliamentary group.

"These women are there to give these parties a more open, modern guise and to appeal to female voters," Elisa Gutsche, who edited the FES study, told *Deutsche Welle*. "These are not progressive parties; there is no real gender equality."[25]

Gutsche said many right-wing populist parties sought to garner female votes by promising to raise child benefit payments and other financial allowances to promote families. White supremacist parties that promise "family benefits" are clearly not interested in just any families. Their main concern is the primacy of white families, and they promote traditional and heterosexual notions of family and center the idea of woman as mother. White supremacy, whether in the US or Europe, is absolutely patriarchal—those far-right parties offer no gender equality. The right-wing party in Poland, much like the Republican party in the US, has fought for a complete ban on abortion. Again, white women who vote for those parties are examples of women who accept crumbs thrown to them in return for limited power in the form of protection and privilege gained via proximity to powerful white men. They whip up xenophobia among white women voters by pitting immigrants against white families, portraying refugees, asylum seekers, and migrants as a drain on resources that should go instead to those white families. They want white women to have more white babies. As with the findings on Brazilian women, women in the European countries studied by FES are more likely to have badly paying jobs and are at higher risk of poverty in their senior years.

"I think women sense they are at the lower rungs of society and find themselves having to compete against refugees and migrants," said Gutsche. Surely, instead of accepting that competition against people disadvantaged and marginalized by the white, capitalist patriarchy, those white women who vote for far-right parties should be asking why they occupy such a lowly place on the ladder. Voting for far-right parties that employ a host of oppressions alongside patriarchy is not the solution. Encouraging white women to see themselves as higher up the ladder—the hierarchy—of oppressions and injustices employed by patriarchy to maintain itself must be seen for the ruse that it is. Those women might be benefitting from proximity to white power, but nothing protects women from patriarchy. We must dismantle the hierarchies that patriarchy uses, not aim to climb our way up its ladder of injustices.

As with the 47 percent of white women voters who voted for Trump, women who support right-wing parties in Europe are white women who allow their race to trump their gender by aligning with a "protect and provide" agenda that emphasizes women's traditional roles as mothers and nurturers and promises them in return "protection." Again, they are foot soldiers of patriarchy. And as in every case where patriarchy tantalizingly holds out protection as a promise, women must ask at what price such protection comes and what happens when women refuse the exchange.

In the case of the far-right parties of Europe, as well as with white supremacists in the US, the protection being offered is from Black and brown men, who have historically been stereotyped as menacing, oversexed would-be rapists of white women. White supremacy promises white women protection from the imagined danger of men of color in return for their loyalty. But the truth is, women around the world are hurt the most by men they know: current or former partners or relatives. In other words, the greater danger for white women who vote for far-right groups is their own misogynists. The *Daily Beast* reported that a meme at a 2017 neo-Nazi rally in Germany claimed immigrants were abusing German women.[26] Yet the news site found that the pictures shown at the rally were not those of white German women brutalized by immigrants but were, rather, those of American and British victims of police brutality and domestic abuse.

Patriarchy too often throws women crumbs in return for a limited form of power. Women who accept those crumbs are expected in return to uphold patriarchy, internalize its dictates, police other women, and never forget that power bestowed is power that can be retracted. Patriarchy will allow a few women into places they have not been allowed before and call it progress, while at the same time demanding that we not point out that power is in the hands of those throwing us such crumbs, and not with those who accept them.

We must refuse those crumbs. Those crumbs are offered as compensation for a host of oppressions that patriarchy employs to maintain itself. I don't want crumbs; I want the whole cake. And I don't want patriarchy's cake—we must bake our own. I believe that is what June Jordan means when she says in the epigraph to this chapter that as a Black woman she has "always had to invent the power my freedom requires."

The goal of feminism cannot be simply the elevation of any and all women. What a vacant and meaningless goal that would be without also destroying patriarchy. To that end, feminism must aim to subvert the oppressions that patriarchy employs for its maintenance. Feminism must aim a Molotov cocktail at the powers that uphold patriarchy and obliterate them. Recognizing that patriarchy has not been dismantled, and working toward that end, we must recognize that the entrance of women into spaces and structures that were created by men and for men is an opportunity to expand power, and not an end in itself. Rather than celebrating exceptional individuals who have been anointed or who have succeeded in securing positions of power—be they via elections or promotions or other paths toward leadership roles wherever they may be—we must nudge and encourage those individuals to expand power beyond themselves. AfD coleader Alice Weidel is an example of a woman who has accepted crumbs of power from patriarchy in return for her own individual benefit while remaining another example of a foot soldier of patriarchy who upholds its oppression. Weidel is a lesbian and belongs to a homophobic party; she's anti-immigrant and illegally employs a Syrian refugee as a housekeeper.[27]

Conservatives and right-wing parties alike, who benefit from a host of oppressions employed by patriarchy, such as white supremacy and the disparities in wealth and income that are maintained by capitalism, will obfuscate from their misogyny by pointing to the appointment by those parties of a woman here or a woman there and smugly exclaim, "See!" Yet the agendas of those women—which are the agendas of those conservative and right-wing parties—invariably cut feminism at the knees. As if by the mere presence of a woman in a position of power, gender equality has been achieved and patriarchy can pack its bags and depart.

We must recognize that disingenuousness for what it is. It is an appropriation of the very thing that conservatives despise: identity politics. When feminists point to patriarchy and its attendant oppressions, conservatives accuse us of being "obsessed" with identity politics. They complain that we play victims by—rightfully—pointing at our various identities that are discriminated against and which are used against us. When we point out that our ethnic and class background, sex, gender, and disabilities are used against us, conservatives will accuse us of playing the identity politics card.

And that is exactly what they played after President Donald Trump nominated Gina Haspel to head the Central Intelligence Agency, boasting in the tweet that announced his decision that she was the "first woman so chosen." The period between her nomination and her eventual Senate confirmation was filled with an unusual amount of focus on Haspel's gender from conservatives who normally bemoan any focus on "identity politics" by those of us on the left or liberal end of the political spectrum. A host of people not known for their feminist credentials, including Trump's spokesperson, Sarah Huckabee Sanders—a woman who lies almost daily for the president—accused anyone who opposed Haspel's nomination of having an anti-feminist agenda. The irony was indeed rich.[28]

It was not lost on those of us who opposed Haspel's nomination that her boosters were so vehemently pressing her as a feminist victory because her gender was a convenient way to deflect scrutiny from her human rights record and involvement in one of the most brutal and shameful episodes of recent US history and, by extension, scrutiny of the CIA's abuse of power and the agency's lack of accountability.

As an Egyptian feminist especially, I was most certainly not celebrating Gina Haspel and for reasons that are reminders of how patriarchy works with a host of oppressions to maintain its power.

Haspel played a direct role in the CIA's global kidnapping, detention, and torture operation known as "extraordinary rendition." Under the program, which was adopted after the 9/11 attacks, suspected militants who were captured in Afghanistan were sent to other countries, which held them in secret detention and allowed CIA personnel to torture them. The first secret prison was in Thailand, where, as an undercover officer in 2002, Haspel oversaw the torture of a terrorism suspect and later helped carry out an order to destroy videotapes that documented the interrogations.[29]

At least fifty-four countries supported the rendition program.[30] As an Egyptian, I am shamefully aware that my country's government was among the most diligent. Egypt, Morocco, Jordan, and Syria were among the most common destinations for rendered suspects.[31] Haspel and others who ran the program could count on Egypt to do the dirty job the CIA required. Annual reports issued by the US State Department and human rights organizations have long documented the systematic use of torture by successive Egyptian governments.[32]

That dirty job, done so well by the regime of President Hosni Mubarak—who was supported by five successive US administrations—was instrumental in providing bogus information used by President George W. Bush's administration to invade Iraq. After Ibn al-Shaykh al-Libi, a Libyan captured in Afghanistan, was rendered by the United States to Egypt in 2002, Egyptian interrogators beat him and subjected him to a "mock burial" by putting him in a cramped box for seventeen hours. Libi fabricated information that Iraq had provided training in chemical and biological weapons to operatives of Al Qaeda. In 2003, Secretary of State Colin Powell cited that information in his speech to the United Nations that made the ultimately debunked "weapons of mass destruction" case for war against Iraq.

Libi recanted the story after being returned to CIA custody in 2004 as the war raged. He was sent back to Libya from American custody in late

2005 or early 2006 and detained there at the Abu Salim prison, where in 2009, at age forty-six, the former preacher who once ran a training camp for armed militants in Afghanistan apparently died of a suicide. His friends were suspicious of his reported cause of death.[33]

The dozens of such "ghost prisoners" who were in American custody overseas were among many shameful examples of collusion between my country and the CIA's rendition program.

How, when it has so readily relied on Egypt to take torture further than its own operatives would or could, can any American administration ever seriously hold our government accountable for its torture against us, the Egyptian people? The answer: It can't, and it doesn't. And successive Egyptian governments count on that. It is less likely to do so with Haspel, whose career is so tainted by torture, at the helm. Furthermore, though previous United States administrations provided at least lip service to condemning torture in Egypt, President Trump has said that he believes torture "absolutely" works, and on the campaign trail in 2015, he vowed to approve waterboarding "in a heartbeat."[34]

Despite Trump's boast of gender advancement, the choice of Haspel for promotion is no victory for women. My feminism does not demand that a woman have an equal opportunity to torture, alongside men. Torture is no less wrong because a woman, not a man, carries it out. I do not celebrate the appointment of women to high positions in regimes where cruelty is a favored tool of governance by a patriarchy; if they accept, they are nothing less than foot soldiers of that patriarchy and the violence it has instituted.

My feminism works to dismantle patriarchy and its violence—whether it is sanctioned by the state, as torture is, or practiced at home, in the form of intimate partner or domestic violence.

I do not subscribe to a feminism that demands perfection or the super-heroic nobility of women. But I do insist that putting women at the service of patriarchy is no victory for us. These are discussions that will come up again and again as women demand inclusion in institutions that have not been friends to women, such as the military, religious institutions, corporations—and the CIA.

Trump is certainly no friend to women. This president has been accused by more than a dozen women of sexual assault. Moreover, the

Guardian newspaper reported that 80 percent of nominations for top jobs in the Trump administration have gone to men, many wealthy white men, putting the president on track to assemble the most male-dominated federal government in nearly a quarter-century.[35] However many women he chooses to promote in his patriarchal government, he is no feminist. Feminism, as I see it, is not about counting women in key jobs.

From his administration's concerted efforts to destroy women's hard-earned reproductive rights to an increasingly homophobic and transphobic agenda; from his racism and bigotry, which has worsened the detention of migrants and asylum seekers at the border, including separating children from their families and placing them in effective concentration camps; to his repeated efforts to enrich the wealthy and to strip away social protections from the poor and vulnerable, it is clear: Trump is no feminist. That is why I refuse to celebrate the move to promote Gina Haspel, a woman with too much experience in cruelty and deception. She and others who tortured for the CIA should have been put on trial and held accountable. Under President Barack Obama's watch, not a single person was charged for authorizing or committing torture.[36] And now President Donald Trump rewarded with a promotion one of those people who should have been held accountable.

Tellingly, in the run-up to Haspel's Senate confirmation hearing, among the attributes that her supporters extolled in articles urging her appointment were that "she is a paragon of humility with zero political ambition," so said the conservative author Mark Thiessen, who has expressed his support for waterboarding and once served as speechwriter for President George W. Bush, under whose presidency Haspel tortured and destroyed evidence of torture. "'She's never lobbied for a job,' one of her former CIA bosses told me. 'The jobs searched for her,'" Thiessen wrote in the *Washington Post*.[37]

Translation: Patriarchy is rewarding Gina Haspel with elevation to an unprecedented position for a woman, but patriarchy understands that Haspel will not threaten it with ambitions of her own. She will take what patriarchy gives her.

Carmen Landa Middleton, former deputy executive director of the CIA, went further in an opinion column in which she begins by saying that Haspel "stands ready to break through one of the most stubborn glass ceilings in the U.S. government."[38] Saying that she had once worked with Haspel at the CIA, Middleton described the nominee to head the agency as a "generous and self-effacing individual."

Translation: The person I am proposing is a great vanquisher of gender hierarchies and is, in fact, without ego and will play nice with the boys.

Patriarchy is reluctant to allow women to be powerful outside the lines that patriarchy has drawn for them and independently of the roles it has assigned to them. Be without ambition, be without ego, be unselfish, and we will extend an unprecedented amount of power (for a girl) to you. It is impossible to imagine a man about to make history by taking an unprecedented position being described the way Thiessen and Middleton described Haspel. One wonders why such a man—without ambition, self-effacing, etc.—would be worthy of elevation to such a history-making position. The woman allowed power by patriarchy must essentially be a blank slate on which patriarchy paints what it wants. It helps of course—especially with the "self-effacing"—that the CIA is such a secretive entity and that much of Haspel's tenure there, including her role in torture and the violations of human rights, is classified. To summarize: When a woman who has proven to patriarchy that she can do the most violent of its bidding just like a man can, she will be considered for promotion to the highest levels, as long as she is not what the boys would consider a "bitch."

When Hillary Clinton lost her bid to become the first American woman to be president, the United States of America behaved as if it had invented the idea of a woman leader. Never mind that women had been elected president or prime minister in other parts of the world. If it had not happened in the US, it had not happened, the message seemed to be at times. Clinton was undoubtedly more qualified than her opponent, and misogyny kept many from voting for her. But much like Gina Haspel, Hillary Clinton became a cipher for those who simply wanted a woman to hold a position never held before. And some of us—even when forced to choose between the lesser of two evils, as we have with so many elections—demanded the right to scrutinize Clinton's record beyond her gender. My politics are much further to the left than Clinton's. I understood the misogyny she was subjected to. And it was particularly galling coming from supporters of Bernie Sanders, whose politics were closer to mine but whose statements and platform lacked a gender and racial perspective. An old white man versus an old white woman: in that crude distilling of the option available as the main candidates for those of us who are not Republican lie the contradictions and conflicts for those who are neither white nor old. A closer look at the 2016 US presidential election is beyond the scope of this book—and several others have been written about it. But it is worth remembering in order to appreciate the 2018 midterm elections.

In the summer of 2016, when Donald Trump was still just the Republican nominee for president, the American Muslim father of a US soldier killed in Iraq launched a scathing critique of Trump's vow to bar Muslims from the US. Standing with his wife, Ghazala, by his side at the Democratic National Convention in Philadelphia, Khizr Khan rebuked Trump by offering to lend him a copy of the US Constitution. "You have sacrificed nothing and no one," an emotional Khan said.[39]

Asked to comment, Trump—in a move we have now come to expect—deflected by way of attack. "His wife . . . if you look at his wife, she was standing there. She had nothing to say," Trump said. "She probably, maybe she wasn't allowed to have anything to say. You tell me."

At the time, I rolled my eyes at Trump's lazy cliché of a submissive and silenced Muslim woman. It was typical of the campaign that he ran: racist, misogynist, and ignorant. But now I like to think that Trump's words conjured a hex. I like to imagine a coven of us American-Muslim women working together to bring about Trump's worst nightmare: not one but two Muslim women—each with plenty to say—elected to the US House of Representatives in November 2018.

The first to be sworn in was Palestinian American Rashida Tlaib, from Michigan's Thirteenth District, who took her oath using a Quran she said was a gift from a best friend of twenty-five years. Tlaib wore a Palestinian thob, a traditional dress with elaborate embroidery, inspiring the novelist Susan Muaddi Darraj to launch #TweetYourThob as a call for Palestinian American women to post pictures wearing it.[40] Ilhan Omar, a Somali American elected to represent Minnesota's Fifth Congressional District, was the second to be sworn in. She posed for pictures wearing a bright orange hijab with her husband wearing traditional Somali garb as they held on to a large copy of the Quran.

I have lost count of how many times I have said or written variations of the following: Muslim women are not monolithic. We are more than our headscarves. Now at last I can point to Tlaib and Omar as examples of this truth.

Neither woman wasted any time in relishing their victories. And why should they?

An estimated 135 million people from seven countries, five of which are Muslim-majority, remain affected by Trump's travel ban, which the US Supreme Court upheld in June 2018.[41]

In her victory speech, Omar—who came to the US as a child refugee—also took jabs at Trump's agenda: "Here in Minnesota, we don't only welcome immigrants; we send them to Washington," she said to loud cheers from her supporters.[42]

Both Tlaib and Omar ran on the kind of progressive platforms that propelled other women of color to electoral victories across the country in the midterms. Tlaib, for example, focused on issues like a $15 minimum wage, Medicare for all, and reducing student debt. Omar's Twitter bio describes her as an "intersectional feminist."

Honestly, though, I celebrate Tlaib and Omar for far more personal reasons. Finally, *finally*, we American Muslim women can be complicated! In a selfie that Tlaib has posted of the two of them, Rashida has her hair up in a ponytail and Ilhan is wearing a brown headscarf.

It reminds me of dozens of selfies I have taken with my sister, who like Ilhan wears hijab. By merely existing next to each other, juxtaposed, Rashida and Ilhan complicate perceptions of Muslim women in a country where many people view us through much the same lens as the one that colored Trump's assumptions of Ghazala Khan.

But Tlaib and Omar complicate more than just the optics of Muslim women. At a time when the patriarchal voting patterns of white American women are finally being scrutinized, these two progressive women of color represent the opposite. I am not embarrassed to say that I am enjoying the Schadenfreude.

Indeed I have lost count of the times I've been asked, mostly by white people, why Muslim women submit to misogyny, as if patriarchy and the misogyny it protects and enables are the sole property of Muslims and not a global social construct.

So now, in the spirit of flipping the House, I am flipping the narrative: Why do Republican white women submit to misogyny? Or, to paraphrase

Trump, maybe they weren't allowed to vote any other way? Exit polls from election night 2018 show that in three key races in Florida, Texas, and Georgia, the majority of white women voters chose Republican candidates over progressive Democratic opponents.[43]

Perhaps the most frustrating example of that was in the close race for governor in Georgia, where CNN exit polls reported that slightly more white women than men chose the Republican candidate Brian Kemp over his opponent, Stacey Abrams, a progressive Black female candidate.[44] Was their reason internalized misogyny? Was it racism? (Spoiler: It was both.)

But who indoctrinated those Republican white women? Who taught them to submit to patriarchy? Those are questions often reserved for Muslim women, but I demand we ask them now of white women—whose votes uphold the benefits of whiteness but hurt the rest of us.

White women are, by nature of their skin color, rarely pathologized or othered in the way that Muslim women of color are. Their acquiescence to patriarchy is rarely presented as indoctrination. Instead, it is portrayed as their choice. And yet, I guarantee that those very same Republican white women are quick to lament the plight of Muslim women and eagerly point to Islam as a source of misogyny, refusing to subject their Christian beliefs to a similar reckoning.

Tlaib and Omar complicate all of that.

In the same way that the elevation of Gina Haspel to head the CIA must in turn not deflect scrutiny of that agency's illegal history of torture and other violations of human rights, which my country of birth is often, and rightfully, scrutinized for, those same white women who vote Republican, who benefit from their proximity to white supremacy and its attendant powers, must be analyzed in the same way Muslim women have been analyzed by Western political scientists for decades. Patriarchy is universal and quotidian, and its foot soldiers everywhere must be called out.

A few days after Trump's remarks about Ghazala Khan, an American Muslim woman, along with twelve other women, disrupted a speech Trump was giving in Detroit.

"American, parent, Muslim, Arab American, and woman. As I thought about my identities, I felt more and more that confronting Trump was the most patriotic and courageous act I could pursue," she later said.[45]

That woman was Rashida Tlaib. She is now the first Palestinian American woman to join the US Congress.

In November 2016, during a campaign stop in Minnesota, Trump said the state had "suffered enough" at the hands of Somali immigrants, and suggested that Somalis were sneaking into the state and spreading extremist views.[46] Two years later, 78 percent of Minnesota's Fifth Congressional District voted to make Ilhan Omar the first Somali American, first Muslim refugee, and first hijab-wearing Muslim woman elected to the US Congress. Racking up one more "first," Omar is also the first woman of color to represent Minnesota in Congress.

When Ilhan Omar says, "I am America's hope and the president's nightmare," I say amen, sister.[47]

It is instructive, and telling of patriarchy's insistence that it and it alone has the right to canonize women into power, that the election of Omar, Tlaib, and other women of color to Congress in the 2018 midterm elections were not celebrated as gender victories as the Haspel nomination and confirmation were. Alexandria Ocasio-Cortez, who became the youngest woman ever elected to Congress, has been the subject of an endless stream of conservative attacks that have questioned her political acumen, even though she beat a ten-year incumbent in her district, which includes parts of the eastern Bronx and northern Queens, during the primaries to become the Democratic Party's nominee for the midterms. Conservatives have also questioned her biography, alleging that she has lied about her working-class background. Even her inability to afford Washington, DC, rents before she was sworn in to the US House of Representatives became fodder in conservative news circles. For too many old, white, wealthy male politicians, young powerful women of color are terrifying because they put patriarchy and its attendant oppressions on notice. But those women of color whose victories in the 2018 midterm elections made them "the firsts" were not heralded for being "self-effacing." Instead, Omar, Tlaib, and Ocasio-Cortez's very existence said they refused to stay in their appointed place. It was a big fuck-you to white supremacists, misogynists, Islamophobes, racists, and those who believe politics are the domain of wealthy white men who seek to maintain the economic and social status quo that keeps the rest of us in our place. These women, unlike Gina

Haspel, were not "utterly lacking in political ambition." Instead, they delighted in it, and they announced loudly that their political ambition included a progressive agenda aimed at free education, universal healthcare, a determination to stall and reverse climate change, and a refusal to be humble, modest, quiet, or anything else patriarchy demanded.

When the conservative pastor E. W. Jackson complained, less than a month after the midterm elections, that "the floor of Congress is now going to look like an Islamic republic," because of the presence of one Muslim woman in a headscarf, that Muslim woman, Ilhan Omar, quipped back perfectly.

"Well sir, the floor of Congress is going to look like America," she wrote on Twitter. "And you're gonna have to just deal."[48]

Omar went on to force the most forthright examination I have seen since I moved to the US of American foreign policy on Israel and the impact the American Israel Public Affairs Committee (AIPAC), which calls itself "America's pro-Israel lobby," has on that policy.[49] Her willingness to question power unaccustomed to being disturbed was on display when she sharply challenged, at a House Foreign Affairs Committee, the Trump administration's new special envoy to Venezuela, Elliott Abrams. Abrams was assistant secretary of state for human rights and assistant secretary of state for inter-American affairs in the Reagan administration, during which, as the *Guardian* reminds us, he was "widely criticized for shrugging off reports about the massacre of a thousand men, women and children by US-funded death squads in El Salvador."[50] In 1991, Abrams admitted he withheld information from Congress about the Iran-Contra affair. President George H. W. Bush pardoned him in 1992. That is what white and privileged patriarchy looks and sounds like. It is rarely, if ever, held accountable, and when it is, there is always a powerful white man to pardon its actions. And then comes along a Black Muslim woman in a headscarf who survived war in her country of birth and arrived in the US as a twelve-year-old refugee and who now had power of her own that she is using to put you on notice that she does not play by the rules that comforted the white and wealthy powerful men.

A few hours after she took her oath, Rashida Tlaib was filmed at a private gathering with friends and supporters celebrating the importance to being true to oneself.

"People are like, 'Rashida, maybe you should put the bullhorn away.' No! 'Maybe you shouldn't wear those gym shoes everywhere.' . . . I say fuck that," she said. " I didn't change or try to run away from being *Arabeyya*, *Muslimah*, *Falestenyya*, and . . . it's such an addition on top of that to being a badass organizer. Don't ever let anyone take away your roots, culture, who you are because when you [don't change] people love you and you win."[51]

Her words will stay with many of us who likewise happily and proudly juggle multiple identities. But what resonated the most, especially with her detractors in the Civility Chorus, was how she ended her moving celebratory speech.

"And when your son looks at you and says 'Mama look you won. Bullies don't win.' And I said 'Baby, they don't. Because we're gonna go in there, we're gonna impeach the motherfucker,'" Tlaib said, signaling to the president that the activist and mother who disrupted his lunch speech in Detroit in 2016 was now a lawmaker.

Women who do not ask for permission are powerful.

■   ■   ■   ■

ON MARCH 18, 2005, I put on my smartest clothes and my favorite jewelry, hailed a cab, and tried my best not to cry as I rode to the Juma'h prayer that marks the highlight of the Muslim week. We are taught to look our best for the weekly prayer, and this was no ordinary Juma'h. It was the first time on record that a woman was to lead a mixed-gender Friday prayer.

Police officers stood guard outside Synod House, next to the Cathedral Church of St. John the Divine in Upper Manhattan. The original venue for the prayer backed out after it received threats. But no security check could dampen our emotions.

For some of the one hundred men and women sitting together on the floor of the prayer hall, the tears flowed early. I could hear the two women next to me quietly sob as they listened to a woman issue the call to prayer. For one of them, a Somali, they were tears of return—in her country, women were not allowed into the local mosque.

When Amina Wadud, at the time an Islamic studies professor at Virginia Commonwealth University, stepped up to the microphone, I let out a long sigh—of relief, of acceptance, and, finally, of peace. For years I had been engaged in a seemingly endless bout over women's rights with a male-dominated Islam, neither one of us able to deal that knockout blow.

Amina Wadud dealt it for me. The struggle would continue, but seeing Wadud give her sermon, I could see the light at the end of the 1,400-year-long tunnel. Hearing her recite verses that addressed men and women as equals and listening as she pointed to the exclusion of women by male jurists from the codification of Islamic law—several decades after the death of the prophet Muhammad—it was clear she was serving notice that female scholars of Islam were done with being on the sidelines. The spiritual equality at the heart of Islam meant nothing less than equality in religious leadership, Wadud was saying. Our presence at Synod House was our collective amen to that.

And then she led us in prayer.

We later heard of protesters outside, but they were a handful and were to be expected.[52] What I had not expected was to look up at Wadud and feel that it was normal to see a woman in her position. Who knew that making history could be so normal? And make history we did. Suddenly, scholars and clerics who have ignored countless atrocities in the name of Islam over the past few years awoke to denounce Wadud and those of us who prayed behind her.[53] Predictably, some saw a Zionist American plot to use women's issues to destabilize the Muslim world. Others irresponsibly accused Wadud of heresy, a word that some consider a death sentence.

A jihadist website urged Osama bin Laden to issue a fatwa calling for our deaths, while the now late Libyan leader Muammar el-Qaddafi complained at the time to an Arab League summit meeting that our prayer would create a million bin Ladens. A woman leading one hundred people in prayer would inspire people to extremist violence, rather than the oppression, torture, and corruption of regimes such as those led by Qaddafi and his fellow dictators at that Arab League summit.[54]

A BBC documentary filmmaker told me that during his interview with the Iraqi cleric Muqtader al-Sadr—usually described as "hardline" and "fiery" in Western media—he asked Sadr what was the worst thing the US had done. This was two years after the US invaded Iraq. Sadr replied, "Allow a woman to lead prayer."

A woman who does not wait for permission is powerful because she has put patriarchy on notice that she is not waiting for its anointment. A few days after our prayer in New York City, in celebrating Amina Wadud's courage, an Indonesian female scholar got straight to the point and urged women to stop waiting for permission.

But I can tell you that the courage of Amina Wadud is impossible to describe. She received so much hate mail and so many death threats that she was asked not to go to campus because her safety could not be guaranteed.[55] With university approval she secretly met with a seminar class on campus once a week but was asked to conduct her other classes from home via videolink. Amina Wadud is a Black Muslim woman who understood how many of her identities would come under attack, and her courage continues to propel and inspire me today, fourteen years later. It was a thrill to stand before God as the spiritual equal of the male congregants.

There is nothing in Islam that bars a woman from giving the Friday sermon or from leading a mixed-gender prayer. The fact that only men have done both for centuries is one of many traditions that Muslims have rarely questioned. It is hard for so many Muslim women to reconcile what they are told is the intrinsic egalitarianism of our religion while encountering the blatant misogyny that centuries of male-dominated interpretation of our religion have wrought.

Since Amina Wadud made history, several other women have led mixed-gender prayer and at least three women-led or solely-for-women mosques have opened around the world. Also, in the intervening years, a growing community of LGBTQ Muslims has courageously come out to further push against patriarchy in the faith.

Too many religions are patriarchal and imbued with misogyny. Because of this I am often asked how I can be a Muslim feminist. My response is that I am both of Muslim descent and a feminist, and the two identities are not connected. One does not depend on the other. My goal is the destruction of patriarchy wherever it exists, be it in the sacred or the secular world. We must all have freedom of faith and freedom from faith. But it is naive to simply say "just leave your religion" as a solution to patriarchal rituals or beliefs. Religions exist across the world in various forms and with various power structures. Most if not all are patriarchal. To "just leave your religion" isn't possible for many women. In fact, the very refrain "Just leave your religion," as a solution to being free of patriarchy, is one that is laden with privilege not available to every woman. What is to be done regarding the patriarchy they face?

Moreover, secular spaces are not free of patriarchy either. It is universal. We cannot abandon women from faith traditions with a simple shrug saying "just leave your religion; all religions are patriarchal anyway." A feminist fight against patriarchy is necessary within and without religion. Having said that, we cannot allow arguments for religious exemptions to become a cover for the continuation of patriarchal traditions within any religion or to serve as excuses to justify misogyny within those religions.

Scholars like Amina Wadud, who identifies as an Islamic feminist, and her equivalents in other faiths are taking that feminist fight to the patriarchy and imbuing their resistance with knowledge that is particular to and necessary for their respective faith communities. My goal is the destruction of patriarchy, and to that end, I will fight anything that hurts women—cis and trans—and queer people. Any institution, secular or sacred, that reserves power and leadership for men only must be condemned and held accountable until it ends such misogyny. When Amina Wadud announced she would lead a mixed-gender Friday prayer in 2005, I was on the board of directors of the Progressive Muslim Union of North America, which cosponsored the prayer. Some people who wanted to join the prayer wrote to us asking for the jurisprudence upon which Wadud assumed the role of imam. Wadud had prepared it, and we sent it to them. For myself and others, though, that proof was unnecessary. I happily supported Amina Wadud as my imam because it was beyond time that women assumed such power for themselves. It was revolutionary, and it was necessary.

When I prayed behind Amina Wadud, I was one of two women who did so without a headscarf and, further, I had my period. A woman leading a mixed-gender congregation was, then and now, taboo enough. Praying without a headscarf and praying while menstruating were double whammies I added as my own revolutionary contributions to Amina Wadud's revolutionary decision. I wanted to add my own ways of defying rules that

I believe place an unfair burden of modesty on women and girls in the case of headscarves, and I was determined in my way to challenge the idea that menstruation is impure or should inhibit women and people who menstruate from partaking in prayer and other faith rituals. Menstruation is taboo globally. It is used to bar women (again, such restrictions are framed around cis-women's bodies) from religious rituals, places of worship, and, at times, from their own homes, as with a Hindu custom that is now illegal in Nepal but which continues to banish women and girls to "menstruation huts" outside their homes. Apart from the ostracization and other indignities, women and girls have died in those huts from snake bites, carbon monoxide poisoning, and other dangers.

In 2015, ten years after Amina Wadud led us in prayer in New York City, while I was in Paris to promote the French edition of my previous book, I mentioned at an event at the Arab World Institute that I had prayed while menstruating. A Muslim man told me, during a Q&A with about four hundred people, that I had "deeply hurt" him by saying that. I was stunned that a man could have such strong feelings about how a woman chooses to pray. It is one thing to know the ways that women and people who menstruate are shamed across the world. It is another to come face to face with that shame from a man who had no shame expressing it in front of a packed hall. How the fuck does what comes out of my body or how and when I choose to pray while my body does a perfectly natural thing "deeply hurt" Mr. Sensitive Feelings? In contrast to that—and as a reminder that when we share our personal rebellions and our moments of seizing power, we find allies who share their personal revolutions—during a panel discussion at the Bradford Literature Festival in 2017, I shared that I had prayed on my period. A Muslim woman later told me that she and her mother have started praying while on their periods too.

To understand the policing of women's bodies that patriarchy enables and protects, and to understand as well how religions cross-pollinate their misogynies, it is instructive to follow the determination of Indian women seeking to pray in temples and mosques barred to them. Their struggle shows that the fight to dismantle patriarchy must occur in every space and that the opposition to that struggle reminds us what is at stake. We must invent the power that our freedom requires, remember!

For centuries, many Hindu temples wouldn't allow women into the innermost chamber where an idol is positioned. The prohibition is at times simply gender-based and at others it is aimed at barring the entrance of women and girls of "menstruating age," which is defined as between the ages of ten and fifty years. Under the banner of #RightToPray, the tactics women have used in their fight to gain access to temples are examples of how we must use a combination of strategies to defy, disobey, and disrupt patriarchy. The ways patriarchy has fought back—at times with the help of women—demonstrates the magnitude of what we are fighting for.

The BBC reported that when lawyer-activist Varsha Deshpande led a group of ten women into a temple for the Hindu god Shani, the temple authorities told them that women "aren't allowed in because Shani doesn't really like women."[56]

"All religions are discriminatory towards women," said Deshpande. "Religion is not meant for women. It's meant to exploit women. We should reject all these religions which are dominated by patriarchy. We should have our own religion—of womanhood."

Demanding their "Right to Worship" and "Right to Pray"—both of which became social media hashtags—Indian feminists began in late 2015 to protest against bans on Hindu temples and a Muslim shrine, attempting to storm them at times, and also filed cases with courts, including the Indian supreme court, against what they described as unconstitutional bans. The prominent Hindu feminist Trupti Desai is a leader of the protesters and member of the women's rights group the Bhumata Brigade (Women Warriors of Mother Earth). She told the BBC that she describes herself as a "practising, believing Hindu" and that she blamed patriarchy for keeping women out of temples and shrines. "These are man-made traditions. God does not differentiate between man and woman," Desai said.[57]

In January 2016 Desai led several hundred women on a march aimed at storming the Shani Shingnapur temple, in the Indian state of Maharashtra. They were stopped and detained en route, but their march made India pay attention to their cause and reminds us all of the importance of protest and civil disobedience as tools to "invent the power [we] require for our freedom." Four months later, in April 2016, Desai and other activists successfully gained entry to the temple after a Bombay High Court ruling forced temple trustees to lift the ban on women of all ages.[58]

Social media has been an important platform for voices that have been marginalized or barred from the mainstream media. It has proven important not just as a place for those voices to say "I count" but also for connecting real life with the virtual world, creating an important call-and-response that serves to fortify protest and help us shore up power as we defy, disobey, and disrupt patriarchy.

This was the case when a temple official at the Sabarimala temple in the southern state of Kerala, which barred women between ten and fifty years of age from entering the shrine, said in November 2016 that women would be allowed access there only if a machine was invented to detect if they were "pure"—meaning that they weren't menstruating. In response, university student Nikita Azad launched a #HappyToBleed campaign on Facebook. Women posted photographs holding placards at times made of sanitary napkins and tampons with the slogan "Happy to Bleed," making the campaign go viral.[59]

The biggest head-to-head confrontation with patriarchy's rules over menstruation came after the Supreme Court of India in September 2018 overturned the Sabarimala temple ban to allow entry to women and girls of all ages. It took more than three months after that decision for any woman to enter the temple. What stopped them? Patriarchy's foot soldiers in the form of men *and* women who violently prevented their entrance.

When Desai announced soon after the ruling that she intended to visit Sabarimala, she said that she received hundreds of death threats. "They said, 'If you come to Kerala, we'll break your limbs. We'll cut you up into pieces,'" she told NPR.[60]

In October 2018 journalist Kavitha Jagdal and social activist Rehana Fathima, in full riot gear and protected by one hundred policemen, were prevented from entering the temple because of violent protesters, men and women.

In November 2018, when Desai landed at an airport ninety-five miles from Sabarimala, protesters blocked airport exits and trapped her inside for thirteen hours, until she eventually turned back. NPR reported that the protesters threatened to attack taxi drivers who might drive her in the direction of the temple.

India is one of many countries that has elected patriarchal authoritarians who are happy to use a mix of right-wing politics and religion to bolster their power. The ruling Hindu nationalist Bharatiya Janata Party (BJP), headed by Prime Minister Narendra Modi, has argued that the Supreme Court of India ruling was an attack on Hindu values. Thousands of protesters, including local politicians from the BJP Party, have been arrested for taking part in violent demonstrations against the court's verdict. When the highest echelon of power unashamedly promotes patriarchy and pits the highest court in the land against "Hindu values," we gain a close-up view of how patriarchy shifts the goalposts to its advantage. Laws are made by male-dominated senates and parliaments around the world, invariably to the advantage of men. But on the few occasions when an ostensibly independent judiciary rules in favor of women, patriarchal powers will step in. The game is always stacked against us. Knowing that, we can either play and hope for the occasional positive ruling or we can upend that game, fight in whatever ways we have at our disposal, and seize permission for ourselves.

There are women who don't want permission: the women who voted for Trump, Bolsonaro, or the candidates of other far-right populist parties; the women who insist they don't need feminism; the women who fight against reproductive rights and insist they don't want those rights; the women who say "We can wait," the slogan under which the foot soldiers of the patriarchy rallied to insist that they are fine with waiting until they're old enough to be beyond the ban age to enter a Hindu temple or shrine.

One such woman told NPR that she visited Sabarimala as a child but then waited until age fifty-three, when she stopped getting her period, before visiting again. "I'll block younger women with my own body if I have to," she told NPR.[61]

It is hard enough to fight patriarchy. That fight is made harder by rules that constantly work against us, goalposts that endlessly shift, and women who sign up to do patriarchy's bidding. The last remind us that patriarchy is not about men, that feminism is not about "hating men." Patriarchy is about power, and feminism is about destroying patriarchy. And we must recognize that some women accept patriarchy's crumbs in exchange for a limited form of power and hollow promises of "protection." Those women—much like white people who insist on civility in the face of racism—must not drain the energy we need to fight patriarchy. Not every woman is my ally or my sister simply by virtue of being a woman. We are sisters and comrades when we share a fight against patriarchy. Patriarchy throws all its efforts at disempowering us. I do not consider as a sister or a comrade anyone who aids in that disempowerment.

I am often asked "How do you justify praying on your period?" which essentially translates to "Which male scholar gave you the permission to break what we believe is not allowed by Islam?" My answer is: I gave myself permission. I took it. When Stella Nyanzi in Uganda is jailed for more than a month essentially for protesting period poverty—a result of taboos on menstruation—and when women in India risk their lives to break a ban that effectively punishes menstruation, we must seize permission for ourselves.

On January 2, 2019, more than three months after the Supreme Court of India ruling, two women finally made it into Sabarimala temple. Bindu Ammini, forty-two, and her friend Kanakadurga, forty-one, successfully entered the temple. Protesters had initially barred them from entering on December 24. The *Washington Post* described their historic entrance thus: "To reach the temple, devotees must walk nearly three miles uphill, and Bindu began the trek at midnight. The group consisted of six men in addition to the two women, who had covered their faces. Four police officers in civilian clothes also accompanied them. At one point, the group was questioned by a couple of protesters but simply continued walking."[62] Soon after the women's victory, the temple's head priest ordered the building closed for "purification" before reopening it. After news of the women's success emerged, violent protests in which at least one person was killed brought Kerala to a standstill. Schools across the state were closed, and public transport was suspended. The BBC reported that at least seven hundred were arrested.[63]

The day before the women's entrance, something historic and incredible happened that beautifully paved the way for the act of seizing power by Ammini and Kanakadurga. Women across Kerala formed a human chain—called the Women's Wall—that extended for 385 miles (620 kilometers) across all national highways from the northern tip of Kasaragod to the southern end, in Thiruvanthapuram. Kerala state's leftist coalition government organized the protest to combat inequality and counter the efforts of right-wing groups that support the Sabarimala ban on women. Kerala officials told the BBC that the Women's Wall comprised five million women.[64] The Indian news site *The News Minute* called the protest "a defining moment for feminist politics in Kerala" that brought together "leaders and members from political parties, socio-political organisations and progressive Hindu organisations."[65] India is a country of more than a billion people, so a wall made up of five million women is not that unimaginable, but I must admit that at first I did a double-take that was quickly followed by asking myself, "When we have such power, when five million women can turn out to protest, who convinced us we had no power?" It was incredible to watch the videos and pictures from the protest. Men who supported the women's protest against right-wing groups formed a corresponding wall across from the Women's Wall.

"This is a great way of saying how powerful women are, and how we can empower ourselves and help each other. Of course, I support the move to allow women of all ages into the temple. I don't think tradition, or any kind of backwardness should stop women. Those who want to pray must have the right to pray," one of the demonstrators told BBC Hindi.[66]

The Communist Party of India's Brinda Karat, a member of the country's Council of States, called the Women's Wall a "historic gathering," adding,

> Very often, religious beliefs and sentiments have been employed to use women in subordinate positions. Today, dear sisters, you have made history. You have resisted against the dark forces that want to push women back into the dark ages. You have built the wall of resilience to take forward the values of social reforms, which are critical for women's advancement in the 21st century. Kerala, you have moved ahead, not only for the women of Kerala but for the women across India.[67]

Revolutions are never about single events. Patriarchy will not be dismantled in one blow. As a reminder of how many blows it will take, Ammini and Kanakadurga went into hiding after entering the temple and were granted twenty-four-hour police protection for almost two weeks after their historic prayer. As a reminder that our biggest fights are often with mothers, families, and other loved ones, Kanakadurga was admitted to a hospital soon after she returned home after her mother-in-law allegedly beat her with a plank of wood. Three weeks after she made history, Kanakadurga, a mother of two, slept in a government-run shelter following her return home from the hospital to find her husband had locked the doors and gone into hiding.[68]

The office of the chief minister of Kerala said that on January 4 a third woman, aged forty-six, had entered the temple since the two women's entry. "Dozens more, including some in men's clothing, have been turned back by demonstrators, backed by the temple's administrators," the *Guardian* reported.[69]

The alliances that turned up for Kerala's Women's Wall are the antithesis of the hierarchies that prop up patriarchy. Too often, women join revolutions and uprisings only to watch their participation erased and diminished as the fight against oppression dwindles to a game of musical chairs among men fighting each other for power. So it is good and vital to see the centering of women's fight against regressive and right-wing forces.

When I talk about the importance of centering the fight against patriarchy and of feminism itself, I often hear "That can wait! Do you know how many x, y, z people are oppressed? War! Political prisoners!" While the fight against various oppressions is, of course, important and necessary, statements like "wait" are actually saying that women are not important enough to center. My response is to remind my interlocutors of what I call the Trifecta of Misogyny. I am told that no one is free, not men and not women, because the state oppresses everyone. Be that as it may, we must remember that the street and the home together also oppress women. That is the Trifecta of Misogyny: state, street, home. And until we recognize how that trifecta is the home of patriarchy and that we must dismantle that trifecta by defying, disobeying, and disrupting patriarchy in the state, the street, and the home, our efforts to be free will fail, because none of us will be free as long as patriarchy remains in place. Women will continue to show up for protests, uprisings, and revolutions for every cause imaginable, but who will turn up for women?

This is an especially vital question for liberatory movements, which claim to be revolutionary but which, along the way, seem to aim only for the right of men in those movements to be free. Upon closer inspection, too many liberatory movements replicate within them the very power dynamics of the oppressions they claim to fight.

In 1974, Elaine Brown became the first and only woman to lead the Black Panther Party, chosen by the Panthers' founder Huey Newton before he went into exile in Cuba. It was a "pivotal moment for a woman in the black power movement," writes DeNeen L. Brown in the *Washington Post*.[70] "Although women had been a dynamic force for social and racial justice, they had often been overshadowed by men. No woman had led the NAACP, the Southern Christian Leadership Conference or the Student Non-Violent Coordinating Committee."

The party was created in 1966 initially to protect Black communities from police brutality but expanded its platform, which was revolutionary— free healthcare, decent housing, and transportation for seniors. The party also created free school-breakfast programs, provided sickle-cell anemia testing, and offered legal aid and adult education.

The naming of a woman in August 1974 to lead, as Elaine Brown writes, "the only armed revolutionary organization operating inside the United States of America" was in and of itself revolutionary. Brown quotes Newton as telling her, "I can't trust anybody else with my party." And during her tenure as party chair, Brown used her position of power to up-end not uphold patriarchy. But that revolutionary act did not extend to the party's gender politics, and Brown angered some men in the party when she installed women in key administrative positions. As she writes in her 1992 memoir *A Taste of Power: A Black Woman's Story*,

> There was one result of all this I had failed to think through. I had in-troduced a number of women in the party's administration. There were too many women in command of the affairs of the Black Panther Party, numerous men were grumbling.
>
> "I hear we can't call them bitches no more," one Brother actually stated to me in the middle of an extraordinarily hectic day.
>
> "No, motherfucker," I responded unendearingly, "you may not call *them* bitches 'no more.'"[71]

Brown goes on to reveal that because of her relationship with Huey Newton, she had "been able to deflect most of the chauvinism of Black Panther
men." She writes:

> It was a given, that the entire Black Power movement was handicapped
> by the limited roles the Brothers allowed the Sisters, and by the outright
> oppressive behavior of men toward women. This had meant little to me
> personally, however. The party was so far to the left of the civil rights
> and black nationalist men, nothing in their philosophies was dreamt of
> in ours. My leadership was secure. Thus, in installing Sisters in key posi-
> tions, I had not considered this business. I had only considered the issue
> of merit, which had no gender.

Brown understood the threat that Black women in leadership positions
posed to patriarchy. Her explanation of why that was the case reminds
me that any movement, no matter how far-left, socialist, antiracist, or
revolutionary it may be, that does not center gender and the fight against
patriarchy becomes, essentially, an arena where men fight other men for
power, on the backs of women.

Writes Brown:

> A woman in the Black Power movement was considered, at best, irrele-
> vant. A woman asserting herself was a pariah. A woman attempting the
> role of leadership was, to my proud black Brothers, making an alliance
> with the "counter-revolutionary man-hating, lesbian, feminist white
> bitches." It was a violation of some Black Power principle that was left
> undefined. If a black woman assumed a role of leadership, this was said
> to be eroding black manhood, to be hindering the progress of the black
> race. She was an enemy of black people.

Brown left the Black Panther Party in 1977 after a female adminis-
trator at the Black Panthers' school was beaten and hospitalized with a
broken jaw. Newton, who had recently returned from exile in Cuba, had
approved the beating of Regina Davis for a minor transgression. He refused to back down when Brown confronted him about it. "The beating
of Regina would be taken as a clear signal that the words 'Panther' and

'comrade' had taken on gender connotations," Brown writes, "denoting an inferiority in the female half of us." Brown resigned and left the party's headquarters in Oakland, California, for Los Angeles. Brown has continued her political activism, with a focus on radical reform of the criminal justice system.

Elaine Brown was the only Black woman to lead a Black Power movement. She used her authority to put other women into positions of power, but ultimately even that proved not enough to combat the misogyny in the Black Panther Party.

And that is exactly why the Combahee River Collective, which developed in 1974 out of the larger National Black Feminist Organization, insisted that the struggles for equality in race, class, gender, and sexuality must be one fight in order to best tackle the multiple oppressions that Black women and women of color experience. The collective's 1977 statement explains why Black feminism remains such a vital source of inspiration and a path to power for many of us. "A combined anti-racist and anti-sexist position drew us together initially, and as we developed politically we addressed ourselves to heterosexism and economic oppression under capitalism," the statement says.[72]

The collective, whose founding members included the radical Black feminist Barbara Smith, her twin sister, Beverly, and Demita Frazier, issued a statement so revolutionary that forty-two years later it remains the ultimate benchmark by which we must hold accountable all who claim to fight for freedom. Freedom is the goal. Destroying patriarchy is the way toward that freedom, but the struggle is also against racism, capitalism, and homophobia. For those of us who are not white or wealthy or heterosexual, the Combahee River Collective laid out the road map for such a struggle.

They write:

> We believe that sexual politics under patriarchy is as pervasive in Black women's lives as are the politics of class and race. We also often find it difficult to separate race from class from sex oppression because in our lives they are most often experienced simultaneously. . . . We realize that the liberation of all oppressed peoples necessitates the destruction of the political-economic systems of capitalism and imperialism as well as

patriarchy. We are socialists because we believe that work must be organized for the collective benefit of those who do the work and create the products, and not for the profit of the bosses. Material resources must be equally distributed among those who create these resources. We are not convinced, however, that a socialist revolution that is not also a feminist and anti-racist revolution will guarantee our liberation.

Women around the world are still being asked to wait our turn because patriarchy protects and enables male dominance. The more women and nonbinary and queer people are affected by the oppressions that patriarchy employs, the more vital a statement from a collective that fought patriarchy, racism, capitalism, and homophobia remains. Remember that these words were written in 1977: "As Black feminists and Lesbians we know that we have a very definite revolutionary task to perform and we are ready for the lifetime of work and struggle before us."

Power for a few exceptional women is not equality or empowerment and is no reason to celebrate. We must define power in a way that liberates us from patriarchy's hierarchies. We must imagine the world we want and redefine what power is, what a powerful woman looks like, and how power can be used to subvert rather than uphold patriarchy. We must imagine better. We can imagine better. We must imagine ways to start wresting power from patriarchy. By imagining that better world, we invent the power required for our freedom.

What does being powerful mean? It must be more than doing what men do or being what men can be. I don't want to be something simply because a man can be that thing. Men are not my yardstick. If men themselves are not free of the ravages of racism, capitalism, and other forms of oppression, it is not enough to say I want to be equal to them. Equal to the ways they themselves are victimized by patriarchy? No thanks! I want to be free. As long as patriarchy remains unchallenged, men will continue to be the default and the standard against which everything is measured. When I imagine what it would look like to invent the power required for our freedom, I know that power for women has often been achieved after a negotiation with patriarchy, as a reward from patriarchy, or as a transaction aimed at diffusing opposition to patriarchy. Recognizing that, we must be strategic in what we do with that power.

The year 2019 began with two relevant events. The inauguration of a far-right misogynist, racist, and homophobic president as president of Latin America's biggest democracy—Brazil—and a protest by five million women in the world's biggest democracy—India—against right-wing groups that believe menstruating women must be banned from temples. The power of patriarchy is strong, and our power to imagine our freedom from it must be even more ferocious.

CHAPTER 6

Violence

Obviously, the most oppressed of any oppressed group will be its women. . . . Obviously, since women, period, are oppressed in society, and if you've got an oppressed group, they're *twice* oppressed. So I should imagine that they react accordingly: as oppression makes people more militant . . . then *twice* militant, because they're *twice oppressed*.

—LORRAINE HANSBERRY, from "An Interview with Lorraine Hansberry by Studs Terkel," May 12, 1959[1]

IMAGINE IF WE DECLARED WAR.
Imagine if we fuck-this-shit snapped, en masse, and systematically killed men, for no reason at all other than for being men. Imagine this culling starting in one country with five men a week. Then each week, this imaginary scenario would add more countries and kill more men in each of them. Fifty a week, then one hundred men, then five hundred.

Imagine an underground movement called Fuck the Patriarchy (FTP), which would claim responsibility and warn that it was putting the world on notice that it would keep killing more and more men until the patriarchy sent a representative to talk. We do not want money, it would say. We do not want a new president or prime minister to replace the current one, this imaginary claimant of responsibility would say. We do not want a few more seats in parliament. We do not want a pay raise. We do not want men to promise to do the laundry or to promise to babysit their own children. We do not want a few more crumbs. So send your representative, patriarchy, this imaginary claimant of responsibility would demand (I can imagine the infighting that would ensue).

Its ultimatum: begin dismantling patriarchy or we will continue killing more and more men every week.

How many men do you think must be killed before patriarchy begins to be dismantled? One thousand? Ten thousand? One million? Is it barbaric? Is it savage? Many millions of men have been killed in wars begun by men against other men. Imagine this our declaration of war against patriarchy.

How long would it take for the world to pay attention to the killings of men? When would it become a global emergency? A month? Five months? How many men would have to be killed—for absolutely no reason whatsoever other than they were men—for the world to wonder: "What the fuck is going on? Who is behind this madness? Who do we talk to so that this savagery can stop? Who do we invade, who should we bomb? What did men ever do to deserve this barbarity?" How many men would have to be killed before the representatives of patriarchy called an emergency summit to bring to a halt the senseless murders of their own? How many men must we kill until we get patriarchy to the table?

How would men feel when they saw so many of their fellow men, murdered simply for being, like them, men? Would they change their behavior—walk together for safety, avoid certain areas of town, make sure they were not out beyond a certain time? How would boys feel, knowing that their gender made them walking targets? How would it make their parents feel? Would it change the way they raised or treated their sons? Would it change the way the boys behaved?

That is an intentionally disturbing scenario. I know. But we are long overdue a fuck-this-shit snapping. It is as if men have hoarded the operating manual for violence and, from boyhood, have been taught the language of that manual, while girls and women are kept illiterate. Violence—daily acts of violence against women simply for being women—benefits men. Patriarchy's copyright over violence has terrorized us into fear and submission. If every act of violence against women were reported on the news, it would be recognized for the epidemic—the war—that it is. Instead, only "especially" violent attacks are reported and not even all of those, which tells you that society does not care and/or is immune to them. A daily war is carried out against women, and yet it is not called "barbaric" or "savage." We are supposed to learn to live with it, accommodate it, never fight it.

Well, enough. Why shouldn't we declare war?

If every murder, rape, sexual assault, beating, and instance of physical and emotional abuse of women were reported, every day, it would force us to see that it is not merely "psychopaths" who are violent toward women but fathers, husbands, brothers, sons, boyfriends, and ordinary men. When only the "especially" violent attacks are reported, you will often hear, "Oh, that's not a real man who did that. That was a psychopath." If we kept a tally of the daily drip of that war women are subjected to, it would deny men the ability to hold the responsibility for that violence at arm's length, to distance themselves from it so they can pretend it was "just a psychopath" who was responsible for the violence that impacts every aspect of the lives of women and girls—at home, in public space, on public transport, at work, school, everywhere. We are not safe from that violence anywhere.

On any given week, I can tell you about the latest political stand-offs, the latest in a war somewhere, or how the "war on _____" (fill in the blank: terror, drugs, etc.) is proceeding. I can tell you, in other words, myriad men's stories: men jostling for power, men killing other men over power, and men negotiating over the spoils of that power.

I cannot, however, tell you how many girls were subjected to sexual assault at home or school during any given week, how many women were beaten or raped by their husbands, nor how many girls and women were subjected to street sexual harassment or worse in the cities of any country. There is no War on Women news bulletin. Imagine hearing nothing but those stories on the news or reading nothing but those stories in the media. It would be overwhelming and suffocating.

In October 2018 I was in Dublin to attend the Safe World Summit, organized by the NGO Safe Ireland as a gathering for activists to discuss and advocate for ways to end violence against women and children. Many of the speakers were themselves survivors who shared their own experience with patriarchal violence: sexual abuse by parents or priests; intimate-partner violence; and incest, rape, and other forms of sexual violence. Some talked of how they survived, others of how they barely have. After two days of listening to the speakers' searing and gutting stories, I wanted to kill men. Two intense days of survivor stories left me wondering, "How can I not hate men?!" It is a challenge—genuinely—and one I often surrender to. It is difficult for me not to hate men.

How would our world be different if the War on Women led every news bulletin? How would we react if each and every single one of the 164 reported rapes per day in Brazil in 2017 were reported on the day they happened? How would we feel if each time a girl in Egypt had her genitals cut it was reported on the news? According to UNICEF, 74 percent of girls in Egypt ages fifteen to seventeen have been subjected to one form or another of genital cutting.[2] What would it be like to hear news reports every time a woman was sexually harassed on the streets of Cairo? According to a 2013 UN survey, 99.3 percent of girls and women in Cairo experience some form of sexual harassment on the streets.[3] Or how about a news report for each one of the 139 women known to have been killed each year by men in the United Kingdom (England, Wales, Northern Ireland, Scotland) in 2017?[4] (Remember, these are just the murders registered in police reports.) Of the 139:

- 105 (76%) knew their killer.
- 64 (46%) were killed by a current/former intimate partner.
- 30 (22%) were killed by strangers, with 21 killed in terrorist attacks.
- 24 (17%) were killed by a man known to them, such as a colleague, neighbor, or friend.
- 17 (12%) were killed by a male family member, including 10 who were killed by their son.

Those figures from the Femicide Census, conducted by Women's Aid and activist Karen Ingala Smith, are grim statistical reminders that it is husbands, fathers, brothers, sons, and lovers—very ordinary men, not "just psychopaths"—whose violence most hurts women.

"Time and time again, we hear of cases where a woman has been killed by a man as an 'isolated incident'; yet the latest Femicide Census report shows yet again that this is not the case. . . . The majority of these cases are not isolated incidents. There are too many similarities in the circumstances where women are killed by men," Katie Ghose, the chief executive of Women's Aid, told the *Guardian*.[5]

Clearly, the daily terrorism of girls and women is akin to the air we breathe: we take it for granted, and we rarely think about it.

"Feminism" is the F-word some hesitate to use, but the word I rarely use is the T-word (for terrorism), because I recognize the ways it is used to distinguish the violence committed by enemies from the violence committed by allies. But if terrorism means violence meant to scare us into changing the way we behave, then surely cutting off healthy parts of a girls' genitals to ensure her chastity, sexually harassing girls and women on the street to maintain male primacy over public spaces, and the startling figure of some three women killed every day in the United States by a current or former partner is terrorism.[6] Add social acceptance on top of the terrorism inflicted on girls and women and ask yourself again why the stories of women rarely make headlines.

Why don't those violations committed against girls and women disturb us as much as stories of explosions and torture? I am not making light of armed militancy, nor of the horrors of torture or police brutality. But by ignoring the hideous violations of women's rights, the daily drip-drip of misogyny, we make light of the crimes committed against girls and women. When acts of militant violence claim the lives of senior politicians, security chiefs are at times fired for failing to do their jobs. Who do we fire for the abject failure of stemming the terrorism that women and girls—cis and trans—are subjected to? Girls and women, half of our society, are always told to wait: wait until elections are held, wait until political prisoners are released, wait until we end torture, wait until we end police brutality, wait, wait, wait. The leitmotif of women's stories and our lives is waiting.

When will the stories of girls and women be elevated and given as much prominence and priority as those about explosions, torture, and cabinet reshuffles?

Unless we impose on societal consciousness just how rife violence against women is and how it is ordinary men who commit it—and not psychopaths—it will continue to benefit ordinary men. Denial of that enables men to distance themselves from the violence. Whether any individual man has ever beaten up or raped a woman is beside the point, because such violence, which is enabled and protected by patriarchy, helps maintain a social construct that privileges all men. They are beneficiaries of that violence because that violence upholds patriarchy. It is the foundation of patriarchy.

Women's violence is considered acceptable when it furthers the cause of patriarchy. The "nurturing" and "motherly" attributes that women are burdened with are essentially propaganda wrought by the patriarchy to keep things exactly as they are. When women rule in the name of patriarchy—remember British prime minister Margaret Thatcher—they are allowed to forgo "nurturing" and "motherly" reductionism and launch wars and pass into effect policy that benefits patriarchy. Countries boast when women begin serving in combat roles in their armed forces. They proudly announce when a woman makes it to a senior position, leading divisions and large numbers of troops. But the wars female combatants will fight are done so in the name of patriarchy; they promote a violence that only the patriarchal state claims a right to. It is time for women to claim that same right to launch wars—not between countries but against patriarchy.

Not only are women socialized into submission, but we are told, essentially, not to be violent even as a form of self-defense but to wait until men can stop being violent toward us. When that would happen exactly is unclear and quite unrealistic, seeing as patriarchy has been using violence to keep us in line for centuries. We are told again and again that it is in men's nature to be violent—surely that should disturb and make those men who refuse violence understand that patriarchal constructs of masculinity confine them too. We are told that women are weak, passive, emotional, submissive, etc. Which women are those things, and which women are excluded from those stereotypes? It matters because race, class, and gender all impact the ways women's violence is punished. We have been socialized into acquiescence ostensibly for our own good.

So, again, how many men would need to be killed in that imaginary scenario for patriarchy to take us seriously? And for how long would we have to wage battle before patriarchy begins to be dismantled?

Are my questions absurd? Yes, deliberately so. But we all must ask the absurd questions to fully take in the scale of violence that women consistently endure. How many women must be killed, raped, beaten, and emotionally abused until we do? And is self-defense the only form of violence allowed to women—if at all? These are disturbing questions. I know. I stand in the disturbance and discomfort caused by the questions I've posed. I insist you do, too, because women, girls, and nonbinary and queer people face more disturbance and discomfort than we can imagine—they are dying, and patriarchy shows little concern.

Consider that many liberatory movements—from the anticolonial to the antioccupation—have used violence as a means to overturn systems of oppression and injustice. People have a right to resist. But which people? It is usually groups and movements led by men and including a few women whose roles are too often erased and conveniently forgotten after the revolution or liberation has succeeded, lest women remember that they, too, can use violence. We can't have women thinking that they, too, know how to use weapons against oppressors! They might turn those weapons used against the foreign occupiers on their local patriarchal occupiers instead. And that's how we must consider patriarchy: as a form of occupation, an oppressive force against which we have a right to use force to liberate ourselves. Is there an older form of occupation?

If violence is the language that patriarchy understands, isn't it time more women speak it, if only for their own safety?

"Society would be better off as a whole if more women were willing to engage in justified violence against men, and fewer men were willing to engage in unjustified violence against women. To that end, women's justified violence against men should be *encouraged, protected, and publicized*."[7] Those words, from the University of Miami School of Law professor Mary Anne Franks in a 2016 law review article, should be enshrined in our declaration of war against patriarchy.

In a necessarily honest and sharp appraisal of what she calls the asymmetry of violence between men and women, Franks explains, "While both men and women can, and do, use violence against each other, men's violence against women is far more common, less justified, and more destructive than women's violence against men."

One of the reasons for that asymmetry is because "men do not fear retaliation for violence against women, whereas women do fear retaliation for their use of violence against men," Franks explains.

EXACTLY THIS!

After I beat the fuck out of the man who groped me in a club in Montreal, I went home on a high. It was glorious. On Twitter, I described what happened under #IBeatMyAssaulter. My tweets were soon shared thousands of times around the world. Women sent me not just support for what I'd done but also stories of the various times they, too, had beaten their assaulter. Years of rage fueled those punches I aimed at that man's face. Like so many women, I knew—because I had been subjected to it for years—that men believe they can do as they like to our bodies without consequences. That was why I did not want to stop punching that man. Each time I punched him I yelled, "Don't you ever touch a woman like that again! Don't you ever touch a woman!" I wanted him to know consequence. I wanted him to remember that this average-height woman, whose ass he believed he could just reach out and grope without fear of retaliation, beat the fuck out of him. I wanted him to wonder—if he ever dared again to want to grope a woman—if she, too, would beat the fuck out of him. We must stop socializing women and girls not to fight back. Stop sending girls only to ballet class. Send them to class to learn to fight too. I am not victim blaming. I am not placing the responsibility of being free from violence on women. I simply want men to know that women can dole out consequences. Patriarchy does not want us to be as fluent in violence as men are. And when we do dare to fight back, women feel patriarchy's full and brutal punishment. And, as always, the more a woman falls between an intersection of oppressions, the worse her punishment.

Three women are killed every day in the United States as a result of intimate-partner violence.[8] Domestic- and intimate-partner violence occurs across race, class, and gender boundaries, but such violence affects Black women disproportionality. African American women are victimized by domestic violence at rates about 35 percent higher than white women, according to Bureau of Justice statistics, and they "only make up about 13 percent of U.S. women, but comprise about half of female homicide victims—the majority of whom were killed by current or former boyfriends or husbands."

The criminal justice system is far from just. A reliance on policing and incarceration as ways to end domestic violence has been shown to be ineffective, as are tools used to further marginalize and discriminate against communities of color, including the very women they are meant to help. On the contrary, calling the police often puts women "at even greater risk of further abuse, criminalization and death," writes Nour Naas in *Huffington Post*.[9]

"Mandatory arrest policies, which require police to make an arrest when responding to a domestic violence call, have been shown to lead to greater fatalities, disproportionately affecting low-income women of color," Naas writes. "Research has shown that victims are 64 percent more likely to be killed if their partners are arrested instead of being warned and permitted to remain in the home. In many cases, domestic violence homicides occur at homes that police have visited multiple times. Calling the police is simply not a viable option for many victims of domestic violence."

Women receive harsher sentences for killing their male partners than men receive for killing their female partners, according to the American Civil Liberties Union (ACLU).[10] In her 1991 article "Rethinking Battered Woman Syndrome: A Black Feminist Perspective," Sharon Angella Allard explains that the ratio of Black women to white women convicted of killing their abusive husbands was nearly two to one.[11] According to the feminist psychotherapist, researcher, and author of *Battered Woman Syndrome* Lenore Walker, who is quoted in Allard's article, "For a battered woman to present a successful defense to a charge of killing her batterer, the woman must not appear angry. If the jury perceives that a woman killed out of anger, rather than fear, the jury is likely to give her a harsher penalty." The stereotype that Black women are angry means that they suffer harsher implications.

"Given that the legal system legitimizes these perceptions, there is a greater likelihood that a jury would believe a prosecutor's story that a battered Black woman acted out of revenge and anger, as opposed to fear, for taking the life of her batterer," writes Allard.

Why can't a Black woman—or any woman—act out of revenge and anger? How else is she supposed to react to abuse and violence? I insist we ask that question. I recognize the danger of asking such a question and demanding that we push beyond self-defense as the only acceptable way for women to respond to patriarchal violence, as imperfect and as almost impossible even self-defense is for many women, especially women of color, who are incarcerated for daring to think they had the right to that self-defense. I know that I will be accused of inciting violence. Still, I insist we do.

I am especially intrigued that in her article "Men, Women, and Optimal Violence," Franks makes room for the countenance of women's violence beyond self-defense: "If men will not refrain from the use of unjust violence against women, and the State refuses to restrain them, then women themselves must be equipped to prevent and preempt this violence."[12] When she says, "Men's disproportionate willingness and ability to use violence against women must be countered, at least in part, by increasing women's willingness and ability to use violence against men," I want to see what lies beyond that "in part." That is why I insist we ask those disturbing questions.

Franks continues: "This is in some ways no more than a claim that women should enjoy an equally robust right to self-defense that men have long enjoyed. Women must be encouraged to respond to violence with proportional force. This is not merely a question of justice but of social efficiency; the more women make use of responsive, justified violence against men, the less men will make use of unjustified violence against women."

But she insists, as I insist on asking disturbing questions, that we consider this too:

> More controversially, perhaps, this Article also argues that an increase in women's violence and aggression must be tolerated *even if such violence violates traditional proportionality principles in individual instances.* However regrettable it may be that in individual cases some women will overreact and perhaps even consciously exploit increased tolerance of their use of violence, creating fear and uncertainty about the possibility of women's retaliatory force serves the overall goal of redistributing violence. (Emphasis mine)

Such a redistribution, she says, should be seen as contributing to what she calls an "inhibiting effect" on men's use of violence.

> Uncertainty about irrational or disproportionate responses has at least a modest inhibiting effect on men's use of violence against other men; the same effect should obtain when women also pose this threat. This solution is justified by the excessive and pernicious nature of the status quo; the force necessary to disrupt social and legal defaults regarding men's violence against women may in some cases be extreme, and individual instances of injustice may be more than compensated by an overall shift

in violence allocation. *The more realistic and salient the possibility of women's violent retaliation or preemption of male violence becomes, the less male violence there will be.* (Emphasis mine)

It is important that a law professor lays down such an argument to consider because, for now, the system is rigged. I have quoted so extensively from Franks's article precisely because she is a law professor who is challenging us with a disturbing idea: that we might need more than just self-defense to stave off patriarchal violence. Staying in an abusive relationship can kill a woman. Leaving an abusive relationship can kill a woman. Calling the police can get you arrested and thrown in jail. Fighting back against your abuser and killing him to defend yourself will get you thrown into prison, where you are likely to be sexually assaulted by staff.

So let's ask those disturbing questions.

THE NATIONAL US AVERAGE prison sentence of men who kill their female partners is two to six years, while women who kill their partners are sentenced on average to fifteen years, despite the fact that most women who kill their partners do so to protect themselves from violence initiated by their partners.[13]

"For a lot of women who do ultimately kill their abusive partners, it's a last-gasp effort," Robert Knechtel, chief operating officer of the Arizona-based Sojourner Center, one of the largest domestic violence shelters in the country.[14] "Many women at the shelter don't have the financial means to move out of the state and have an either neutral or negative relationship with the police." That sentiment is echoed by Rita Smith, executive director of the National Coalition Against Domestic Violence: "When a woman or minority is claiming they are defending themselves, they don't get the benefit of the doubt. Most battered women who kill in self-defense end up in prison. There is a well-documented bias against women [in these cases]."[15]

Women are the fastest-growing segment of the incarcerated population in the United States.[16] According to the ACLU, as many as 90 percent of the women who are incarcerated for killing a man were battered by that same person and 79 percent of those in prison have suffered physical abuse before their arrest.[17] Two-thirds of the women in jail are of color, and the majority of that population is also low-income, according to a 2016 Vera Institute of Justice report, *Overlooked: Women and Jails in an Era of Reform*. Further, according to the report, women represented just 13 percent of the jail population between 2009 and 2011, yet they represented 67 percent of the victims of staff-on-inmate sexual victimization.

"The legal system is designed to protect men from the superior power of the state but not to protect women or children from the superior power of men," wrote the feminist psychiatrist Judith Herman in her book *Trauma and Recovery: The Aftermath of Violence—from Domestic Abuse to Political Terror*.[18]

It is a never-ending vicious cycle of violence. We can't win. So when are we going to terrify the fuck out of patriarchy and those who benefit from the rotten structures it has created? The vicious cycle of violence from patriarchy and its institutions contributes to what Franks, in "Men, Women, and Optimal Violence," calls a "suboptimal" distribution of violence between the genders. Franks sent me her article after I started #IBeatMyAssaulter on Twitter and described how I beat up the man who sexually assaulted me in the Montreal club. She called the way I beat up the man an "instructive example of . . . optimal violence."[19]

My story of beating up that man elicited hundreds of responses from women all over the world, who shared the times they, too, had punched or kicked or beaten a man who had assaulted or threatened them.

> "First time, I was 15 and it happened in school with an older student. I remember the power I felt in throwing that first punch. And the ones after. Glad I was taught to fight."[20]
> "A man once approached me at a bus stop, stood behind me & then slowly tried to touch me, because it was dark. I pushed him away, hit him with my bag and kicked him twice in the balls. Whilst he was groaning on the floor, I took the bus & left."
> "A few months ago, a drunk ex friend cornered me and put his hands on me. I said no repeatedly but he kept touching me so I kicked him hard and got away. I have absolutely no regrets and would do it again to any man who doesn't take my no for a concrete answer."

"Years ago, a guy followed me into the lobby of my apartment late
    at night. He pushed me to the floor. I used all the power in my
    legs to kick the crap out of him (I was learning karate). He ran off
    when he realized it wasn't going to be as easy as he fantasized."

"When I was in 7th grade this guy kept snapping my bra in gym class   .
    and the teachers wouldn't do anything, so I told him if he did it
    again I'd roundhouse kick him. He didn't believe me, did it again,
    and ended up with two broken ribs and a punctured lung."

When a law professor clearly states that an asymmetry in violence between genders does not benefit society, what are we waiting for to remedy
the situation? We would be better, Franks stresses, if "women's justified
violence against men [was] encouraged, protected, and publicized."[21] To
address the asymmetry of violence, Franks writes, we must reverse "the
current trend in legal and social practices, which is to tolerate and encourage men's unjustified violence against women while discouraging and
legally restricting women's violence against men."

Teach them to fight. Teach girls early to fight. This is war.

Fighting back comes with risk, I know. Every woman must take into
account where she is, who else is there, how big the man is, the possibility
that he might be armed, etc. I understand, and the priority must always
be a woman's safety and survival. We have to survive in order to take on
that ultimate fight against patriarchy, but that fight is ultimately won one
confrontation at a time. The threat of violence from women is necessary.
Men must know that a woman can and will fight back. Just as they do when
and if they consider violence against another man. But we must also take
into account, as Franks reminds us, that we may need more than just the
notion that women can and will fight back. Patriarchy must also be put on
notice that women can fight, period, and not just as a form of self-defense.
If the system is so rigged against us and there is little justice in the criminal
justice system, how else do we, as women, instill as much fear in men as
they instill in each other?

And for the "But what about the innocent men?" Franks minces no
words: "Even if encouraging an increase in women's justified violence
against men may sometimes result in unjustified or disproportionate

violence in individual situations, the overall effects of the redistribution of
violence will be preferable to the current asymmetry."

How much longer are we going to wait?

How many rapists must women kill before rape is erased? Imagine if
fifty, one hundred, five hundred women killed their rapists. What would
the world look like if women openly declared that we would kill any man
who raped us? How long would it take before men stopped raping us?
How many rapists would need to be killed in order for men to stop raping
women? How many rapists must be killed before a man thinks twice before raping or sexually assaulting women and girls? And I am not talking
here of state-imposed death penalties. I am talking about the end of rape
because men are sufficiently scared of women that they would never dare
to rape or try to rape them. Again, this is not victim blaming. I insist we
push the conversation until we get to the part where men fear women
enough that rape becomes an anomaly. I don't want the state to protect
me, because as I have stated several times already, protection from the
patriarchy is conditional. I want to be free of patriarchy, not at its mercy.

IN 2016 I VISITED BOSNIA for the first time to speak at the Bookstan literature
festival in Sarajevo. After one of my events, Bosnian journalist Nidzara
Ahmetasevic struck up a conversation with me during which she told
me I had to visit the town of Višegrad and a spa hotel there called Vilina
Vlas. I had heard snippets here and there since I had been in Sarajevo
about a former rape camp that was now a spa.[22] It had been one of several where Serb troops sexually enslaved Muslim women and girls. The
thought of it horrified me, but I had to go to learn about what happened
there and see for myself how violations of women and girls are erased.
I was grateful that a Bosnian woman so kindly offered to take me. War
is begun by men; it is ended by men. Women and children are rarely
consulted when wars are started nor when men are trying to end them
around a peace table. And the story of war is written not just by the vic-
tor, as the adage goes, but by the men who fought that war, regardless of
their side. I looked for books about the Bosnian war written by women
and found very few. There were several by men, several more by foreign
correspondents, mostly male, but I struggled to collect recommendations

for further reading by women. So the chance to travel to Višegrad with a Bosnian woman who had survived the war and who was willing to take me to the site of such a gutting reminder of the use of sexual violence as a weapon of war against women and girls was welcome. It would be like hearing Nidzara narrate in real time the book she must one day write about the Bosnian war, because the world needs books by Bosnian women about what happened to their country.

I did not know about Vilina Vlas before I arrived in Bosnia. During the 1992–1995 Bosnian war, I was a Reuters correspondent in Cairo. Writing for a news agency means that you read breaking news before anyone. I remembered well the harrowing stories that came across the wires. I had planned on visiting Srebrenica, where Serb forces killed eight thousand Muslim men and boys in July 1995 in Europe's worst atrocity since the Second World War. The UN International Criminal Tribunal for the former Yugoslavia (ICTY) and the International Court of Justice have ruled that the atrocity qualified as genocide. But the murders prompted Western airstrikes on Serbian forces, which ended the war in 1995. I knew about the mass rape and sexual violence that Bosnian Muslims had been subjected to by Serbian forces, but I did not know of the names of cities or specific sites of camps where women and girls were sexually enslaved in the way that I did Srebrenica.

In 1992 Vilina Vlas was used as headquarters for murder and rape by Milan Lukic, the leader of the Serb paramilitary group the White Eagles. A judgement at the ICTY confirmed the hotel had been used as a rape center. Nidzara told me that two hundred women and girls were sexually enslaved there, tied to the furniture in rooms where they were raped. At the end of each day, Nidzara told me, they would be mass raped in the swimming pool. After one such mass rape, a fourteen-year-old girl killed herself by jumping out of the window of her room.[23]

Nidzara told me these stories as we drove through some of the most beautiful vistas I have ever seen in my life. Bosnia is a beautiful country. The juxtaposition of the details I heard from Nidzara inside the car and the breathtaking scenes around us magnified the horror. By the time we arrived at the hotel, our driver, a Bosnian man who was a child during the war, said he would wait for us in the parking lot because he could not enter the hotel after all he had heard.

Inside the building, Nidzara told the receptionist that I was a tourist from New York who was interested in staying at the hotel. Nidzara translated for me as the front-desk receptionist gave us a tour. The woman told us that she had started working at Vilina Vlas as soon as it had reopened. She must have known its history. The whole town must have known. As she led us to the elevator on our way to see the guestrooms, I saw guests milling around in robes, on their way to the hotel's spa and hot springs. I wanted to yell at them, "Don't you know women were raped in this hotel? How could you stay here as if nothing had happened?"

And they might indeed have had no idea, because for all intents and purposes, there is a concerted effort by the hotel itself and the Višegrad government, not to let anyone know. There are no memorials outside the hotel. Travel sites in English make no mention that the place was a rape concentration camp. The front-desk receptionist told us that the hotel is administered by the Višegrad municipality, which is led and dominated by Serbs who are not interested in what happened to Muslim women and girls in the hotel during the war.

I rarely use the word "evil." But there is no other word to describe Vilina Vlas. As the receptionist showed us the kind of rooms available, I remembered that Nidzara had told me in the car on the way that some of the rooms still had the same furniture from the days when women were imprisoned and raped in them. The receptionist led us into one room, and I wondered as we looked out the window which one the fourteen-year-old had used as her exit from hell.

As I followed Nidzara and the receptionist through the corridors, I could feel the spirit of the women and the girls who had been kept prisoner in that concentration camp. I have a tattoo on my right forearm of Sekhmet, the ancient Egyptian goddess of retribution and sex. I touched her image with my left hand, like reaching for a talisman for strength, and kept muttering to myself, "We remember you, sisters. We honor you, sisters." It was my promise to honor them by continuing to remind the world of what they endured, to avenge them as I am now by insisting that you hear what happened to them.

After seeing two rooms, we took the elevator to the lobby level, and the receptionist breezily told us we could make our own way to the pool. Along the way, I saw the hair salon to our left. One woman was having her hair blow-dried. The more mundane the activities we encountered, the more the deliberate amnesia and erasure sickened me.

At the pool, guests splashed in the water; some reclined on the side enjoying the warmth of the sun shining through the windows. Some two decades earlier, women were subjected to mass rape in this very pool. Nidzara and I quickly left to use the bathroom. I asked her how many times she had been to Vilina Vlas. As she told me that this visit was her third, I could see her hands were shaking. On the way out, Nidzara asked for brochures from the receptionist so that I could take home with me documents to the surreal depiction of evil.

As soon as we exited the building, I asked Nidzara if I could hug her, and I sobbed as I did. I could not stop crying as we got in the car and drove away. Nidzara, who was sitting in the passenger seat by the driver, reached to the back seat to hold my hand.

As we drove away, our driver, Edin, who had waited for us outside the hotel where he could see guests eating and drinking on the terrace, shared his horror at how oblivious guests were. "I wanted to yell at the people having tea on the terrace, 'How could you be here?' I wanted to scream at the woman having tea with her daughter, 'Don't you know what happened to women and girls here?'"

I wanted to burn the building down. I wanted to destroy it, brick by brick.

We drove to Srebrenica, where we had a tour of the memorial for the men and boys massacred in that town. There are photographs and some personal possessions of those whose remains have been identified. It was heart-wrenching to read personal details that fleshed out their individuality, but it is a beautiful memorial. At the burial site across the street is a plaque in honor of the men and the boys. There are white headstones as far as the eye can see and a list of the names of the victims whose remains were identified and buried there. In many cases, victims had the same surname, testament to the massive toll on the same families that the massacre had taken.

How different Vilina Vlas would be if the names of the women and girls who were raped and killed there were listed on a plaque outside the building. In Srebrenica, the men and boys have a moving and fitting memorial that acknowledges the horror they were subjected to. In Višegrad, women and girls have a spa, where all memory of the atrocities committed in the war's biggest rape camp has been erased. The hotel brochure for this former site of crime against humanity, where rape was used as a weapon of war, promotes the place as a "healthy" retreat. The memories of those women and girls that patriarchy has erased has been left to other women to honor. The Association of the Women Victims of War has been fighting to have a memorial plate put on the front wall of Vilina Vlas hotel and spa, and the Bosnian filmmaker Jasmila Zbanic has made a narrative film about Vilina Vlas called *For Those Who Can Tell No Tales*.

It is believed that between twelve thousand and fifty thousand women were raped during the Bosnian war.[24] No one has been held accountable for the rape of women and girls in Vilina Vlas.[25] A 2001 ruling by the International Criminal Tribunal for the former Yugoslavia against three Bosnian Serbs declared systemic rape and sexual enslavement a crime against humanity for the first time.

I am forever grateful that Nidzara, who knows and has befriended several women who survived rape during their countries' war, took me to Vilina Vlas.[26] I could not imagine being taken there by a man or being told by a man the stories that Nidzara told me. Men are too often both heroes and villains during the narration of war. Women get one or two lines in the story. For too long, rape has been considered an almost natural result of war—as if soldiers and rebels and fighters just stumbled upon it, as if it were something that was inevitable rather than deliberate.

The 2018 Nobel Peace Prize committee recognized that rape was a deliberately used weapon of war and honored a woman who is a survivor and a man who helps survivors: Nadia Murad, a Yazidi woman from the northern Iraqi town of Sinjar, who was sexually enslaved by ISIS, and Dr. Dennis Mukwege, a gynecologist and surgeon who treats women and girls affected by rape and sexual violence in the Democratic Republic of Congo.[27]

In 2017 I went with France-based antiracist activists from European Grassroots Antiracist Movement (EGAM) to Rwanda to take part in the commemoration of the genocide against the Tutsis. In 1994, during just a hundred days, some 800,000 people were slaughtered in Rwanda by ethnic Hutu extremists. The assailants raped an estimated 250,000 women, many of whom were mutilated or killed.[28]

Rape and sexual violence have *always* been used—deliberately, systematically, intentionally—in conflict and war to terrorize women (and sometimes to emasculate men)—and it is done both by "our troops" and "their troops." Women's bodies are considered proxy battlegrounds. It is yet another reminder of patriarchy's insistence that it and it alone owns our bodies.

It is imperative that the world acknowledge that rape and sexual violence are used as weapons in war and conflict everywhere. And in doing so, we must connect the use of sexual violence as a weapon of war to the more mundane and daily use of sexual violence globally as a weapon of patriarchy's war on women and girls. Because when we connect that wartime systematic use of rape and sexual violence to its use against women in non-war zones, we connect the ways that patriarchy protects and enables misogyny via sexual violence as a weapon, a weapon of war and its more quotidian uses as a weapon. That weapon is meant to terrorize us and keep us in our place. It's a weapon used to control where and when we can go and how we can behave, a weapon that patriarchy wants us to think will damage and destroy us forever. The world finally sees how that weapon works during war. Let's recognize it in the everyday too. Today, we read about rape as a weapon of war being used against Rohingya women by troops in Myanmar, in the war in Syria, in every conflict zone. Know that whether you read about it in headlines or not, it is happening. And women are often silenced by its shame, stigma, and trauma.

And as we celebrate Nadia Murad and Denis Mukwege, let's remember that in the most powerful country in the world a man accused of sexual assault by more than a dozen women was elected US president and that he nominated to the Supreme Court a man also accused of sexual assault. That man, Brett Kavanaugh, was confirmed and joined another justice on the court—Clarence Thomas—who was accused of sexual harassment.

Patriarchy has enabled and protected sexual violence and assault in every aspect of our lives. The Nobel Peace Prize is usually given with a political purpose, and I believe that in 2018 it highlighted sexual violence for a reason. I wish that #MeToo founder Tarana Burke had also been a recipient, along with Murad and Mukwege, because honoring her would have made that connection between sexual violence as a weapon of war in conflict zones and sexual violence as a weapon of war in the more day-to-day war that patriarchy perpetrates against us.

And what Tarana Burke, #MeToo, and Black women in the US have been telling us for centuries is that the state has always used sexual violence against them with impunity—from the days of slavery to more recent times. And now Trump and Kavanaugh remind us that the state continues to enable and protect men at the highest levels who commit such violence. What could be higher: the president of the most powerful country in the world and a justice for life on the highest court in the land?

During Kavanaugh's hearing, dozens of women flooded the US Congress to protest, disrupt the confirmation session, and confront senators with stories of their experiences with sexual violence. They sought to make Republican senators in particular, since they held the majority on the Judiciary Committee, more sympathetic to the concerns of women and also to urge them to take seriously Christine Blasey Ford, who testified that Kavanaugh had tried to rape her when they were in high school.

In one incident that took place during the days of the confirmation hearing, two women confronted Republican senator Jeff Flake in an elevator, urging him with a combination of tears and recounting their experience of sexual violence, to reject Kavanaugh's nomination. Those few moments in the elevator went viral on social media and became emblematic of exactly what was wrong with Kavanaugh's nomination: the attempts, in vain, by women who cried as they shared traumatic experiences of sexual violence in the hope to move male politicians to vote against Kavanaugh. Again and again, women cry and share trauma to no avail. Flake, his pained expression in the elevator notwithstanding, ultimately voted to confirm Kavanaugh.[29] In another incident, as his security detail stood between him and female protesters who wanted to talk to him, Republican senator Orrin Hatch literally shooed the women away as he hurriedly got into an elevator, telling them he would talk to them when they "grow up."[30] Pause for a minute and take stock of the disrespect, the diminishment, the mockery of women's trauma and their courage in so publicly confronting lawmakers. The rage you should feel should be equivalent to the immunity that patriarchy guarantees those men who shoo us away, with little regard to our pain and demands to be safe from patriarchal violence.

I could barely watch any of those scenes of women crying. Always women are required to cry as we slit open a metaphorical vein to let out stories of assaults and abuse—and in return for what? How much longer must our ostensibly most powerful weapon be to recount our stories of pain and abuse? It was clear that so many of those representatives had neither respect nor compassion for women. In the days leading up to Kavanaugh's confirmation, Americans urged each other, "Call your senator!" Women's groups organized and protested. And for what? To have the representatives of patriarchy mock us and shoo us as they stand behind their security detail?

At the time of the Kavanagh hearing, there had never been a woman Republican senator on the Judiciary Committee, which eventually confirmed Kavanaugh. In fact, in 2018 the Republican senators were all white men, whose average age was sixty-two; the oldest member was eighty-five.[31] At the start of 2019, the GOP finally named two women to the committee.

I watched the patriarchal victory fest over what was the Kavanaugh hearing and all I could think was this: I am done crying. I am done begging for compassion. I am done calling my senator. It is time to make patriarchy fear us.

We must make patriarchy fear us.

Until and unless women are ready and able to use violence as a form of defense, as a deterrence, as a weapon, patriarchy will never fear us. And patriarchal violence will continue unabated, every day, week, month, year. It will continue to shoo us! What are we waiting for? Do we think that men—enabled and protected by patriarchy, which guarantees their dominance and privilege—will suddenly, overnight, miraculously stop killing and abusing us? Why would they do that? After centuries of counting on their violence against us to keep themselves in power and us in our place, why would they stop?

After my assault by Egyptian riot police in 2011, a feminist NGO in Egypt asked me if I would take the Interior Ministry to court with the help of their legal team. They told me that twelve other women had been assaulted in an almost identical manner as that I was subjected to—beating, sexual assault, threats of gang rape. But none had spoken out, either from shame or because their families had prevented them from speaking out, again from shame. I agreed to do it. I collected copies of the X-rays from my orthopedic surgeon and information about the operation he had performed on my left arm, during which he had inserted a titanium plate and five screws. The NGO filed a complaint to the prosecutor general, a man who had been appointed by the Mubarak regime, that is, a regime loyalist. Our complaint was never approved. Some people have suggested that I sue the Egyptian regime in a US court, but I refuse. I am a dual citizen, it is true. But I want justice in an Egyptian court for what was done to me by the Egyptian regime's riot police, who are among the poorest and least-educated Egyptians and are themselves victims of that regime, which abuses them and has trained them to abuse us in the ways the regime orders. I recognize my wish for justice in an Egyptian court is a wish that is years away from being fulfilled, if ever. When the *Wall Street Journal* correspondent in Egypt called the Interior Ministry spokesman for a response to my description of my assaults, the spokesman replied, laughing: "How many kids does she have because of that?"[32]

"Nobody in the world, nobody in history, has ever gotten their freedom by appealing to the moral sense of the people who were oppressing them," Assata Shakur, founding member of the Black Liberation Army and former Black Panther, writes in her autobiography.[33]

It is the right of women and girls to not just fight back against the crimes of patriarchy, but surely it should also be our right to fight to dismantle patriarchy itself. Surely violence is a legitimate form of resistance. This book is not a road map for making peace with patriarchy. It is a manifesto for destroying patriarchy and ending its crimes.

We have a right to declare war on patriarchy. As long as patriarchy holds the patent to violence, it knows it can rely on women's real and legitimate fear of patriarchal violence. It counts on its use of violence to keep women scared shitless.

We must make patriarchy fear us. We must consider how best to do that. We should declare war if we must. And to those who protest, I again offer the words of Mary Anne Franks: "To move the use of violence between men and women closer to optimal level, women must increase their willingness and ability to use violence against men."

CHAPTER 7

Lust

Bodily truth is the frontline of existence in the world. I'm given to potty talk, menstruation talk and sex talk. I use my vagina the way I want to, and I am not ashamed of being a sexual being.

—MITALI SARAN, in *Walking Towards Ourselves:
Indian Women Tell Their Stories*[1]

I OWN MY BODY.

I own my body: not the state, not the street, and not the home.

I own my body: not the temple, not the church, not the mosque, not any other house of worship.

It is my right to have sex whenever I choose, with whomever I choose—obviously, with their consent. It is my right to have sex with a woman or a man; with multiple women or multiple men, cis- or transgender; and with people whose gender identity is fluid or nonbinary. It is my right to decide how I express my sexuality, as it is the right of every consenting adult. How consenting adults express their sexuality is nobody's business because the keywords here are "consenting" and "adults."

When I say "I own my body," it is a revolutionary statement. It is deceptively simple but resolutely powerful because the beating heart of any revolution must be the twin forces of consent and agency. The revolution is incomplete if it focuses on our autonomy only from the state. The state is not the only entity that exercises power over us, especially if we do not identify as cisgender, heterosexual men.

Who we can desire, how we can express that desire, who has the right to desire, and our right to determine for ourselves whose desire we can and cannot accept or reject: all those go to the heart of defying, disobeying, and disrupting patriarchy. In a keynote address that was published as an essay in 1991, poet and essayist June Jordan explains why "deeper and more pervasive than any other oppression, than any other bitterly contested human domain, is the oppression of sexuality, the exploitation of the human domain of sexuality for power."[2]

> From China to Iran, from Nigeria to Czechoslovakia, from Chile to California, the politics of sexuality—enforced by traditions of state-sanctioned violence plus religion and the law—reduces to male domination of women, heterosexist tyranny, and, among those of us who are in any case deemed despicable or deviant by the powerful, we find intolerance for those who choose a different, a more complicated—for example, an interracial or bisexual—mode of rebellion and freedom.

Jordan's writing powerfully interwove the personal oppressions she fought as a Black and bisexual woman to the global oppressions millions fight. In her keynote address, Jordan brings her revolutionary and astute analysis, which insists that when it comes to the politics of sexuality, complexity is a powerful weapon against patriarchy.

Before explaining the revolutionary potential of bisexuality, Jordan lays out her definitions of "sexuality":

"When I say sexuality, I mean gender: I mean male subjugation of human beings because they are female. When I say sexuality, I mean heterosexual institutionalization of rights and privileges denied to homosexual men and women. When I say sexuality I mean gay or lesbian contempt for bisexual modes of human relationship," Jordan writes.

I would add rights and privileges denied to transgender and nonbinary people and to those who reject monogamy.

As a woman who was born in Egypt to a Muslim family who has lived in several countries and for whom the path to owning my sexuality was one resolutely paved with complexity, I read this June Jordan essay like a personal manifesto. I identify myself among the "many men and women, especially young men and women, who seek to embrace the complexity of their total, always changing social and political circumstance." Such people "seek to embrace our increasing global complexity on the basis of the heart and on the basis of an honest human body. Not according to ideology. Not according to group pressure. Not according to anybody's concept of 'correct.'"[3]

Dubbing this freedom a "New Politics of Sexuality," Jordan explains the political and revolutionary power of bisexuality, which, she says, "invalidates either/or formulation, either/or analysis."

"Bisexuality means I am free and I am as likely to want and to love a woman as I am likely to want and to love a man, and what about that? Isn't that what freedom implies?" Jordan says.

> If you are free, you are not predictable and you are not controllable. To my mind, that is the keenly positive, politicizing significance of bisexual affirmation: To insist upon complexity, to insist upon the validity of all of the components of social/sexual complexity, to insist upon the equal validity of all of the components of social/sexual complexity. This seems to me a unifying, 1990s mandate for revolutionary Americans planning to make it into the twenty-first century on the basis of the heart, on the basis of an honest human body, consecrated to every struggle for justice, every struggle for equality, every struggle for freedom.[4]

I live to complicate because I walk through many identities, each one of them subject to control by patriarchy and its allied forces. I most identify with the narratives of women of color and queer folks—especially when they are all those identities, as Jordan was—because their understanding of those multiple levels of oppression and control extend much further than the narratives of white, heterosexual men or women, for whom misogyny is the only demon to slay. My demons are many and like Kali, the Indian goddess of war, I have had to develop multiple arms (complex identities) to slay them.

We need more spaces where we can express the revolutionary identities we can fashion free of patriarchy and its attendant chokeholds. It is always a thrill when heroes and mentors create those spaces and invite us in. The Black feminist theorist bell hooks did just that at a panel discussion she moderated at the New School in New York City in 2014 called Transgression: Whose Booty Is This? She asked the audience how we, as people of color, can break out of the framing of our sexualities. That is, Who owns our booty? and, just as importantly, Who owns and directs the expression and narration of how and when and with whom we share (or not) that booty? Have Black women and women of color figured out progressive ways to see our sexualities, hooks asked us.

"Desire disrupts rules," hooks told us.

Fuck, yes! Hearing a panel of people of color talking about sexual transgression is important for me because where I come from, and because of how I identify, that complexity is necessary. At the panel an educator who identified herself as being of West Indian and Catholic descent asked hooks and the panel she had assembled a question that the educator ended with "Where I come from, just this question is transgressive!" That's what I mean!

On creating spaces of risk and vulnerability to explore transgression, panelist Marci Blackman, a lesbian whose fiction explores issues of race and sadomasochism, asked, "Do we want to live life or do we want life to live us?"

The challenge that hooks gave us is one I carry with me wherever I travel to lecture. "What does it mean to have spaces of radical openness?" Everywhere I go, my priority is to meet feminist and LGBTQ activists, be it Lagos, Johannesburg, Sarajevo, or Mumbai. And I have determined to open the events I speak or read at by being as honest—as radically open—about my own path to owning my body and my sexuality. The response has always been worth it.

After I gave a reading in Britain in 2015 while promoting my first book, I spoke to a woman who said she was from a British Muslim family of Arab origin. I was seated at a table signing books, so she knelt down to speak with me so that we were at eye level.

"I, too, am fed up with waiting to have sex," she said, referring to the experience I had related in the reading. "I'm thirty-two and there's no one I want to marry. How do I get over the fear that God will hate me if I have sex before marriage?"

I hear this a lot. My email inbox is jammed with messages from women who, like me, are of Middle Eastern and Muslim descent. They write to vent about how to "get rid of this burden of virginity," or to ask about hymen reconstruction surgery if they're planning to marry someone who doesn't know their sexual history, or just to share their thoughts about sex.

Countless articles have been written on the sexual frustration of men in the Middle East—from the jihadi supposedly drawn to armed militancy by the promise of virgins in the afterlife to ordinary Arab men unable to afford marriage.[5] Far fewer stories have given voice to the sexual frustration of women in the region or to an honest account of women's sexual experiences, either within or outside marriage.

I am not a cleric, and I am not here to argue over what religion says about sex. I am an Egyptian woman of Muslim descent who waited until she was twenty-nine to have sex and has been making up for lost time. My upbringing and faith taught me that I should abstain until I married. I obeyed this until I could not find anyone I wanted to marry and grew impatient. I have come to regret that it took my younger self so long to rebel and experience something that gives me so much pleasure. And as for the guilt that I initially felt about that transgression: I fucked it out of my system.

We barely acknowledge the sexual straitjacket we force upon women. When it comes to women, especially Muslim women in the Middle East, the story seems to begin and end with the debate about the veil. Always the veil. As if we don't exist unless it's to express a position on the veil.

So where are the stories on women's sexual frustrations and experiences? I spent much of 2015 on a book tour that took me to twelve countries. Everywhere I went—from Europe and North America to India, Nigeria, and Pakistan—women, including Muslim women, readily shared with me their stories of guilt, shame, denial, and desire. They shared because I shared.

Many cultures and religions prescribe the abstinence that was indoctrinated in me. When I was teaching at the University of Oklahoma in 2010, one of my students told the class that she had signed a purity pledge for her father, vowing to him that she would wait until marriage before she had sex.[6] It was a useful reminder that a cult of virginity is specific neither to Egypt, my birthplace, nor to Islam, my religion. Remembering my struggles with abstinence and being alone with that, I determined to talk honestly about the sexual frustration of my twenties, how I overcame the initial guilt of disobedience, and how I made my way through that guilt to a positive attitude toward sex.

It has not been easy for my parents to hear their daughter talk so frankly about sex, but it has opened up a world of other women's experiences. In many non-Western countries, speaking about such things is scorned as "white" or "Western" behavior. But this is a conversation that I insist on having because when sex is surrounded by silence and taboo, it is the most vulnerable who are hurt, especially girls and nonbinary people.

During the book tour for *Headscarves and Hymens*, many women shared stories that were stark reminders of these taboos. In New York, a Christian Egyptian American woman told me how hard it was for her to come out as gay to her family. In Washington, a young Egyptian woman told the audience that her family didn't know she was a lesbian. In Jaipur, a young Indian talked about the challenge of being gender nonconforming, and in Lahore, I met a young woman who shared what it was like to be queer in Pakistan. My notebooks are full of stories like these. I tell friends I could write the manual on how to lose your virginity.

Many of the women who share them with me, I realize, enjoy some privilege, be it education or an independent income. It is striking that such privilege does not always translate to sexual freedom, nor protect these women if they transgress cultural norms. But the issue of sex affects all women, not just those with money or a college degree. Sometimes I hear the argument that women in the Middle East have enough to worry about simply struggling with literacy and employment. To which my response is, "So, because someone is poor or can't read, she shouldn't have consent and agency, the right to enjoy sex and her own body?"

The answer to that question is already out there, in places like the blog *Adventures from the Bedrooms of African Women*, founded by the Ghana-based writer Nana Darkoa Sekyiamah, and the Mumbai-based *Agents of Ishq*, a digital project on sex education and sexual life founded by filmmaker and writer Paromita Vohra.[7] These initiatives prove that sex-positive attitudes are not the province only of so-called white feminism. As the writer Mitali Saran put it, in an anthology of Indian women's writing: "I am not ashamed of being a sexual being."[8]

My revolution has been to develop from a twenty-nine-year-old virgin to the fifty-plus-year-old woman who declares, on any platform I get: "It is I who own my body." Not the state, the mosque, the street, or my family. And it is my right to have sex whenever, and with whomever, I choose.

I have been a feminist since I was nineteen years old. Truth be told, I became a feminist when my family moved to Saudi Arabia from the United Kingdom when I was fifteen. I didn't have the word "feminist" then, but the extreme form of patriarchy enforced in Saudi Arabia, where girls and women must have a male guardian from birth to death, rendering adult women perpetual minors, traumatized me into feminism. I discovered the F-word thanks to feminist journals on the shelves of the university in Saudi Arabia that I attended.

Before I left Egypt for the United States in 2000, my feminism had focused solely on misogyny, which I understood was protected and enabled by patriarchy. I knew there was an LGBTQ community in Egypt, as there is in all countries. When I attended a conference in 2004 for LGBTQ Muslims organized by al-Fatiha, one of the first ever organizations for queer Muslims, I began to better understand the need to combine feminism with the fight for LGBTQ rights. Our enemy was the same: patriarchy, specifically a cisgender and heteronormative patriarchy that privileged heterosexual relationships. There are several more Muslim LGBTQ organizations that have worked hard to create those spaces of radical openness that bell hooks talks of, so that queer Muslims do not feel they have to choose between any of their identities because, as June Jordan says, the revolution lives within that complexity.

Across the Middle East and North Africa, increasingly bold expressions of sexual freedom are clearly unsettling regimes accustomed to being guardians not just of "national security" but also of our bodies and sexualities. Although an insurgency that has killed hundreds of troops and police officers in northern Sinai continues, and judges and police officers in Cairo have been attacked, the Egyptian regime under the leadership of former army chief Abdul-Fattah el-Sisi in 2017 carried out an unprecedented crackdown on Egypt's LGBTQ community.[9]

Aided by a team of media personalities and religious authorities, the regime undertook what can best be described as hysterical homophobia during which more than sixty-five people, mostly gay men, were arrested in the crackdown against LGBTQ Egyptians. At least twenty people received prison sentences, ranging from six months to six years. Several men were subjected to anal examinations, which human rights groups describe as a form of torture, ostensibly to determine whether they have engaged in anal sex.

This wave of arrests and raids began after gay-pride rainbow flags were flown at a concert by a Lebanese indie-rock band, Mashrou' Leila, whose lead singer, Hamed Sinno, is openly gay.[10] It was not the first time fans displayed rainbow flags at a Mashrou' Leila concert, a gay friend who has attended some of the band's previous concerts in Cairo reminds me. He also reminds me that rainbow flags were flown in Tahrir Square during the eighteen days of protest that toppled President Hosni Mubarak in 2011.

Same-sex relationships are not illegal in Egypt, but the LGBTQ community is targeted by "debauchery" laws. So why now? Why the parade of men "confessing" to being gay and "repenting" on TV talk shows, and the psychiatrists touting "conversion therapy"?

It would have been easy to label the crackdown a distraction. There is much that Egyptians need distracting from: disastrous economic austerity policies, the insurgency in Sinai, sixty thousand political prisoners. And it does make for a convenient topic. Egypt's political parties might disagree on how to remedy any or all of those issues—but homophobia cuts across disagreement. "All political parties here, even the 'leftist' ones, think homosexuality is a disgrace," my friend told me. "Some people think gay people should be stoned, others recommend burning them after stoning, while some sheikhs are saying their hands and legs should be cut on opposite sides of their bodies, and ask in the softest of voices for their imprisonment or deportation."

But there is more than just distraction at play. An Egyptian talk-show host who suggested that both terrorism and homosexuality were being used to "ruin our youth" by a nameless external enemy offered perhaps the most honest explanation for this vicious round of homophobia in Egypt: the conflation of a security threat with a "moral" threat.

After the Mashrou' Leila concert—attended by an estimated thirty-five thousand—a parade of TV personalities pleaded with the regime to "save our youth" from homosexuality. Egyptian authorities promptly barred the group from performing again. In June 2017 Jordan had done the same.[11]

Sinno is unapologetically "brown, queer and from a Muslim family" by his own description. Mashrou' Leila's sexually subversive songs include references to gender fluidity and Abu Nuwas, an eighth-century poet, and Sappho (both known for poems that celebrate same-sex love)—and the band, especially Sinno, has become an icon for a beleaguered but determined LGBTQ community and a lightning rod for our moral guardians.

Armed with social media and audacity, more people are questioning taboos around religion and sexuality. There are online LGBTQ accounts offering information and solidarity, in Arabic and English. Three are the newly formed Alliance of Queer Egyptian Organizations, Solidarity with Egypt LGBT, and NoH8 Egypt, which coordinated protests outside Egyptian embassies and consulates to protest the crackdown.[12]

My.Kali, one of the region's first LGBTQ magazines, started publishing in 2008.[13] In July 2017 a *BuzzFeed* video interview with an Egyptian lesbian (who lives in the United States) talking about her relationship with a woman and her father's reaction to her coming out went viral.[14]

Egypt, of course, is far from alone in its witch hunt. From Chechnya to Azerbaijan, from Tanzania to Indonesia, there are similar crackdowns by governments obsessed with policing people's sexuality.[15] And let's not forget that President Sisi's booster, President Trump—and his Evangelical Christian vice president, Mike Pence, especially—is no friend to LGBTQ rights.

Morality crusades unite military regimes and religious zealots alike. Sisi, a former army general who became president after forcing out former Egyptian president Mohamed Morsi, of the Muslim Brotherhood, understands the potency of connecting the catchall "national security" to "inciting debauchery" as a deliberate reminder that the Islamists do not hold the copyright on piety. (Long-time dictator Mubarak, too, often vaunted his regime's religiosity to outdo its Islamist rivals.)

October 19, 2017, was dubbed a day of global solidarity for LGBTQ Egyptians. To commemorate it, a protest was held outside the Egyptian consulate in Montreal. Later that day, I saw Mashrou' Leila in concert in that city, and some concertgoers flew an Egyptian flag alongside a rainbow flag. Sinno told the audience that the best way to fight the crackdown in Egypt is to keep up international pressure. He understood the importance of visibility—for safety and for solidarity. And Egypt was not the first country in the region to ban the band from performing there again.

"Getting just one email from some queer kid in Tunisia who says something super emotional, even just one of those messages, justifies taking on the Jordanian state," Sinno told me that summer, after he and his band were banned from performing in Jordan. He can now add Egypt to that list of states he's taking on.

In 2018, in Sinno and Mashrou' Leila's Lebanon, to coincide with International Women's Day, March 8, Lebanese feminists and queer activists held the Solidarity and Rage march in the capital, Beirut. Rainbow pride flags and the flag for transgender pride flew among banners and placards, some of which read: "Our issues are many but our anger is one and the same," "Trans women are women," and "Trans, bi, or gay, together against patriarchy."[16]

It is imperative to see how feminist and queer activists around the world work together so that we can counter transphobic hate that insists on excluding trans women. Such hate—and the energy expended on it— is wrong and a waste of time, and energy that would be better invested in fighting our common enemy: patriarchy, as the placard in the Beirut march reminds us. A life expectancy of just thirty-five in the US is a reminder that trans women, particularly of color, are especially vulnerable to violence.[17]

Pop stars who are openly queer, like Hamed Sinno of Mashrou' Leila, are important for defying, disobeying, and disrupting patriarchy all over the world. Halsey, who shook to the core a concert hall in Montreal when she led the audience of mostly young women and nonbinary people in a chant of "I'm a fucking hurricane," is openly bisexual. Although some initially accused her record label of trying to force her into a heteronormative persona, Halsey has emerged as proudly queer. She recorded "Strangers" with Lauren Jauregui from Fifth Harmony, the first-ever duet with two openly bisexual female singers and which *Billboard* described as a "long-overdue bisexual milestone in mainstream music."[18] And Halsey's song "Bad at Love" alternates between a male love interest in one verse and a female love interest in the next.

When actor and recording artist Janelle Monáe told *Rolling Stone* in 2018 that she was pansexual, her already iconic status among queer people of color across the world was bolstered. "I want young girls, young boys, nonbinary, gay, straight, queer people who are having a hard time dealing with their sexuality, dealing with feeling ostracized or bullied for just being their unique selves, to know that I see you," she said.[19]

The liberatory and revolutionary potential of queerness became especially poignant for me when I first visited Sarajevo in 2016. The night before I went to Vilina Vlas hotel and spa, which had been used as the largest rape concentration camp during the Bosnian War, and to Srebrenica, site of the worst massacre in modern European history, I went to a queer club in the Bosnian capital with queer friends. It was a small club that played a mix of Western pop and dance songs along with domestic folk dance music. The dance floor was packed with mostly men who frequently kissed. I held onto those images—the men kissing all around me as I danced with my friends—the next day when I was reeling at the atrocities that had been committed at the places I visited. It was worth getting just a few hours of sleep because I had spent most of the night in that small queer club. The queerness I carried out of that radical space of openness and the transgressive sexualities that surrounded me were the perfect antidote to the horror of militarism that had been unleashed at Vilina Vlas and Srebrenica. Men should kiss each other more often and kill less, much less.

After I attended the 2004 al-Fatiha conference for LGBTQ Muslims, I began to more consciously link my fight against misogyny to the fight against homophobia, with the growing understanding that both oppressions spring from patriarchy. And the more I linked those fights, the more I resolved to undo how I had been socialized into heteronormativity. I wondered: Why and how was I socialized into compulsory heterosexuality? Why and how was I socialized into compulsory monogamy? What would my life be without the compulsory? As someone whose goal is always to be free, it would be a life of being free of the compulsory, a life of freedom.

The older I get, the more I identify as queer. How feminism and queerness have made me the woman I am is beyond the scope of this book. But I will share a few reasons as examples of the importance of feminism and queerness to informing the ways I subvert patriarchy.

In my first book, *Headscarves and Hymens*, I write about my struggle to stop wearing hijab and the ensuing struggle to have sex before getting married, contrary to how I was raised. The burdens of "modesty" and "purity" are always much heavier on women and girls than on men and boys, but we must remember that patriarchy has defined in very narrow ways how to be a "man," which often excludes anyone but a conservative, heterosexual, married man. Depending on where you live, that man usually belongs to the most powerful group in a given culture. So in the United States, it would be a heterosexual and monogamous white man; in Egypt, it would be a heterosexual Muslim man, allowed to be nonmonogamous according to Islamic teachings that permit up to four wives for each Muslim man.

Such definitions of "man" are usually associated not just with the group in power but are also invested in creating a further hierarchy that privileges "masculinity" (in men, never in cis- or trans women) with power and all things to be aspired to, and associating "femininity" (especially in cisgender men) with weakness and inferiority.

Given those narrow and unforgiving gender binaries, subversion of those binaries and refusal to conform to the dictates of patriarchy and heteronormativity, as well as the ensuing monogamy, are forms of rebellion. That is why queerness is powerful.

When I finally had intercourse, I was forced to deal with the guilt that ensued from knowing that I had broken a once unquestioned taboo. I hated that I was still held hostage by that guilt, which I considered a mark of patriarchal dictates about how and when a woman could express herself sexually. "I own my body" was a mantra that was long in the making, and I earned the right to say it out loud as I do now. And I insist on saying that I fucked the guilt out of my system, because being brazen and shameless are not powers I am supposed to wield so easily. But I have seized them for myself, and I wield them joyfully. When I talk about sex and my own journey, I talk openly and with joy about lust, pleasure, and desire, because they are "sins" for those of us dispossessed by patriarchy of the right to enjoy our bodies when and how we want. It is especially important for me to talk about joy, pleasure, lust, and desire because I survived state-sanctioned sexual assault in Egypt in November 2011, as well as having experienced daily onslaughts sanctioned by the street and by society, which does nothing to stop them because public space is a privilege that patriarchy has awarded to men. It is especially the state-sanctioned sexual assault that I highlight when I talk about the power of seizing and wielding brazenness and shamelessness. Every woman must deal with surviving sexual assault in the way that she best finds healing. When I talk about my healing, I insist that the conversation does not end with my assault but rather continues into how part of my healing was to have a lot of consensual and joyful sex, the antithesis of the assault I was subjected to and the gang rape I was threatened with. I enjoyed my body, and it was important for me to find joy again through pleasure and desire. That is not to exclude those who identify as asexual from the declaration of "I own my body," nor does it exclude them from finding joy in their identity. In fact, the power of that declaration ensures that whether we choose to have sex or not, regardless of how we identify, it is *our* choice and not one imposed by patriarchy and its attendant oppressions.

In May 2016 the South African feminist Nthabiseng Nooe launched a nationwide campaign called #FillUpThisPussy to get South Africans talking about consent, slut-shaming, and women's pleasure, with the vision "to have a world of people who get toe-curling orgasms and experience that party that sex is."[20]

Nooe told *OkayAfrica*, "I decided I could have a conversation on women being subjects in sex, and making sure they get what they want out of sex with their consent. This discussion includes conversations on slut-shaming, and sexual liberation includes both wanting and not wanting sex without that affecting how a woman is valued. I wanted to speak about the politics of sex, and sensuality, and transactional sexual relations, and everything else. And I knew that I would need to allow people to contribute in ways they felt comfortable."

Asked what she felt South Africa needed when it came to conversations about women and sex, Nooe's response was one that will resonate with women globally.

What I felt lacked in my elementary sexual education was the important discussion of consent. I was given abstinence and fear sexual education. So I am familiar with the notion that I should not openly want to have sex, and that I must be pursued and persuaded into sex. . . . And this is, according to me, a result of the social conditioning of patriarchy. What I lacked in my sexual education was an extensive conversation on consent, agency and sexuality in all its forms. I could have benefited from under-standing what constitutes harassment, that some people desire sex and some don't. Sex isn't simply the penetration of a vagina by a penis. Sex can be enjoyed, and there is nothing "loose" about being a woman who craves sex.

It is important to hear the voices of women around the world owning desire and pleasure. It is especially important for me to find nonwhite and non-Western voices that challenge heteronormativity and mononorma-tivity, used to refer to the assumption that "normal" romantic or sexual relationships are those limited to two monogamous people.

Over the years I have also spoken more openly about my move away from monogamy. One of the reasons I waited for so long to have sex was that I was bound by patriarchal dictates about purity and modesty that unfairly burden women and girls. Once I smashed those dictates, I determined to be free. I wanted nothing to do with those dictates, which spring from patriarchy and therefore privilege male dominance in the arena of what June Jordan called the politics of sexuality. I had not come across Jordan's essay on the revolutionary potential of bisexuality when I determined to reject monogamy and identify as polyamorous—sometimes referred to as being ethically nonmonogamous. But I do so in the understanding that what Jordan called "the oppression of sexual-ity" was indeed, as she said, "deeper and more pervasive than any other oppression."[21]

I cannot be anyone's possession nor do I want to possess anyone. I am in a loving primary relationship in which my partner and I have openly dis-cussed boundaries and our requirements to feel loved and respected while not demanding of each other a monogamy that denies us freedom. I iden-tify as queer mostly because of my polyamory. I consider it as part of my defiance, disobedience, and disruption of patriarchal dictates around sex.

"The term 'queer' implies resistance to the 'normal,' where 'normal' is what seems natural and intrinsic," writes Susan Song in her essay "Poly-amory and Queer Anarchism: Infinite Possibilities for Resistance."[22]

In the essay, Song discusses "queer theory's relevance to anarchist sexual practice and why anarchists might critique *compulsory* monog-amy as a relationship form" (emphasis hers). She defines polyamory (in a way that I agree with) as "the practice of openly and honestly having more than one intimate relationship simultaneously with the awareness and knowledge of all participants. . . . The open and honest aspect of polyamory points to anarchist conceptions of voluntary association and mutual aid. Polyamory also allows for free love in a way that monogamous state conceptions of sexuality don't allow."

"In contrast to compulsory monogamy, polyamory can allow for more than one partner, which can challenge state conceptions of what is a normal/natural relationship and enacts a queer form of relation," Song adds. "Compulsory monogamy is a concept that's pervasive in our laws and institutions, where the expectation and pressure to conform to monogamy is awarded by material and social gain."

Declaring that "we want more than class liberation alone," Song goes on to create a manifesto that I happily share when I explain why I am polyamorous: "We want to be liberated from the bourgeois expectations that we should be married, that there is only a binary of men and women in rigid normative roles who can date monogamously and express their gender in normative, restrictive ways. We should fight for gender liberation for our gender-transgressive friends and comrades and fight for freedom of consensual sexual expressions and love. This fight isn't just in the streets."

Echoing my assertion that too many men who claim to be engaged in liberatory work are, in fact, engaged in a struggle with other men for more power, rather than in what I consider the true revolutionary struggle to destroy patriarchy, Song is clear about the fight: "It's in our meetings and movements where critical voices that don't belong to straight, white, cisgender men are marginalized. We should create new, different ways of living and allow for queerer forms of relating and being."

It is especially important to me to meet activists whose work does just that. It's an incredible privilege to be invited to speak in so many places around the world. Whether I'm at a literary festival or a conference on human rights, my goal is always to meet as many feminist and LGBTQ activists as possible. The work of those activists to dismantle patriarchy, misogyny, homophobia, transphobia, and all kinds of bigotry around the world is inspiring and a reminder that feminism and LGBTQ activism is global.

In 2018 I met two Chinese activists whose feminism and queerness have combined to create a movement that has become so popular that it represents a threat to the authoritarian patriarchal Chinese Communist Party, which has been in power for almost seventy years. I met Zheng Churan and Liang Xiaowen in New York City through author Leta Hong Fincher, whose book *Betraying Big Brother: The Feminist Awakening in China* tells the story of the two activists and the movement they belong to as part of her examination of feminism in contemporary China.[23]

Churan, who goes by the nickname Datu (Big Rabbit), is one of China's Feminist Five, who were detained for thirty-seven days in the run-up to International Women's Day in 2015 for planning to hand out stickers against sexual harassment on public transport. I first read about them soon after their arrest. During my book tour that year, I always mentioned their activism and arrest as an important reminder of the power of feminist movements, of the reminder of transnational movements against patriarchy.

Churan and Xiaowen met in 2011 when they were volunteers for an LGBT youth organization. I interviewed them seven years later for *Sister-hood*, an online magazine for women of Muslim descent founded by Deeyah Khan, a documentary filmmaker, activist, and UNESCO Goodwill Ambassador for artistic freedom and creativity. I asked how their queerness is connected to their feminism, and Churan told me: "A lot of lesbian activists feel like a lot of LGBT organizations, even though they [the organizations] don't agree with a heterosexual norm, are patriarchal inside the organization. I wasn't satisfied with how the organization was run and that it never talked about gender equality. I was angry and left the organization and started my own organization."[24] Xiaowen explained that she was a cofounder of that new organization, which she and Churan called SinnerB Feminist and Lesbian Group.

"Sinner because we admit we're sinners because we decided to be non-conforming women," Xiaowen explained in an instant of synchronicity with the "sins" of which I write in this book. "B was for Bitch," added Churan.

They eventually left SinnerB to focus on feminist activism, which would eventually get Zheng Churan detained along with four other activists. Their identities as both feminist and queer give these young activists a depth and reach with other young queer women in a way that distinguishes them from male-dominated and patriarchal activism circles.

"Within the [Chinese] human rights and LGBTQ rights communities, male activists often showed that they did not truly see women's rights as human rights. Several of the feminist activists I interviewed complained about the sexism of men who were rights activists," Fincher explains in *Betraying Big Brother*, a foundational text that captures the power and scope of those feminist activists and which serves notice that we must pay attention to and learn from feminists around the world.

I witnessed the power of expanding LGBTQ conversations beyond male voices during several visits to Nigeria for the Ake Arts and Book Festival, which was founded by the author Lola Shoneyin. In 2014, a year before my first visit, Nigeria's then president, Goodluck Jonathan, signed the Same Sex Marriage Prohibition Act (SSMPA).[25] Known as the "Jail the Gays" law, it includes penalties of up to fourteen years in jail for same-sex marriage and up to ten years' imprisonment for membership or encouragement of LGBTQ clubs, societies, and organizations. After lobbying and financial support by American white Evangelical homophobic groups, several countries on the African continent have criminalized homosexuality.

I visited Nigeria in 2015 and again in 2017 and in 2018. I have seen how the Ake Arts and Book Festival has become a space, as bell hooks would say, of radical openness where LGBTQ Nigerians can meet authors and creators, some queer, others heterosexual. During my first visit to the festival, in 2015, a film was shown about the LGBTQ community in Africa and the panel that followed was dominated by male voices. It was good to hear openly gay men bravely talk on a stage about their sexuality in a country where they could have been arrested on the spot under the SSMPA, but women's and nonbinary people's voices were conspicuously absent from the discussion. So distraught were some of the activists and audience members in attendance that they organized an informal side event to discuss "Where are women and nonbinary people?" Compare that to a panel at the Ake festival just three years later, in 2018, on which three queer women and a nonbinary person discussed queerness. It was testament to the work put in by Shoneyin, the Ake team, and Nigeria's feminist and queer activists. Further, the panel included Azeenarh Mohammed and

Chitra Nagarajan, two of three coeditors (the third is Rafeeat Aliyu) of *She Called Me Woman: Nigeria's Queer Women Speak*, the country's first anthology of lesbian, bisexual, and trans women.[26] The anthology—which, full disclosure, I blurbed with great excitement—was published by the Nigerian publisher Cassava Republic. Its cofounder, Bibi Bakare-Yusuf, was the moderator of that 2015 panel on LGBTQ communities. It is clear that the anthology Bakare-Yusuf published was a necessary and direct response to that informal side event, which Nagarajan was involved in organizing.

"We decided to put together this collection of thirty narratives to correct the invisibility, the confusion, the caricaturizing and the writing out of history," *She Called Me Woman*'s editors say in the introduction.[27]

It is imperative that queer voices of color that transgress against patriarchy are recognized around the world. For too long, they have been dominated by a white-centric and cisgender perspective. It is important to me that I amplify queer voices that stretch beyond those identities. At that first Ake festival I attended, I made many lifelong friends with fellow authors and other creators from across the continent, including Nigerian LGBTQ activist Bisi Alimi and journalism professor Chike Frankie Edozien, who I am proud to know and to consider fellow African comrades in the fight to subvert patriarchy.

Alimi made history in 2004 when he became the first Nigerian to come out as a gay man on a popular television show.[28] He told me the show was yanked from the air mid-broadcast and he was forced to go into exile after attacks and threats that followed. Alimi's wedding, when he married his husband, Anthony, an Australian, was the first same-sex marriage I attended. It happened in England, because in 2017 neither one's country of birth allowed same-sex marriage. Same sex marriage has since come into effect in Australia.

Edozien's memoir, *Lives of Great Men: Living and Loving as an African Gay Man*, has been published in several countries and won the 2018 LAMBDA award for gay memoir.[29]

At the 2018 Ake festival, Shoneyin and her team screened to a packed audience the Kenyan film *Rafiki*, directed by Wanuri Kahiu. Dubbed Africa's first lesbian love film, *Rafiki*—the Swahili word for "friend"—was banned in April 2017 on the grounds that it promoted homosexuality, which is a criminal offense in Kenya, under a British colonial-era law.[30]

In May 2018 *Rafiki* became the first Kenyan film to be selected for screening at the Cannes Film Festival in France. A judge lifted the ban in Kenya for a week after the film's director, Kahiu, sued to allow a domestic screening so *Rafiki* could qualify for entrance into the Foreign Language Oscar category. The ban was lifted, but only for daytime screenings at a particular Nairobi cinema, which quickly sold out. Reuters news agency reported that the Kenyan censor said it still considered *Rafiki* morally subversive.

But for those at the screenings, *Rafiki* was important and affirming. "This week means so much to so many people," said Vicky, a Nairobi photographer who chose to be identified by her first name only. She told Reuters she was part of the LGBTQ community, adding, "People can see themselves on screen and they can know that it is okay to express themselves in that way."[31] Kenyan LGBTQ rights activists are fighting to decriminalize same-sex relations in their country. They were encouraged by the decriminalization of homosexuality in India in 2018.[32]

In colonial India, as in Kenya and many other countries that were colonized by Britain, homosexuality was considered immoral and criminalized by conservative and prudish white Christians. "India's fluid gender and sexual norms did not fit into Britain's strict Victorian conceptions of appropriate sexual behavior," writes Amy Bhatt, associate professor of gender and women's studies at the University of Maryland, Baltimore County.[33] The ruling decriminalizing same-sex relations "is more than a human rights win," she says. "It is also a restoration of ancient Indian sexual norms."

When India finally abolished Section 377 of the Indian Penal Code, an "unnatural offences" law introduced during the colonial era, it was not "making progress" or "modernizing" but rather ridding itself of a homophobia enshrined in laws imposed on it by empire.

Same-sex relationships have always existed across time and across the globe. When Britain exported its conservative Christian homophobia to its colonies, while stealing their resources, assets, and antiquities, it was a way for the white heteronormative patriarchy to police bodies and their expressions of lust, desire, and pleasure. Remember that radical rudeness was used to rebel against British colonizers in Uganda. Imposing laws of civility is often accompanied by codes of behavior that control more than language.

They control bodies and expressions of sexuality and gender that threaten privilege, whiteness, and heterosexuality—that essentially threaten patriarchy. The modern-day equivalent of those colonial-era homophobes are the white American Christian Evangelicals who have helped push recent statutes that criminalize homosexuality on the African continent. During the British Empire it was white, Christian, and prudish Victorians who codified who can fuck and with who. Today, during the era of American Empire, it is white, Christian Evangelical Americans who are the moral guardians of sex and gender.

It is increasingly apparent around the world that feminist and queer alliances are particularly effective and necessary in the fight against patriarchy. "I own my body" is their revolutionary declaration, and sexual liberation is an important goal. In Argentina, one such alliance came about in the campaign to allow elective abortion in the first fourteen weeks of pregnancy, although lawmakers narrowly voted against a bill to legalize abortion, in August 2019.[34] Under the banner of the #NiUnaMenos Movement (Not One More), which fights gender-based violence in Latin America, a statement published the day before the vote celebrated the power of their alliance, regardless of the Argentinian Senate's decision: "For us, women, men, and trans people, there has already been a collective triumph: we have brought our bodies, our abortions, and our desires out of hiding and we will not go back."[35]

> During these months of debate, our voices have been amplified everywhere: from Congress to our homes, from schools to unions, from neighborhood organizations to campesino territories, and what we discussed was our autonomy. An autonomy that does not understand the body as private property but that recognizes the community web that all people rely on to be able to live and develop ourselves, to collectively care for each other. To exercise our right to liberated sexuality and to design the families that we want, when we want, with the people we want.

Regardless of the law's outcome, Ni Una Menos stressed they would not leave the streets until legal, safe, and free abortion became available in Argentina, where 60 percent of public opinion favored the bill and forty-one abortions are carried out per hour, according to official statistics in the country.[36]

Abortion is not made less rare because it is illegal. On the contrary, making it legal and easily available is the best way to do that. "If the law is not passed, we will not leave the streets, and they will not be able to leave the Congress building, because in the street Legal Abortion is already the law," vowed Ni Una Menos.

They ended their statement with a rallying cry so powerful that I have adopted it as the conclusion to my public talks. I begin with "Fuck the patriarchy." I end with this:

"We will not let ourselves be burned because this time the fire is ours."

CONCLUSION

AS I SAID AT THE BEGINNING, I wrote this book with enough rage to fuel a rocket. And just as I was wrapping it up, somewhere between the chapter on violence and the one on lust, an eighteen-year-old woman launched her own rocket with such a breathtaking amount of defiance, disobedience, and disruption on board that she forced the world to look and bask in the audacity of a woman who knew she deserved to be free.

That woman is a Saudi Arabian called Rahaf Mohamed. How she got from Saudi Arabia—where she said her family was abusive and from where she said it was especially urgent for her to escape because she had renounced Islam—to Canada—where she has been granted refugee status—is a story worthy of a superhero. If every single one of the "sins" I write about in this book could manifest in one person, Rahaf would be their perfect embodiment. (Soon after her escape, Rahaf's family publicly denounced and disowned her, after which she dropped her family name. So captivating was her plight on social media that she is known to many simply as Rahaf, and that is why I refer to her by her first name.)

I first heard of Rahaf when a Saudi feminist who herself is an asylee wrote to me on Twitter asking for my help in spreading the word about Rahaf's plight. While on vacation in Kuwait with her family in January 2019, Rahaf took a flight to Thailand en route to Australia, where she had planned on seeking asylum. Upon arriving in Thailand's Bangkok airport, an official with the Saudi embassy confiscated Rahaf's passport, and Rahaf was told that she would be deported back to Kuwait and forcibly repatriated to Saudi Arabia.

Patriarchy is global. In Saudi Arabia, it takes an especially extreme version due to the guardianship system that gives men the ability to control almost every aspect of the lives of girls and women. Under the system, as explained by Human Rights Watch, every woman must have a male guardian to be issued a passport, to travel abroad, to marry, to study abroad if she gets a government scholarship, or to exit prison, and she may require a male guardian's permission to work and to access healthcare.[1]

There are no exceptions. Every Saudi woman is subject to the guardianship system, which effectively renders her a minor for her entire life. Her guardian could be her father, husband, brother, or even her son. This must be called what it is: gender apartheid.[2]

Due to racial apartheid, South Africa was justifiably rendered a pariah, boycotted by much of the world until it dismantled that heinous system. And yet, Saudi Arabia is subjecting half of its population to gender apartheid with little consequence or accountability. If you are a Saudi woman like Rahaf who tries to escape gender apartheid in that country, forcible repatriation can be devastating. Her male guardian can file a legal complaint of "disobedience" against her. She could face criminal charges and punishment, including imprisonment, which could mean indefinite confinement since a woman needs a guardian's permission to leave prison. It could also mean a return to her guardian's home, even if that guardian is abusive and was the reason for her attempted escape in the first place, as was the case for Rahaf.[3]

Foremost on my mind when I first heard about Rahaf was another Saudi woman, Dina Ali Lasloom, who tried a similar escape to Australia in 2017 when she was twenty-four years old. Lasloom traveled via the Philippines rather than Thailand. Authorities at the Manila airport confiscated Lasloom's passport and her onward ticket to Sydney and detained her at an airport lounge until two of her uncles arrived, beat her, and dragged her onto a plane to Saudi Arabia with her mouth taped shut and her arms and legs bound together. Activists say that after her forcible repatriation, Lasloom was held at a women's prison in Saudi Arabia. We don't know what happened to her after that.[4]

I had no way of knowing if Rahaf was real or if the person who was tweeting using the name Rahaf asking the world to help her was trolling all of us, but I could not live with myself if she were real and I had not done anything about her plight. So I translated into English her tweets describing what was happening at the airport and alerted human rights activists and journalists I knew to help. The least I could do was galvanize my large social media following to help in any way they could. I was especially struck by Rahaf's tweet in which she stated, clearly and forth-rightly, her demands: "I should be able to live alone, freely, independently of anyone who does not respect my dignity and who doesn't respect me as a woman."[5]

Fuck, yes! I was just fifteen years old when my family moved to Saudi Arabia, and here was a Saudi teenager courageous enough for an army of teenage me's, giving word to the fire that sparked feminism in me when I lived in her country. Those words of hers are revolutionary.

One of these days, Rahaf will write a book about how she saved herself. When we eventually met in Toronto eight days after I first translated her tweets from the Bangkok airport, she told me she was the last of her circle of friends to escape. She had wanted to escape for two years. For a few desperate hours, the entire world had a front-row seat to her deter-mined bid for freedom. She barricaded herself into her hotel room and refused to exit until the United Nations High Commission for Refugees (UNHCR) came to her hotel to take her under its supervision until it assessed her case. Australian journalist Sophie McNeill flew on her own dime from Sydney to Bangkok to be with Rahaf, whom she had never met before, to act as witness in case Thai authorities tried to make good on Rahaf's deportation.[6]

In the end, Rahaf won. She saved herself. She took that initial jump to escape—hers was the courage that fueled that flight—and an incredible network amplified and advocated for her. Three of Rahaf's friends—Saudi women who themselves had also escaped and were awaiting asylum in Aus-tralia, Canada, and Sweden, respectively—were incredible advocates for Rahaf on Twitter, spreading the word about her and further amplifying her plight. And what a thrill to watch the ways that Saudi feminists on Twitter uplifted Rahaf and fought off vicious and orchestrated regime cyber trolls who tried to discredit Rahaf. The ways those Saudi feminists use social me-dia is nothing short of revolutionary. Daily and despite state intimidation, they take on gender apartheid and say, "We are here. We exist."

An eighteen-year-old wrong-footed and embarrassed the Saudi abso-lute monarchy. While her individual crisis was poignant, ultimately, what Rahaf did was force Saudi Arabia's gender apartheid onto the global con-sciousness. She forced the world to ask, "What the fuck is Saudi Arabia doing to women that they are escaping?"

Those of us familiar with that country have long known about its cruel treatment of women, but the Saudi regime too often gets a pass because of geopolitics. For the West, it sells oil and buys weapons, making it a valuable friend to successive US administrations—Republican and Democratic—as well as various European countries. And as home to Islam's two holiest sites, the kingdom's human rights violations, including its gender apartheid, do not elicit condemnation from Muslim-majority countries.

To understand the magnitude of what Rahaf did, it is imperative to see the guardianship system as central to the Trifecta of Misogyny, which upholds patriarchy. The Saudi absolute monarchy most certainly oppresses everyone in the kingdom, which is named after the patriarch of that royal family. But by enforcing the guardianship system, the state enlists the street and the home in enforcing misogyny. To understand how central the guardianship system is to the regime, remember that when Rahaf made her escape in January 2019, eighteen women's rights activists were in Saudi prisons for advocating against the guardianship system. Crown Prince Mohammed bin Salman, the de facto leader of the kingdom, began detaining them in May 2018, just a few weeks before he lifted the world's only driving ban for women. Those women's rights activists had long fought the ban, with several having been arrested in the past for defying it by driving while friends in passenger seats filmed them. The crown prince clearly wanted to claim all credit for the end of the ban, to signal that activism and defiance do not work, to say that rights are given by the regime and not taken by defiant protests. When Rahaf escaped, none of the imprisoned women's rights activists had been charged with anything. Instead, Saudi state-sanctioned media smeared them as "traitors." In March 2019 the activists were charged—although it was not clear with what—and were referred to trial.[7] Human rights groups quoting relatives of the detainees revealed that at least eight had been subjected to various forms of torture, including electric shocks, flogging, and threats of rape. One had been waterboarded, a punishment usually associated with terrorism suspects.[8]

Feminism gets treated like terrorism.

As absurd as that sounds, that was exactly the message the Saudi regime hammered home after Rahaf's escape. Her successful escape had not only unhinged the absolute monarchy but also galvanized countless Saudi women. Days after Rahaf's escape, the hashtag "End Guardianship Or We

Will All Seek Asylum" trended in Saudi Arabia and neighboring countries. Cognizant of the dangers of one brave woman, the Saudi regime spared no effort to conflate feminism with terrorism, to paint feminists as dangerous as the violent rapists and murderers of the so-called Islamic State and as dangerous as al-Qaeda and its recruiters. A Saudi government counter-extremist agency produced a video that begins with a split screen: on the left is a man holding a rifle; on the right is a woman with a suitcase. Imagine! A Saudi woman determined to escape gender apartheid is considered as dangerous as a man who joins a violent extremist group! It should be the right of every woman in Saudi Arabia to "live alone, freely, independently of anyone who does not respect [her] dignity and who doesn't respect [her] as a woman," without escaping into asylum. We associate asylum seekers and refugees with the need to escape oppression and war. Saudi Arabia's gender apartheid represents both of those threats to women. Women should not have to flee to live freely and with dignity.

For my part in amplifying Rahaf's voice, by translating her tweets and asking my followers to help raise her plea, I became effectively one of the most hated women of the Saudi regime. I was subjected to an orchestrated and sustained attack by the regime's "electronic flies," as the troll farms they use to stifle dissent and opposition are known. Tellingly, the attacks centered on my looks. Interviews I'd given several years ago about my views on sexual freedom were used to slut-shame me in an attempt to discredit me. My face was Photoshopped onto the body of a woman standing next to an adult film star to suggest that I was involved with the adult film industry. At least five Saudi newspapers carried articles with headlines such as "Porn Activist Welcomes Rahaf in Canada: 12 Facts About the Red-Haired Woman."[9] And the Arab world's largest media company, Middle East Broadcasting Corporation (MBC), which is believed to be owned by the crown prince, broadcast a "news segment" about what it called the "use by radical feminist movements" of Rahaf's "family troubles" as a political weapon against the family and the Saudi state, in which I was the "star."[10]

"Mona Eltahawy is a woman who identifies herself as a defender of women's rights, who says in her statements that she hates men and calls for sex in the streets," it was reported in the segment, which also suggested that I had masterminded Rahaf's escape. It was a stunning and bold-faced example of incitement and propaganda—and I will forever be proud that I caused it.

Imagine: an eighteen-year-old woman's successful escape into freedom and a fifty-one-year-old woman's help in that bid so discombobulated the Saudi regime that it orchestrated propaganda claiming we were dangerous to the royal family and to the state.

Feminism terrifies authoritarians.

Lest the finger-pointing at the Saudi patriarchy becomes too comfortable, let me remind you that some of the very same white American women who most full-heartedly supported Rahaf's bid for freedom were Trump supporters who conveniently forgot their own support for patriarchy at home. It is always easier and more comfortable to point to patriarchy "over there" and to ignore its manifestations "over here." Saudi women who support the guardianship system—they sadly exist—are foot soldiers of the patriarchy in the same way that white American women voters who voted for Trump uphold white supremacy and its attendant misogyny. Both groups of women mistakenly believe their proximity to power in their respective countries will protect them from the worst ravages of patriarchy. What's more, in my social media feeds, some of the same white American women so upset by my reminder that supporting Trump made them foot soldiers of the patriarchy told me, on social media, that they would stop caring about Rahaf and Saudi women altogether. It was as if their support was incumbent on telling only half of patriarchy's story, as if solidarity with Saudi women were contingent upon ensuring that the finger that points at patriarchy must point only "over there" and never "over here," and that feminism must occupy itself only with "saving" women of color rather than destroying patriarchy wherever it exists, including in the United States of America.

Many white American men joined the social media fray with shouts of "That's the real feminist struggle over there in Saudi Arabia, not here in the US, where feminists just complain about trivial things like manspreading," referring to the habit of men on public transport spreading their legs widely while seated, thus taking up more space than they should.

Tellingly, the orchestrated Saudi regime trolling against Rahaf and anyone who supported her had a similar refrain that is commonly described as "whataboutery," in which, to derail the subject at hand, they ask, "What about X, Y, and Z?" The Saudi misogynists, too, just wanted to focus on "over there"—be it domestic-violence rates or rates of homelessness in Canada, as if it were impossible to fight all these injustices at once.

As the US political climate grows more and more fraught, it is imperative that we are agile in the ways we confront patriarchy and the host of oppressions it employs, including whataboutery. It is increasingly obvious that the women of color elected to the US Congress in 2018 have proven disruptive for patriarchy and other powers unaccustomed to challenge. It is clear that much of the outrage and many of the headlines have less to do with what the lawmakers actually have said and more to do with who said it.

It is easy to forget that Rahaf was just eighteen years old when she escaped. As you marvel at her courage, ask yourself if you could have done what she did when you were that age. "I wish I had done it," several much older women told me as we all cheered on Rahaf. In this young woman, the older women saw their younger selves—their braver selves. And I love that Rahaf is not the only brave teenage girl changing the world right now.

In 2018 sixteen-year-old Swedish climate activist Greta Thunberg began weekly protests outside her country's parliament. Teenage girls in several European countries and Australia have since emerged as part of a determined movement staging climate strikes during which they walk out of school in protest and demand that their governments take climate change seriously.

CNN reported that in several of their respective countries, the teenage girls are falsely rumored to be pawns of political parties or older, established male activists.[11] "Many people love to spread rumors saying that I have people 'behind me' or that I'm being 'paid' or 'used' to do what I'm doing. But there is no one 'behind' me except for myself," Thunberg wrote on Facebook.[12] "I am not part of any organization. I sometimes support and cooperate with several NGOs that work with the climate and environment."

In Belgium a student-led climate march organized by schoolgirl Anuna De Wever and her best friend, Kyra Gantois, drew thirty-five thousand people in January 2019. CNN said that "false claims against [De Wever's] marches . . . led to the resignation of an environment minister, who incorrectly said the country's intelligence service had evidence that unnamed powers were behind the protests."[13] The schoolgirl told CNN that she thought "the disbelief stems from an ingrained patriarchal attitude in society, where people find it hard to believe that young women [can] inspire and run their own movements. 'And I think that is an insult.'" De Wever's mother said, "People find it hard to imagine young women with power. . . . They think there must be some adult males behind the scenes pulling the strings."

Think about that. In the same way that Rahaf's escape was blamed on brainwashing and sinister "masterminds," the increasingly powerful global climate movement that teenage girls have established is said to be "masterminded" by others. Patriarchy refuses to believe that girls and young women have the audacity to look it in the eye and to say, "Enough!" Patriarchy refuses to believe that girls and young women can be angry, attention-seeking, profane, ambitious, powerful, violent, and lustful.

Rahaf defied, disobeyed, and disrupted her way to freedom. Teenage girls worldwide are defying, disobeying, and disrupting in their fight to ensure they have a future on the planet they will inherit.

Let us celebrate the audacity of teenage girls who save themselves and teenage girls who will save the planet. Let us celebrate teenage girls whose ability to "sin" catapulted them above the derision too often directed toward their cohort.

Let us celebrate women and girls who sin!

ACKNOWLEDGMENTS

I WROTE THIS BOOK with my mind on fire, and it is thanks to the support of these wonderful people that I am still here, ready for more:

Thank you Jessica Papin, my agent, for knowing where my book would find the best home.

Thank you Rakia Clark, my editor, for reading an explosive proposal and saying I want to help this book erupt.

Thank you Louis Roe and Carol Chu, the design team at Beacon Press, for a cover that spins me with delight every time I look at it.

Thank you the entire team at Beacon Press for believing in my book with an enthusiasm an author yearns for.

Thank you friends whose warmth is my home in cities across the world.

Thank you my parents, my siblings, their spouses, and their children for love and always love.

Thank you Robert E. Rutledge, my beloved: I adore you and our magnificent adventure of love.

NOTES

INTRODUCTION

1. Audre Lorde, "The Transformation of Silence into Language and Action," in Lorde, *Sister Outsider: Essays and Speeches* (Berkeley, CA: Crossing Press, 2007).

2. Mona Eltahawy, *Headscarves and Hymens: Why the Middle East Needs a Sexual Revolution* (New York: Farrar, Straus and Giroux, 2015).

3. Libby Nelson and Sarah Frostenson, "A Brief Guide to the 17 Women Trump Has Allegedly Assaulted, Groped or Harassed," *Vox*, October 20, 2016, https:// www.vox.com/2016/10/13/13269448/trump-sexual-assault-allegations.

4. Mona Eltahawy, "These 'Virginity Tests' Will Spark Egypt's Next Revolution," *Guardian*, June 2, 2011, http://www.theguardian.com/commentisfree/2011 /jun/02/egypt-next-revolution-virginity-tests.

5. Mona Eltahawy, "The American Sisi," *New York Times*, January 20, 2017, https://www.nytimes.com/interactive/projects/cp/opinion/presidential -inauguration-2017/the-american-sisi.

6. Jung Hawon, "'Spycam Porn' Sparks Record Protests in South Korea," Agence France Presse, August 4, 2018, https://sg.news.yahoo.com/spycam-porn -sparks-record-protests-south-korea-063841341.html.

7. Ni Una Menos, "The Fire Is Ours: A Statement from Ni Una Menos," Verso blog, August 7, 2018, https://www.versobooks.com/blogs/3966-the-fire-is-ours-a -statement-from-ni-una-menos.

CHAPTER I: ANGER

1. Ntozake Shange, *For Colored Girls who Have Considered Suicide/When the Rainbow is Enuf* (1975) (New York: Simon and Schuster, 2010).

2. Belinda Luscombe, "Kids Believe Gender Stereotypes by Age 10, Global Study Says," *Time*, September 20, 2017, http://time.com/4948607/gender-stereotypes-roles.

3. Luscombe, "Kids Believe Gender Stereotypes by Age 10."

4. "Teen Girls Twice as Likely to Suffer Depression Than Boys, Research Shows," Australian Broadcasting Corporation, January 16, 2014, https://www.abc .net.au/news/2014-01-16/teen-girls-twice-as-likely-to-suffer-depression-than -boys2c-re/5203626.

5. "Q & A: Child Marriage and Violations of Girls' Rights," Human Rights Watch, June 14, 2013, https://www.hrw.org/news/2013/06/14/q-child-marriage -and-violations-girls-rights.

6. "Women and Girls, HIV and AIDS," AVERT, July 21, 2015, https://www .avert.org/professionals/hiv-social-issues/key-affected-populations/women.

7. Jacqueline Howard, "Adults View Black Girls as 'Less Innocent,' Study Says," CNN.com, June 28, 2017, https://www.cnn.com/2017/06/28/health/black-girls -adultification-racial-bias-study/index.html.

8. Howard, "Adults View Black Girls as 'Less Innocent,' Study Says."

9. Owethu Makhatini, "A Lot to Be Mad About: Advocating for the Legitimacy of a Black Woman's Anger," in *Feminism Is: South Africans Speak Their Truth*, ed. Jen Thorpe (Kwela Books, 2018), Kindle ed., https://www.litnet.co.za/feminism-south -africans-speak-truth-edited-jen-thorpe-book-review.

10. Makhatini, "A Lot to Be Mad About."

11. Will Hobson "At Larry Nassar Sentencing Hearing, a Parade of Horror and Catharsis," *Washington Post*, January 18, 2018, https://www.washingtonpost .com/sports/olympics/at-larry-nassar-sentencing-hearing-a-parade-of-horror -and-catharsis/2018/01/18/19bed832-fc55-11e7-8f66-2df0b94bb98a_story .html.

12. Nawal El Saadawi, *The Hidden Face of Eve* (London: ZED Books, 2007).

13. Hobson "At Larry Nassar Sentencing Hearing, a Parade of Horror and Catharsis."

14. Ursula K. Le Guin, "Bryn Mawr Commencement Address," in *Dancing at the Edge of the World: Thoughts on Words, Women, Places* (New York: Grove Atlantic, 1997), Kindle ed.

15. June Jordan, "Poem About My Rights," in *Directed by Desire: The Collected Poems of June Jordan* (Port Townsend, WA: Copper Canyon Press, 2007).

16. June Jordan, introduction, *Some of Us Did Not Die: New and Selected Essays of June Jordan* (New York: Civitas Books, 2003).

17. June Jordan, "Where Is the Rage?," in *Life as Activism: June Jordan's Writings from the* Progressive (Sacramento: Litwin Books, 2014).

18. Alex Frank, "Stream a New Song from Alt-Pop Artist Halsey," Vogue.com, September 25, 2014, https://www.vogue.com/article/singer-halsey-new-song -hurricane.

19. Audre Lorde, "The Uses of Anger: Women Responding to Racism," in *Sister Outsider*.

20. Pew Research Center, *For Most Trump Voters, "Very Warm" Feelings for Him Endured* (August 2018), http://www.people-press.org/2018/08/09/an-examination -of-the-2016-electorate-based-on-validated-voters.

CHAPTER 2: ATTENTION

1. Virgie Tovar, *You Have the Right to Remain Fat* (New York: Feminist Press, 2018), Kindle ed.

2. Sigal Samuel, "Battle of the Subway Ads," *Daily Beast*, October 9, 2012, https:// www.thedailybeast.com/battle-of-the-subway-ads.

3. Jennifer Hansler and Maegan Vazquez, "Wilson Hits Back at Trump: Niger Is His Benghazi," CNN.com, October 22, 2017, https://www.cnn.com/2017/10/22 /politics/frederica-wilson-tweets-trump/index.html.

4. Dr. Gina Loudon, "Rep. Frederica Wilson Desperately Seeking Attention?," Fox News.com, October 19, 2017, https://www.foxnews.com/opinion/rep-frederica -wilson-desperately-seeking-attention.

5. Moya Bailey and Trudy, "On Misogynoir: Citation, Erasure, and Plagiarism," *Feminist Media Studies* 18, no. 4 (2018): 762–68, https://www.tandfonline.com/doi /abs/10.1080/14680777.2018.1447395.

6. "Piers Morgan Slams Amber Rose for Baring It All for Feminism," *Just Jared*, June 11, 2017, http://www.justjared.com/2017/06/11/piers-morgan-slams-amber -rose-for-baring-it-all-for-feminism.

7. Sarah Millar, "Police Officer's Remarks at York Inspire 'SlutWalk,'" *Toronto Star*, March 17, 2011, https://www.thestar.com/news/gta/2011/03/17/police _officers_remarks_at_york_inspire_slutwalk.html.

8. "Women Journalists Report Less News Than Men; TV Gender Gap Most Stark," press release, Women's Media Center, March 22, 2017, http://www.womens mediacenter.com/about/press/press-releases/womens-media-center-report-women -journalists-report-less-news-than-men-tv-g.

9. Stacy L. Smith, Marc Choueiti, Katherine Pieper, Ariana Case, and Angel Choi, *Inequality in 1,100 Popular Films: Examining Portrayals of Gender, Race/Ethnicity, LGBT & Disability from 2007 to 2017* (Los Angeles: Annenberg Foundation, July 2018), http://assets.uscannenberg.org/docs/inequality-in-1100-popular-films.pdf.

10. Brett Lang, "Despite Diversity Push, Women and Minorities Aren't Getting Better Movie Roles (Study)," *Variety*, July 31, 2018, https://variety.com/2018/film /news/women-minorities-hollywood-movie-roles-study-1202890199.

11. "Happy to Fire, Reluctant to Hire: Hollywood Inclusion Remains Un-changed," USC Annenberg, July 30, 2018, updated October 17, 2018, https:// annenberg.usc.edu/news/research/happy-fire-reluctant-hire-hollywood-inclusion -remains-unchanged.

12. Inter-American Commission on Human Rights, An Overview of Vio-lence Against LGBTI Persons: A Registry Documenting Acts of Violence Between January 1, 2013 and March 31, 2014 (Washington, DC: IACHR, December 2014), http://www.oas.org/en/iachr/lgtbi/docs/Annex-Registry-Violence-LGBTI.pdf.

13. "Exit Poll Indicates Large Majority Vote to Change Abortion Laws," RTE, May 30, 2018, https://www.rte.ie/news/politics/2018/0526/966120-eighth -amendment-referendum.

14. "Killings of High-Profile Women in Iraq Spark Outrage," DW.com, Octo-ber 2, 2018, https://www.dw.com/en/killings-of-high-profile-women-in-iraq -spark-outrage/a-45732835.

15. "Killings of High-Profile Women in Iraq Spark Outrage."

16. Juliet Perry and Sophia Saifi, "Brother 'Proud' of Killing Pakistan Social Media Star," CNN.com, July 18, 2016, https://www.cnn.com/2016/07/18/asia /pakistan-qandeel-baloch-brother-confession/index.html.

17. Issam Ahmed, "I Wish I'd Sent That Message," Agence France Correspon-dent, July 20, 2016, https://correspondent.afp.com/i-wish-id-sent-message.

18. Juliet Perry and Sophia Saifi, "Brother of Pakistan's Qandeel Baloch Charged with Crime Against State," CNN.com, July 19, 2016, https://www.cnn.com/2016 /07/19/asia/pakistan-qandeel-baloch-brother-charged/index.html.

19. Jon Boone, "'She Feared No One': The Life and Death of Qandeel Baloch," *Guardian*, September 22, 2017, http://www.theguardian.com/world/2017/sep/22 /qandeel-baloch-feared-no-one-life-and-death.

20. Tovar, *You Have the Right to Remain Fat.*

CHAPTER 3: PROFANITY

1. Julia Reinstein, "Cardi B Wants the Government to Tell Her 'What You're Doing with My Fucking Tax Money,'" *BuzzFeed News*, March 23, 2018, https:// www.buzzfeednews.com/article/juliareinstein/cardi-b-taxes.

2. Emily Stewart, "The Past 72 Hours in Sarah Sanders's Dinner and the Civility Debate, Explained," *Vox*, June 25, 2018, https://www.vox.com/policy-and-politics /2018/6/25/17500988/sarah-sanders-red-hen-civility.

3. "Comic Michelle Wolf Responds to Backlash: 'I'm Glad I Stuck to My Guns,'" *Fresh Air*, NPR.org, May 1, 2018, https://www.npr.org/2018/05/01/607262463 /comic-michelle-wolf-responds-to-backlash-im-glad-i-stuck-to-my-guns.

4. Chris Cillizza, "5 Takeaways on Michelle Wolf's Hugely Controversial Speech at the White House Correspondents' Dinner," CNN.com, April 29, 2018, https:// www.cnn.com/2018/04/29/politics/michelle-wolf-whcd-takeaways/index.html.

5. April Ryan, "April Ryan: I'm a Black Woman. Trump Loves Insulting People Like Me," *Washington Post*, November 10, 2018, https://www.washingtonpost .com/outlook/2018/11/10/im-black-woman-white-house-reporter-trump-loves -insulting-people-like-me.

6. Stella Nyanzi, @drstellanyanzi, Twitter account, https://twitter.com /drstellanyanzi?lang=en; Patience Akumu, "How Insults and a Campaign over Sanitary Towels Landed Activist in Jail," *Guardian*, April 22, 2017, http://www .theguardian.com/world/2017/apr/22/activist-uganda-president-buttocks-jail -stella-nyanzi.

7. "30% of Girls Leaving School for Lack of Sanitary Pads," New Vision, August 4, 2013, http://www.newvision.co.ug/new_vision/news/1328198/-girls-leaving -school-lack-sanitary-pads.

8. Geoffrey York, "Stella Nyanzi: The Woman Who Used Facebook to Take On Uganda's President," *Globe and Mail*, May 30, 2017, https://www.theglobeand mail.com/news/world/ugandan-scholar-stella-nyanzi-the-woman-who-tickled -the-leopard/article35159152.

9. Nicola Slawson, "Fury over Arrest of Academic Who Called Uganda's President a Pair of Buttocks," *Guardian*, April 13, 2017, http://www.theguardian.com /global-development/2017/apr/13/stella-nyanzi-fury-arrest-uganda-president-a -pair-of-buttocks-yoweri-museveni-cyber-harassment.

10. Akumu, "How Insults and a Campaign over Sanitary Towels Landed Activist in Jail."

11. York, "Stella Nyanzi."

12. Carol Summers, "Radical Rudeness: Ugandan Social Critiques in the 1940s," *Journal of Social History* 39, no. 3 (2006): 741–70, http://www.jstor.org/stable/3790288.

13. Emma Batha, "Ugandan Girls Forced into Child Marriage Because They Can't Afford Sanitary Pads," Reuters, October 24, 2017, https://www.reuters.com /article/us-uganda-girls-childmarriage-idUSKBN1CT01R.

14. Akumu, "How Insults and a Campaign over Sanitary Towels Landed Activist in Jail."

15. Slawson, "Fury over Arrest of Academic Who Called Uganda's President a Pair of Buttocks."

16. Slawson, "Fury over Arrest of Academic Who Called Uganda's President a Pair of Buttocks."

17. "Uganda's BBC Documentary Actor of 'My Mad World' Joseph Atukunda Visits Dr Stella Nyanzi in Prison, Calls Her 'Extraordinary,'" Alleastafrica.com, April 15, 2017, https://www.alleastafrica.com/2017/04/15/ugandas-bbc-documentary -actor-of-my-mad-world-joseph-atukunda-visits-dr-stella-nyanzi-in-prison-calls -her-extraordinary.

18. Haggai Matsiko, "Stella Nyanzi's Obscenity War," *Independent*, April 17, 2017, https://www.independent.co.ug/stella-nyanzis-obscenity-war.

19. York, "Stella Nyanzi."

20. York, "Stella Nyanzi."

21. Sumi Sadurni, "Women Activists Take to the Streets of Kampala to Demand More Police Action," Public Radio International, July 3, 2018, https://www.pri .org/stories/2018-07-03/women-activists-take-streets-kampala-demand-more -police-action.

22. Jackline Kemigisa, "The Homophobic Backlash That Followed the Ugandan Women's March," Women's Media Center, August 22, 2018, http://www.womens mediacenter.com/fbomb/the-homophobic-backlash-that-followed-the-ugandan -womens-march.

23. Kemigisa, "The Homophobic Backlash That Followed the Ugandan Women's March."

24. Mary Serumaga, "'You Should Have Died at Birth, Oh Dirty Delinquent Dictator': A Poet's Rage Against Museveni in the Bobi Wine Age," *East African Review*, September 22, 2018, https://www.theeastafricanreview.info/op-eds/2018 /09/22/you-should-have-died-at-birth-oh-dirty-delinquent-dictator-a-poets-rage -against-museveni-in-the-bobi-wine-age.

25. Sam Jones, "Vaginagate: US Politician Banned for Saying 'Vagina' in Abortion Bill Debate," *Guardian*, June 15, 2012, http://www.theguardian.com/world /2012/jun/15/michigan-politician-banned-using-word-vagina.

26. "Pussy Riot: The Story So Far," BBC News.com, December 23, 2013, https://www.bbc.com/news/world-europe-25490161.

27. Nadya Tolokonnikova, *Read & Riot: A Pussy Riot Guide to Activism* (New York: HarperOne, 2018).

28. "One of my favorite . . . ," Angela (@ducgummybuns), Twitter, February 16, 2018, https://twitter.com/ducgummybuns/status/964562324228136960.

29. "Because 'fuck' . . . ," M. (@Mandy_RN13), Twitter, February 16, 2018, https://twitter.com/Mandy_RN13/status/964626969274077184.

30. "For me a reaction . . . ," Michele McKenzie (@McolvinMcKenzie), Twitter, February 16, 2018, https://twitter.com/search?f=tweets&q=For%20me%20a %20reaction%20to%20being%20expected%20to%20be%20quiet%20and%20 ladylike&src=typd.

31. Mona Eltahawy, "I Swear to Make the Patriarchy Uncomfortable. And I'm Proud of It," *Think*, NBCNews.com, May 6, 2018, https://www.nbcnews .com/think/opinion/i-swear-make-patriarchy-uncomfortable-i-m-proud-it-ncna 870736.

32. Doreen St. Félix, "Cardi B, the Female Rapper Who Ousted Taylor Swift from the Top of the Charts," *New Yorker*, September 27, 2017, https://www.new yorker.com/culture/culture-desk/cardi-b-the-female-rapper-who-ousted-taylor -swift-from-the-top-of-the-charts-bodak-yellow.

33. Cardi B Defends Cursing to High Schoolers—"I'm Real. They Can Relate," MTO News, November 29, 2018, https://mtonews.com/cardi-b-defends-cursing -to-high-schoolers-im-real-they-can-relate.

34. Jasmine BRAND, "#CardiB Responds to Criticism of Her Using Profanity While Speaking to High School Kids," Instagram, November 29, 2018, https:// www.instagram.com/p/BqxMPdOrDh1.

35. Evelyn Brooks Higginbotham, *Righteous Discontent: The Women's Movement in the Black Baptist Church, 1880–1920* (Cambridge, MA: Harvard University Press, 1994).

36. Ashley Iasimone, "Cardi B Responds to Critics of Her Nude Photo, Talks Plastic Surgery Plans & More," *Billboard*, August 26, 2018, https://www.billboard .com/articles/columns/hip-hop/8472202/cardi-b-nude-photo-plastic-surgery -trump-taxes-instagram-video.

37. Eltahawy, Headscarves and Hymens.

38. In Cherrie Moraga and Gloria Anzaldua, eds., *This Bridge Called My Back: Writings by Radical Women of Color* (New York: Kitchen Table/Women of Color Press, 1994).

39. Melanie Mignucci, "Helen Mirren Would Have Taught Her Daughter to Say, 'Fuck Off!,'" *BUST*, https://bust.com/feminism/10306-helen-mirren-would -have-taught-her-daughter-to-say-fuck-off.html; originally published *Daily Mail*, July 20, 2013.

CHAPTER 4: AMBITION

1. Mindy Kaling, *Why Not Me?* (New York: Crown Archetype, 2015), 220–21.

2. Octavia E. Butler, *Parable of the Sower* (New York: Four Walls Eight Windows, 1993).

3. Desiree Martinez, "Dear High School Teacher Who Tried to Discourage Me from Applying to UCLA, I'm a BRUIN Now!," *La Comadre*, August 15, 2017, http://lacomadre.org/2017/08/dear-high-school-teacher-tried-discourage-applying -ucla-im-bruin-now.

4. Desiree Martinez, "Students Don't Enroll in School to Make a Political Statement, They Go to Learn," *La Comadre*, October 26, 2018, http://lacomadre.org/2018 /10/students-dont-enroll-in-school-to-make-a-political-statement-they-go-to-learn.

5. Seth Gershenson, Stephen B. Holt, and Nicholas W. Papageorge, "'Who Believes in Me?' The Effect of Student-Teacher Demographic Match on Teacher Expectations," Upjohn Institute Working Paper 15-231, 2015, https://doi.org /10.17848/wp15-231.

6. Scott Jaschik, "Study Finds High School Teachers Have Differing Expectations of Black and White Students," *Inside Higher Ed*, October 24, 2017, https:// www.insidehighered.com/news/2017/10/24/study-finds-high-school-teachers -have-differing-expectations-black-and-white.

7. Martinez, "Dear High School Teacher Who Tried to Discourage Me from Applying to UCLA."

8. Louisa Loveluck, "Education in Egypt: Key Challenges," background paper, Middle East and North Africa Programme, Chatham House (London), March 2012, https://www.chathamhouse.org/sites/default/files/public/Research/Middle%20 East/0312egyptedu_background.pdf.

9. "Japan Says 10 Med Schools Altered Admissions, Some Kept Out Women," *France24*, December 14, 2018, https://www.france24.com/en/20181214-japan-says -10-med-schools-altered-admissions-kept-out-women.

10. "Medical Schools 'Rigged Women's Results,'" BBC News.com, December 14, 2018, https://www.bbc.com/news/world-asia-46568975.

11. "Japan Says 10 Med Schools Altered Admissions, Some Kept Out Women," AFP, December 14, 2018, https://www.france24.com/en/20181214-japan-says-10 -med-schools-altered-admissions-kept-out-women.

12. Jake Sturmer, "This Japanese University Penalised Women Because It Believed They Were 'Too Mature,'" Australian Broadcasting Corporation, Decem-

ber 11, 2018, https://www.abc.net.au/news/2018-12-12/japanese-universities-rig
-entrance-exams-to-keep-women-out/10608548.

13. Joya Bahaar, "What Ambition Gap? Women as Ambitious as Men Unless
Companies Block Them: Study," Reuters, April 5, 2017, https://www.reuters.com
/article/us-women-ambition-study/what-ambition-gap-women-as-ambitious-as
-men-unless-companies-block-them-study-idUSKBN1772AB.

14. Jake Sturmer, "Japan's Juntendo University Admits Rigging Interviews to
Keep Women Out," Australian Broadcasting, December 11, 2018,
https://www.abc.net.au/news/2018-12-12/japanese-universities-rig-entrance
-exams-to keep-women-out/10608548.

15. Bahaar, "What Ambition Gap?"

16. Katie Abouzahr et al. "Dispelling the Myths of the Gender 'Ambition
Gap,'" BCG.com, April 5, 2017, https://www.bcg.com/en-ca/publications/2017
/peopleorganization-leadership-change-dispelling-the-myths-of-the-gender-ambition
-gap.aspx.

17. Bahaar, "What Ambition Gap?"

18. Dorothy Sue Cobble, Linda Gordon, and Astrid Henry, prologue, *Feminism
Unfinished: A Short, Surprising History of American Women's Movements* (New York:
Liveright, 2015), Kindle ed.

19. Erika L. Sánchez, "Crying in the Bathroom," in *Double Bind: Women on
Ambition*, ed. Robin Romm (New York: Liveright, 2018).

20. Diana Tourjée, "Men Are Losing Their Minds over the New Female 'Doctor Who,'" *Broadly*, July 17, 2017, https://broadly.vice.com/en_us/article/evdq8z
/men-are-losing-their-minds-over-the-new-female-doctor-who; David Sims, "The
Outcry Against the All-Female 'Ghostbusters' Remake Gets Louder," *Atlantic*, May
18, 2016, https://www.theatlantic.com/entertainment/archive/2016/05/the-sexist
-outcry-against-the-ghostbusters-remake-gets-louder/483270.

21. Isaac Stanley-Becker, "'I Prefer to Hear a Male Voice': Female Commenta-
tors Find Harsh Judgment at World Cup," *Washington Post*, June 26, 2018, https://
www.washingtonpost.com/news/morning-mix/wp/2018/06/26/i-prefer-to-hear
-a-male-voice-women-commentators-find-harsh-judgment-at-world-cup.

22. Aditya Kalra, "India Triumphs in Maiden Mars Mission, Sets Record in
Space Race," Reuters, September 4, 2014, https://www.reuters.com/article/us
-india-mars-idUSKCN0HJ05J20140924.

23. Tracey Bashkoff, "Hilma af Klint: Paintings for the Future," Guggenheim
press kit, August 17, 2017, https://www.guggenheim.org/wp-content/uploads
/2018/10/Gugg-Press-Hilma-af-Klint-Paintings-for-the-Future-Press-Kit.pdf.

24. Ghada Amer, "We are the granddaughters . . ," #WomensArt (@womens
art1), Twitter, October 31, 2017, https://twitter.com/womensart1/status/92527034
9314494464.

CHAPTER 5: POWER

1. June Jordan, *On Call: Political Essays* (Boston: South End Press, 1985).

2. Kara Cooney, preface, *The Woman Who Would Be King: Hatshepsut's Rise to
Power in Ancient Egypt* (New York: Crown, 2014), Kindle ed.

3. Adriana Carranca, "The Women-Led Opposition to Brazil's Far-Right
Leader," *Atlantic*, November 2, 2018, https://www.theatlantic.com/international
/archive/2018/11/brazil-women-bolsonaro-haddad-election/574792.

4. Jonathan Watts, "Dilma Rousseff Impeachment: What You Need to Know," *Guardian*, August 31, 2016, http://www.theguardian.com/news/2016/aug/31/dilma -rousseff-impeachment-brazil-what-you-need-to-know.

5. Dom Phillips, "Bolsonaro Declares Brazil's 'Liberation from Socialism' as He Is Sworn In," *Guardian*, January 1, 2019,http://www.theguardian.com/world/2019 /jan/01/jair-bolsonaro-inauguration-brazil-president.

6. Chayenne Polimédio, "Women for Bolsonaro: What Drives Female Support for Brazil's Far Right," *Foreign Affairs*, October 26, 2018, https://www.foreignaffairs .com/articles/brazil/2018-10-26/women-bolsonaro.

7. "Congratulations . . . ," Donald J. Trump (@realDonaldTrump), Twitter, January 1, 2019, https://twitter.com/realDonaldTrump.

8. Anna Jean Kaiser, "'I Don't See Any Reason for Feminism': The Women Backing Brazil's Bolsonaro," *Guardian*, October 14, 2018, http://www.theguardian .com/world/2018/oct/14/bolsonaro-brazil-presidential-candidate-women-voters -anti-feminism.

9. Anna Jean Kaiser, "Woman Who Bolsonaro Insulted: 'Our President-Elect Encourages Rape,'" *Guardian*, December 23, 2018, http://www.theguardian.com /world/2018/dec/23/maria-do-rosario-jair-bolsonaro-brazil-rape.

10. Kaiser, "Woman Who Bolsonaro Insulted."

11. Kaiser, "Woman Who Bolsonaro Insulted."

12. Carranca, "The Women-Led Opposition to Brazil's Far-Right Leader."

13. Pablo Uchoa, "Why Brazilian Women Are Saying #NotHim," BBC News, September 21, 2018, https://www.bbc.com/news/world-latin-america-45579635.

14. Kaiser, "Woman Who Bolsonaro Insulted."

15. Dom Phillips, "Bolsonaro to Abolish Human Rights Ministry in Favour of Family Values," *Guardian*, December 10, 2018, https://www.theguardian.com /world/2018/dec/06/outcry-over-bolsonaros-plan-to-put-conservative-in-charge -of-new-family-and-women-ministry.

16. Phillips, "Bolsonaro to Abolish Human Rights Ministry in Favour of Family Values."

17. Polimédio, "Women for Bolsonaro."

18. "Brazil's New Far-Right Leader Urges Unity," BBC News, January 1, 2019, https://www.bbc.com/news/world-latin-america-46720899.

19. Carranca, "The Women-Led Opposition to Brazil's Far-Right Leader."

20. Polimédio, "Women for Bolsonaro."

21. Uchoa, "Why Brazilian Women Are Saying #NotHim."

22. Jill Langlois, "Brazil Condemns Violence Against a Candidate, but Marielle Franco's Killers Remain Free," *Washington Post*, September 12, 2018, https://www .washingtonpost.com/news/global-opinions/wp/2018/09/12/brazil-condemns -violence-against-a-candidate-but-marielle-francos-killers-remain-free.

23. Amy Gunia, "Two Former Police Officers Have Been Arrested for Brazilian Activist Marielle Franco's Murder," *Time*, March 13, 2019, http://time.com /5550428/brazil-marielle-franco-murder-arrests.

24. Elisa Gutsche, ed., *Triumph of the Women? The Female Face of the Populist & Far Right in Europe* (Berlin: Friedrich Ebert Stiftung, 2018).

25. Friedel Taube, "Women Increasingly Drawn to Right-Wing Populist Parties, Study Shows," *Deutsche Welle*, August 30, 2018, https://www.dw.com/en/women -increasingly-drawn-to-right-wing-populist-parties-study-shows/a-45284465.

26. Kelly Weill, "German Neo-Nazis Say These Women Were Abused by Muslim Immigrants. They're Actually American Victims of Domestic Violence," *Daily Beast*, August 30, 2018, https://www.thedailybeast.com/german-neo-nazis-say-these-women-were-abused-by-muslim-immigrants-theyre-actually-american-victims-of-domestic-violence.

27. Paul Hockenos, "Meet the Lesbian Goldman Sachs Economist Who Just Led Germany's Far Right to Victory," *Foreign Policy*, September 24, 2017, https://foreignpolicy.com/2017/09/24/meet-the-lesbian-goldman-sachs-economist-who-just-lead-germanys-far-right-to-victory.

28. Eugene Scott, "White House Is Playing the "Woman" Card in Response to Concerns About Gina Haspel," *Washington Post*, May 7, 2018, https://www.washingtonpost.com/news/the-fix/wp/2018/05/07/the-white-house-is-playing-the-woman-card-in-its-response-to-concerns-about-gina-haspel.

29. Jennifer Williams, "Gina Haspel, Trump's Controversial Pick for CIA Director, Explained," *Vox*, May 8, 2018, https://www.vox.com/policy-and-politics/2018/5/8/17326638/gina-haspel-bio-new-cia-director-nominee-torture-war-crimes-trump-bush-confirmation.

30. Ian Cobain, "CIA Rendition: More Than a Quarter of Countries 'Offered Covert Support,'" *Guardian*, February 5, 2013, http://www.theguardian.com/world/2013/feb/05/cia-rendition-countries-covert-support.

31. Max Fisher, "A Staggering Map of the 54 Countries That Reportedly Participated in the CIA's Rendition Program," *Washington Post*, February 5, 2013, https://www.washingtonpost.com/news/worldviews/wp/2013/02/05/a-staggering-map-of-the-54-countries-that-reportedly-participated-in-the-cias-rendition-program.

32. Jane Mayer, "Outsourcing Torture," *New Yorker*, February 7, 2005, https://www.newyorker.com/magazine/2005/02/14/outsourcing-torture.

33. Peter Finn, "Detainee Who Gave False Iraq Data Dies in Prison in Libya," *Washington Post*, May 12, 2009, http://www.washingtonpost.com/wp-dyn/content/article/2009/05/11/AR2009051103412.html.

34. Jenna Johnson, "Trump Says 'Torture Works,' Backs Waterboarding and 'Much Worse,'" *Washington Post*, February 17, 2016, https://www.washingtonpost.com/politics/trump-says-torture-works-backs-waterboarding-and-much-worse/2016/02/17/4c9277be-d59c-11e5-b195-2e29a4e13425_story.html.

35. Molly Redden, "Trump Is Assembling the Most Male-Dominated Government in Decades," *Guardian*, September 21, 2017, http://www.theguardian.com/us-news/2017/sep/21/trump-is-assembling-the-most-male-dominated-government-in-decades.

36. Juan E. Méndez, "I Was Tortured. I Know How Important It Is to Hold the CIA Accountable," *Politico*, June 23, 2015, https://www.politico.com/magazine/story/2015/06/cia-torturers-should-be-held-accountable-119345.

37. Marc A. Thiessen, "Gina Haspel Is Too Qualified to Pass Up," *Washington Post*, May 8, 2018, https://www.washingtonpost.com/opinions/gina-haspel-is-too-qualified-to-pass-up/2018/05/08/3cf5b7ba-52dd-11e8-9c91-7dab596e8252_story.html.

38. Carmen Landa Middleton, "Gina Haspel Stands Ready to Break the Glass Ceiling. Let Her," *Cipher Brief*, April 3, 2018, https://www.thecipherbrief.com/column_article/gina-haspel-stands-ready-break-glass-ceiling-let.

39. Philip Bump, "Donald Trump Responds to the Khan Family: 'Maybe She Wasn't Allowed to Have Anything to Say,'" *Washington Post*, July 30, 2016, https://www.washingtonpost.com/news/the-fix/wp/2016/07/30/donald-trump-responds-to-the-khan-family-maybe-she-wasnt-allowed-to-have-anything-to-say.

40. Karen Zraick, "As Rashida Tlaib Is Sworn In, Palestinian-Americans Respond With #TweetYourThobe," *New York Times*, January 3, 2019, https://www.nytimes.com/2019/01/03/us/politics/rashida-tlaib-palestinian-thobe.html.

41. Pete Williams, "Supreme Court Upholds Trump Travel Ban, President Claims Vindication from 'Hysterical' Critics," NBC News.com, June 26, 2018, https://www.nbcnews.com/politics/supreme-court/supreme-court-upholds-trump-travel-ban-n873441.

42. Erin Golden, "Ilhan Omar Makes History, Becoming First Somali-American Elected to U.S. House," *Star Tribune*, November 7, 2018, http://www.startribune.com/ilhan-omar-becomes-first-somali-american-elected-u-s-house/499708271.

43. Treva B. Lindsey, "The Betrayal of White Women Voters: In Pivotal State Races, They Still Backed the GOP," *Vox*, November 9, 2018, https://www.vox.com/first-person/2018/11/9/18075390/election-2018-midterms-white-women-voters.

44. "2018 Midterms: Exit Polling," CNN.com, November 6, 2018, https://www.cnn.com/election/2018/exit-polls/georgia.

45. Rashida Tlaib, "Why I Disrupted Donald Trump," *Detroit Free Press*, August 24, 2016, https://www.freep.com/story/opinion/contributors/2016/08/24/rashida-tlaib-why-disrupted-donald-trump/89251860.

46. Doualy Xaykaothao, "Trump's Comments on MN Somalis Draw Sharp Response," MPRNews, November 7, 2016, https://www.mprnews.org/story/2016/11/07/trumps-comments-on-mn-somalis-draw-sharp-response.

47. Mona Eltahawy, "Rashida Tlaib and Ilhan Omar Make Midterms History While Complicating Stereotypes of Muslim American Women," *Think*, November 9, 2018, https://www.nbcnews.com/think/opinion/rashida-tlaib-ilhan-omar-make-midterms-history-while-complicating-stereotypes-ncna934561.

48. Katie Mettler, "'Just Deal,' Muslim Lawmaker Ilhan Omar Says to Pastor Who Complained About Hijabs on House Floor," *Washington Post*, December 7, 2018, https://www.washingtonpost.com/religion/2018/12/07/just-deal-muslim-lawmaker-ilhan-omar-says-pastor-who-complained-about-hijabs-house-floor.

49. Cody Nelson, "Minnesota Congressswoman Ignites Debate on Israel and Anti-Semitism," NPR, March 7, 2019, https://www.npr.org/2019/03/07/700901834/minnesota-congresswoman-ignites-debate-on-israel-and-anti-semitism.

50. Vivian Ho, "Ilhan Omar Takes Trump's Venezuela Envoy to Task over His Political Past," *Guardian*, February 13, 2019, https://www.theguardian.com/politics/2019/feb/13/ilhan-omar-elliott-abrams-trump-venezuela.

51. "Bullies Don't Win," posted by demsocialism, YouTube, posted January 3, 2019, https://www.youtube.com/watch?v=Bub4bRNy8YQ.

52. Lisa Anderson, "Woman Leads Prayer for Muslims in NYC," *Chicago Tribune*, March 19, 2005, https://www.chicagotribune.com/news/ct-xpm-2005-03-19-0503190168-story.html.

53. "Woman Leads Controversial US Prayer," *Al Jazeera*, March 19, 2005, https://www.aljazeera.com/archive/2005/03/200849145527855944.html.

54. Nadia Abou El-Magd, "Muslims in Middle East Outraged After a Woman Conducts Mixed-Gender Islamic Prayer Service in New York," *Seattle Times*, March 19, 2005, https://www.seattletimes.com/nation-world/muslims-in-middle-east -outraged-after-a-woman-conducts-mixed-gender-islamic-prayer-service-in-new -york; Andrea Elliott, "Woman Leads Muslim Prayer Service in New York," *New York Times*, March 19, 2005, https://www.nytimes.com/2005/03/19/nyregion /woman-leads-muslim-prayer-service-in-new-york.html.

55. "Singing a Song Many Women Have Been Humming," *Richmond Times-Dispatch*, October 7, 2005, https://www.dailypress.com/news/dp-xpm-20051007 -2005-10-07-0510070026-story.html.

56. "Enough Is Enough: India Women Fight to Enter Temples," BBC News, February 18, 2016, https://www.bbc.com/news/world-asia-india-35595501.

57. "Enough Is Enough."

58. "Shani Shingnapur Temple Lifts Ban on Women's Entry," *Hindu*, April 8, 2016, https://www.thehindu.com/news/national/other-states/shani-shingnapur -temple-lifts-ban-on-womens-entry/article8451406.ece.

59. "Enough Is Enough."

60. Lauren Frayer and Sushmita Pathak, "India's Supreme Court Orders Hindu Temple to Open Doors to Women, but Devotees Object," NPR, December 22, 2018, https://www.npr.org/2018/12/22/675548304/indias-supreme-court-orders -hindu-temple-to-open-doors-to-women-but-devotees-obj.

61. "Shani Shingnapur Temple Lifts Ban on Women's Entry."

62. Niha Masih, "In India, Two Women Defy Protests," *Washington Post*, January 3, 2019, https://www.washingtonpost.com/world/asia_pacific/protesters -kept-women-out-of-a-prominent-indian-temple-for-months--until-today /2019/01/02/f01304e0-0e64-11e9-831f-3aa2c2be4cbd_story.html?utm_term= .c0b84603a65f.

63. "Sabarimala: India's Kerala Paralysed amid Protests over Temple Entry," BBCNews.com, January 3, 2019, https://www.bbc.com/news/world-asia-india -46744142.

64. "Indian Women in '620km Human Chain' Protest," BBC News, January 1, 2019, https://www.bbc.com/news/world-asia-india-46728521.

65. Cris and Saritha S. Balan, "Kerala's Wall of Resistance: Lakhs of Women Stand Up Against Patriarchy," *News Minute*, January 1, 2019, https://www.thenews minute.com/article/keralas-wall-resistance-lakhs-women-stand-against-patriarchy -94314.

66. "Indian Women in '620km Human Chain' Protest."

67. Balan, "Kerala's Wall of Resistance."

68. "Sabarimala: India Woman Who Defied Temple Ban 'Abandoned' by Family," BBC News, January 23, 2019, https://www.bbc.com/news/world-asia-india -46969160.

69. Michael Safi, "Woman Who Defied Indian Temple Ban 'Shunned' by Family," *Guardian*, January 23, 2019, http://www.theguardian.com/world/2019/jan/23 /woman-indian-temple-family-sabarimala-kerala.

70. DeNeen L. Brown, "'I Have All the Guns and Money': When a Woman Led the Black Panther Party," *Washington Post*, May 22, 2018, https://www.washington post.com/news/retropolis/wp/2018/01/09/i-have-all-the-guns-and-money-when -a-woman-led-the-black-panther-party.

71. Elaine Brown, *A Taste of Power: A Black Woman's Story* (New York: Anchor, 1993), Kindle ed.

72. Combahee River Collective Statement, April 1977, https://americanstudies .yale.edu/sites/default/files/files/Keyword%20Coalition_Readings.pdf.

CHAPTER 6: VIOLENCE

1. "Lorraine Hansberry: Sighted Eyes/Feeling Heart," interview, May 12, 1959, Studs Terkel Radio Archive, https://studsterkel.wfmt.com/digital-bughouse /lorraine-hansberry-sighted-eyesfeeling-heart, accessed March 21, 2019.

2. "Female Genital Mutilation Among Egyptian Teenage Girls Drops By 27 Percent," *Egyptian Streets*, February 5, 2016, https://egyptianstreets.com/2016 /02/05/female-genital-mutilation-among-egyptian-teenage-girls-drops-by -27-percent.

3. Seif El Mashad, "The Moral Epidemic of Egypt: 99% of Women Are Sexually Harassed," *Egyptian Streets*, March 5, 2015, https://egyptianstreets.com/2015/03/05 /the-moral-epidemic-of-egypt-99-of-women-are-sexually-harassed.

4. Frances Perraudin, "Femicide in UK: 76% of Women Killed by Men in 2017 Knew Their Killer," *Guardian*, December 18, 2018, http://www.theguardian.com /uk-news/2018/dec/18/femicide-in-uk-76-of-women-killed-by-men-in-2017 -knew-their-killer.

5. Perraudin, "Femicide in UK."

6. Mary Emily O'Hara, "Domestic Violence: Nearly Three U.S. Women Killed Every Day by Intimate Partners," NBC News.com, April 11, 2017, https://www .nbcnews.com/news/us-news/domestic-violence-nearly-three-u-s-women-killed -every-day-n745166.

7. Mary Anne Franks, "Men, Women, and Optimal Violence," *University of Illinois Law Review* (2016): 929, https://repository.law.miami.edu/fac_articles/200. Emphasis added.

8. O'Hara, "Domestic Violence."

9. Nour Naas, "When the Only Legal Option for Domestic Violence Victims Is to Not Survive," *Huffington Post*, May 8, 2018, https://www.huffingtonpost.com /entry/opinion-naas-domestic-violence-police_us_5af0645ce4b0c4f19324d6e4.

10. "Words from Prison—Did You Know . . . ?," American Civil Liberties Union, https://www.aclu.org/other/words-prison-did-you-know, accessed February 4, 2019.

11. Sharon Angella Allard, "Rethinking Battered Woman Syndrome: A Black Feminist Perspective," *UCLA Women's Law Journal* 1 (1991), https://escholarship .org/content/qt62z1s13j/qt62z1s13j.pdf, accessed January 30, 2019.

12. Franks, "Men, Women, and Optimal Violence," 958.

13. "Words from Prison—Did You Know . . . ?"

14. Rebecca McCray, "When Battered Women Are Punished with Prison," *TakePart*, September 24, 2015, http://www.takepart.com/article/2015/09/24 /battered-women-prison.

15. Kirsten Powers, "Angela Corey's Overzealous Prosecution of Marissa Alexander," *Daily Beast*, July 19, 2013, https://www.thedailybeast.com/articles/2013 /07/19/angela-corey-s-overzealous-prosecution-of-marissa-alexander.

16. Elizabeth Swavola, Kristi Riley, and Ram Subramanian, *Overlooked: Women and Jails in an Era of Reform* (New York: Vera Institute of Justice, August 2016), https://www.vera.org/publications/overlooked-women-and-jails-report.

17. "Words from Prison—Did You Know . . . ?"

18. Judith Herman, *Trauma and Recovery: The Aftermath of Violence—from Domestic Abuse to Political Terror* (New York: Basic Books, 1997), Kindle ed., chapter 3.

19. "An instructive example . . . ," Mary Anne Franks, @ma_franks, Twitter, February 10, 2018, https://twitter.com/ma_franks/status/962385300642304000.

20. Examples are from the following tweets: "Loving . . . ," Sunny Singh (@sunnysingh_n6), Twitter, February 10, 2018, https://twitter.com/sunnysingh _n6/status/962445068870307840; "A man . . . ," Samia Khan (@samiakhan183), Twitter, February 10, 2018, https://twitter.com/samiakhan183/status/96242084 8060784640; "A few . . . ," Nikita Gill is on hiatus (@nktgill), Twitter, February 10, 2018, https://twitter.com/nktgill/status/962450036536827904; "Years ago . . . ," Francie Meeting You Here (@Francie_one), Twitter, February 10, 2018, https:// twitter.com/Francie_one/status/962422628974809088; "When I was . . . ," Yikes (@KaleyW408), Twitter, February 10, 2018, https://twitter.com/KaleyW408 /status/962425813680435201.

21. Franks, "Men, Women, and Optimal Violence," 929.

22. Emma Graham-Harrison, "Back on the Tourist Trail: The Hotel Where Women Were Raped and Tortured," *Guardian*, January 28, 2018, http://www .theguardian.com/world/2018/jan/28/bosnia-hotel-rape-murder-war-crimes.

23. Graham-Harrison, "Back on the Tourist Trail"; Nidzara Ahmetasevic, Nerma Jelacic, and Selma Boracic, "Visegrad Rape Victims Say Their Cries Go Unheard," *Balkan Insight*, December 10, 2007, http://www.balkaninsight.com/en /article/visegrad-rape-victims-say-their-cries-go-unheard.

24. Carlo Angerer and Vladimir Banic, "Hotel, Hospital Where War Crimes Occurred Remain Open in Bosnia-Herzegovina," NBC News.com, June 3, 2018, https://www.nbcnews.com/news/world/hotel-hospital-where-war-crimes-occurred -remain-open-bosnia-herzegovina-n878086.

25. Graham-Harrison, "Back on the Tourist Trail."

26. Ahmetasevic, Jelacic, and Boracic, "Visegrad Rape Victims Say Their Cries Go Unheard."

27. Laura Smith-Spark, "Denis Mukwege and Nadia Murad Win Nobel Peace Prize," CNN.com, October 5, 2018, https://edition.cnn.com/2018/10/05/europe /nobel-peace-prize-intl/index.html.

28. Danielle Paquette, "Thousands of Women Were Raped During Rwanda's Genocide. Now Their Kids Are Coming of Age," *Washington Post*, June 11, 2017, http://www.washingtonpost.com/sf/world/2017/06/11/rwandas-children-of-rape -are-coming-of-age-against-the-odds.

29. Abby Vesoulis, "Meet the Woman Who Helped Change Jeff Flake's Mind in a Senate Elevator," *Time*, October 2, 2018, http://time.com/5412444/jeff-flake -elevator-protester.

30. Eli Rosenberg, "'Grow Up': Orrin Hatch Waves Off Female Protesters Demanding to Speak with Him," *Washington Post*, October 5, 2018, https://www .washingtonpost.com/politics/2018/10/05/grow-up-orrin-hatch-waves-off-female -protesters-demanding-speak-with-him.

31. Alexander Nazaryan, "Republican Men—and Not a Single GOP Woman— Will Be Christine Blasey Ford's Interrogators on the Senate Judiciary Committee," Yahoo News, September 18, 2018, https://ca.news.yahoo.com/republican-men-not -single-gop-woman-will-christine-blasey-fords-interrogators-senate-judiciary -committee-212116316.html.

32. "I called MOI for response . . . ," Matt Bradley, @MattMcBradley, Twitter, November 25, 2011, https://twitter.com/MattMcBradley/status/1400659796 60111872.

33. Assata Shakur, *Assata: An Autobiography* (Chicago: Lawrence Hill Books, 1999).

CHAPTER 7: LUST

1. Mitali Saran, "Square Peg, Round Hole," *Walking Towards Ourselves: Indian Women Tell Their Stories*, ed. Catriona Mitchell (Melbourne: Hardie Grant Books, 2016), Kindle ed.

2. Jordan, *Some of Us Did Not Die*, 132.

3. Jordan, *Some of Us Did Not Die*, 135.

4. Jordan, *Some of Us Did Not Die*, 135–36.

5. Heather Murdock, "'Delayed' Marriage Frustrates Middle East Youth," Voice of America.com, February 23, 2011, https://www.voanews.com/a/delayed-marriage -frustrates-middle-east-youth-116744384/172742.html.

6. Mark Oppenheimer, "Purity Balls: Local Tradition or National Trend?," *New York Times*, July 20, 2012, https://www.nytimes.com/2012/07/21/us/purity-balls -local-tradition-or-national-trend.html.

7. Adventures from the Bedrooms of African Women, https://adventuresfrom. com, accessed February 4, 2019; Agents of Ishq, http://agentsofishq.com/home-2, accessed February 4, 2019.

8. Mitchell, ed., *Walking Towards Ourselves.*

9. Mona Eltahawy, "Why Is the Egyptian Government So Afraid of a Rainbow Flag?," *New York Times*, October 26, 2017, https://www.nytimes.com/2017/10/26 /opinion/egypt-gay-lgbt-rights.html.

10. Declan Walsh, "Egyptian Concertgoers Wave a Flag, and Land in Jail," *New York Times*, September 26, 2017, https://www.nytimes.com/2017/09/26/world /middleeast/egypt-mashrou-leila-gays-concert.html.

11. Tamara Qiblawi, "Jordan Bans Lebanese Rock Band," CNN.com, June 16, 2017, https://www.cnn.com/2017/06/16/middleeast/jordan-bans-lebanese-rock -band/index.html.

12. Alliance of Queer Egyptian Organizations Facebook page, accessed March 21, 2019. https://www.facebook.com/AQEO2017.

13. *My.Kali*, https://medium.com/my-kali-magazine, accessed February 4, 2019.

14. "This Woman Is The Most Hated Lesbian In Egypt," BuzzFeedVideo, YouTube, posted August 24, 2017, https://www.youtube.com/watch?v=hWh1srps128.

15. Nick Cumming-Bruce, "U.N. Officials Condemn Arrests of Gays in Azerbaijan, Egypt and Indonesia," *New York Times*, October 13, 2017, https://www .nytimes.com/2017/10/13/world/asia/azerbaijan-indonesia-egypt-arrests-gays -un.html.

16. "Trans women are women too . . . ," Mona Eltahawy, @monaeltahawy, Twitter, posted March 12, 2018, https://twitter.com/monaeltahawy/status /973266946799099904.

17. Jen Richards, "It's Time for Trans Lives to Truly Matter to Us All," op-ed, *Advocate*, February 18, 2015, https://www.advocate.com/commentary/2015/02/18 /op-ed-its-time-trans-lives-truly-matter-us-all; Joaquín Carcaño, National Transgender HIV Testing Day, blog post, North Carolina AIDS Training & Education

Center, https://www.med.unc.edu/ncaidstraining/clincian-resources/blog/national
-transgender-hiv-testing-day-blog-post, accessed March 26, 2019.

18. Alexa Shouneyia, "Halsey & Lauren Jauregui's 'Strangers' Is a
Long-Overdue Bisexual Milestone in Mainstream Music," *Billboard*, June 6, 2017,
https://www.billboard.com/articles/columns/pop/7824521/halsey-lauren-jauregui
-strangers-lgbtq-representation.

19. Brittany Spanos, "Janelle Monáe Frees Herself," *Rolling Stone*, April 26, 2018,
https://www.rollingstone.com/music/music-features/janelle-monae-frees
-herself-629204.

20. Selam Wabi, "Meet the Feminist Calling for South Africans to Talk About
the Politics of Sex," *OkayAfrica*, August 17, 2016, https://www.okayafrica.com/south
-african-feminist-sex-politics.

21. Jordan, *Some of Us Did Not Die*.

22. Susan Song, "Polyamory and Queer Anarchism: Infinite Possibilities for Resistance," in *Queering Anarchism: Addressing and Undressing Power and Desire*, ed. C. B.
Daring et al. (Oakland: AK Press, 2012), Kindle ed.

23. Leta Hong Fincher, *Betraying Big Brother: The Feminist Awakening in China*
(London: Verso, 2018).

24. Mona Eltahawy, "#MonaTalksTo: Zheng Churan and Liang Xiaowen,"
sister-hood, February 13, 2018, http://sister-hood.com/mona-eltahawy/monatalksto
-zheng-churan-and-liang-xiaowen/.

25. Owen Bowcott, "Nigeria Arrests Dozens as Anti-Gay Law Comes into
Force," *Guardian*, January 14, 2014, http://www.theguardian.com/world/2014/jan
/14/nigeria-arrests-dozens-anti-gay-law.

26. Azeenarh Mohammed, Chitra Nagarajan, and Rafeeat Aliyu, eds., *She Called
Me Woman: Nigeria's Queer Women Speak* (Abuja: Cassava Republic Press, 2018).

27. *She Called Me Woman* book page, Cassava Republic Press, https://cassava
republicpress.biz/shop-2/non-fiction/she-called-me-woman/?v=3e8d115eb4b3,
accessed March 21, 2019.

28. James Michael Nichols, "Meet The First And Only Man To Ever Publicly
Come Out In Nigeria," *Huffington Post*, March 1, 2016, https://www.huffington
post.ca/entry/boy-from-mushin-kickstarter_us_56d5ea33e4b0bf0dab338eaf.

29. Chike Frankie Edozien, *Lives of Great Men: Living and Loving as an African
Gay Man* (London: Team Angelica Publishing, 2017).

30. "Kenya Briefly Lifts Ban on Lesbian Film," BBC News.com, September 21,
2018, https://www.bbc.com/news/world-africa-45605758.

31. Cecilie Kallestrup, "Lesbian Romance Film Shows to Sell-Out Crowd in
Nairobi After Court Lifts Ban," Reuters, September 23, 2018, https://www.reuters
.com/article/us-kenya-films-idUSKCN1M30NK.

32. John Ndiso and Cecilie Kallestrup, "In Legal Battle over Gay Sex, Kenya
Court to Consider Indian Ruling," Reuters, September 27, 2018, https://www
.reuters.com/article/us-kenya-lgbt-idUSKCN1M71LU.

33. Amy Bhatt, "India's Sodomy Ban, Now Ruled Illegal, Was a British Colonial Legacy," *Conversation*, September 18, 2018, http://theconversation.com/indias
-sodomy-ban-now-ruled-illegal-was-a-british-colonial-legacy-103052.

34. Uki Goñi, "Argentina Senate Rejects Bill to Legalise Abortion," *Guardian*,
August 9, 2018, http://www.theguardian.com/world/2018/aug/09/argentina-senate
-rejects-bill-legalise-abortion.

35. Ni Una Menos, "The Fire Is Ours."

36. Goni, "Argentina Senate Rejects Bill to Legalise Abortion."

CONCLUSION

1. Human Rights Watch, *Boxed In: Women and Saudi Arabia's Male Guardianship System* (New York: July 2016), https://www.hrw.org/report/2016/07/16/boxed /women-and-saudi-arabias-male-guardianship-system#

2. Human Rights Watch, *Boxed In.*

3. Human Rights Watch, "Thailand: Allow Fleeing Saudi Woman to Seek Refuge," January 6, 2019, https://www.hrw.org/news/2019/01/06/thailand-allow -fleeing-saudi-woman-seek-refuge.

4. Mona Eltahawy, "Why Saudi Women Are Literally Living 'The Handmaid's Tale,'" *New York Times*, May 24, 2017, https://www.nytimes.com/2017/05/24 /opinion/why-saudi-women-are-literally-living-the-handmaids-tale.html.

5. Mona Eltahawy, retweet of Rahaf Mohamed tweet, @monaeltahawy, Twitter, January 5, 2019, https://twitter.com/monaeltahawy/status/1081660044729552896 ?lang=en.

6. Sunai Phasuk, "Saudi Woman Had Courage, Perseverance and Global Support," Human Rights Watch.org, January 12, 2019, https://www.hrw.org/news /2019/01/12/saudi-woman-had-courage-perseverance-and-global-support.

7. Stephen Kalin, "Saudi Women's Rights Activists Stand Trial in Criminal Court," Reuters, March 13, 2019, https://www.reuters.com/article/us-saudi -arrests/saudi-womens-rights-activists-stand-trial-in-criminal-court-idUSKBN 1QU0WN.

8. Margherita Stancati and Summer Said, "Jailed Women's Rights Activists Tell Saudi Investigators of Torture," *Wall Street Journal*, March 21, 2019, https://www .wsj.com/articles/jailed-womens-rights-activists-tell-saudi-investigators-of-torture -11545074461.

9. Abtahaj Meniaoui, "A 'Pornographic' Activist Embraces Rahaf in Canada," *Al Madinah*, January 17, 2019, https://www.al-madina.com/article/609797; "There is al-Madinah newspaper . . . ," Mona Eltahawy tweet, posted January 19, 2019, https://twitter.com/monaeltahawy/status/1086636497397342212?lang=en.

10. "I was accused of masterminding . . . " Mona Eltahawy, @monaeltahawy, Twitter, February 8, 2019, https://twitter.com/monaeltahawy/status/1093882099 067686913?s=12.

11. Tara John, "How Teenage Girls Defied Skeptics to Build a New Global Climate Movement," CNN.com, February 13, 2019, https://www.cnn.com/2019/02 /13/uk/student-climate-strike-girls-gbr-scli-intl/index.html.

12. Greta Thunberg Facebook post, February 11, 2019, https://www.facebook .com/gretathunbergsweden/photos/as-the-rumours-lies-and-constant-leaving-out -of-well-established-facts-continue-/773673599667129.

13. John, "How Teenage Girls Defied Skeptics to Build a New Global Climate Movement."